Leadership Blind Spots
And What to Do about Them

From everyone who has been given much, much will be demanded; and from the one who has been entrusted with much, much more will be asked.

Luke 12:48

"I have tried to do my best"

Tony Blair, February 2007

Leadership Blind Spots

And What to Do about Them

Karen Blakeley

JOSSEY-BASS
A Wiley Imprint
www.josseybass.com

Other Wiley Editorial Offices

John Wiley & Sons Inc., 111 River Street, Hoboken, NJ 07030, USA

Jossey-Bass, 989 Market Street, San Francisco, CA 94103-1741, USA

Wiley-VCH Verlag GmbH, Boschstr. 12, D-69469 Weinheim, Germany

John Wiley & Sons Australia Ltd, 42 McDougall Street, Milton, Queensland 4064, Australia

John Wiley & Sons (Asia) Pte Ltd, 2 Clementi Loop #02-01, Jin Xing Distripark, Singapore 129809

John Wiley & Sons Canada Ltd, 6045 Freemont Blvd, Mississauga, ONT, L5R 4J3, Canada

Wiley also publishes its books in a variety of electronic formats. Some content that appears in print may
not be available in electronic books.

Anniversary Logo Design: Richard J. Pacifico

Library of Congress Cataloging-in-Publication Data

Blakeley, Karen.
   Leadership blind spots – and what to do about them / Karen Blakeley.
      p.   cm.
   Includdes bibliographical references and index.
   ISBN 978-0-470-03193-3 (cloth : alk. paper)
   1. Leadership – Psychological aspects.   2. Management – Psychological aspects.   3. Perception.
4. Attitude (Psychology)   5. Behavior modification.   I. Title.
   HD57.7.B554 2007
   658.4′092 – dc22

                                                                              2007004232

British Library Cataloguing in Publication Data

A catalogue record for this book is available from the British Library

ISBN 978-0-470-03193-3 (HB)

Typeset in 11/13pt Plantin by SNP Best-set Typesetter Ltd., Hong Kong
Printed and bound in Great Britain by TJ International Ltd, Padstow, Cornwall, UK
This book is printed on acid-free paper responsibly manufactured from sustainable forestry
in which at least two trees are planted for each one used for paper production.

Dedicated to my parents, Ken and Doreen Weaving, and, of course, Chris, without whom this book would not have been written.

Contents

Preface

WE LIVE IN COMPLEX TIMES. EVERY DAY, LEADERS MAKE decisions that affect thousands, or even hundreds of thousands, of people. Yet, due to the complex nature of our organizations, the outcomes of these decisions are often unintended and even unknown. There is a school of thought that suggests that many of today's senior jobs are unfeasible. The scope of these jobs and the constant, all-pervasive nature of change places an almost intolerable burden on decision makers.

Yet, despite the complexity, important decisions have to be made. And the more senior the decision maker, the greater the number of people affected by their decisions. It is difficult to make good decisions in situations characterized by:

- fragile, dispersed relationships;

- paucity or excess of information;

- high levels of uncertainty;

- clashes in cultural values and beliefs;

- complex, interdependent social and economic systems.

In these circumstances it is easy to miss important events or to dismiss alternative ideas or opinions. It is easy to get caught on the treadmill with no time to make sense of what is happening, no time to experiment and no time to develop the range and depth of your leadership style. In other words, in these circumstances it is easy to develop blind spots.

Blind spots emerge when, for a variety of reasons, we do not want to listen or learn. The reason for this is that learning can be both painful and time-consuming; as a result, we often avoid it. We all tend to learn what suits us and the temptation to do this once in a leadership position is great. The clique that often surrounds a leader suggests that many leaders consciously limit the people who influence them. Leaders, too, can be highly resistant to change.

Whilst leaders have always had blind spots, the stakes today seem higher. It is not unusual for leaders' decisions to have a global impact – for good or bad. It seems right, therefore, to bring out a book that looks at these blind spots in more detail, exploring where they come from and what can be done to address them.

This book is based upon an extensive research project that looked at how leaders and their staff learned and adapted when their organizations went through change. The 21 people who participated in this research completed learning diaries over the period of a year and underwent a number of in-depth interviews. Their stories have contributed towards a model that helps us to better understand when and how people learn and when and how they develop blind spots. However, this book is not simply about understanding blind spots – it also seeks to address them. We have identified eight learning practices, which, if implemented on-the-job, will help leaders to improve their decisions, increase their learning agility and boost both their personal and their organization's performance.

The first part of this book explores some of the sources and possible impact of leadership blind spots. Chapter 1 provides a definition of blind spots and looks at how the blind spots of three leaders affected their decision making and performance. Chapter 2 introduces a new theory of learning and blind spots. It draws on the stories of the participants in the original research to bring the theory to life. This chapter also presents the eight learning practices that form the basis for the second part of the book. Chapter 3 looks at the impact of leaders' blind spots using real life examples, showing just how important this whole area is. Chapter 4 looks at a different kind of leadership blind spot. We identify some of the reasons that people throughout organizations avoid taking leadership, despite the need and opportunity for them to do so.

The second part of the book looks at each of the eight learning practices in depth. The last chapter offers some exercises to support each practice, many of which can be applied on-the-job.

There are two areas where some controversial choices were made. First, the focus is almost exclusively on individuals. We look at individual blind spots and individual learning. This is based on an assumption that a more thorough understanding of how individuals learn and overcome blind spots will provide a sound base for exploring more about how groups and organizations learn. Second, we have used the term *leader* to describe people in formal, senior leadership positions. Of course, leaders exist throughout the system – in both formal and informal positions. However, the focus of this book is on people in senior positions who are making decisions that affect large numbers of people. They may not be leaders in the true sense of the word – they may simply be senior managers in positions of leadership, who may or may not inspire followership. However, their power and influence suggest that their blind spots could have major ramifications. For this reason, we have focused on those in senior positions and have referred to them as 'leaders'. Nevertheless, the model and the ideas described here are relevant to everyone.

This book offers those in leadership positions a challenge. It has often been said that learning is a company's only sustainable competitive advantage. This is particularly true today, when business models and markets can change every few years. Knowledge and skills that we build up over a lifetime can be made redundant within a few years. In a rapidly changing and complex world, the leaders who succeed will need to be able to accelerate learning – both their own and their organization's. Central to this will be the ability to know, face and overcome both personal and organizational blind spots. This is not easy. It takes character, integrity, resilience and determination. Many leaders, for a number of reasons, will not rise to the challenge. Yet, without a doubt, the ability to learn rapidly and effectively will be the hallmark of successful leaders in the 21st century. This book hopes to encourage debate and learning around these issues. It is a tentative step in offering ideas, techniques and models whilst recognizing that the best learning comes when many people join the debate. I look forward to the ongoing dialogue I hope these ideas will inspire.

Acknowledgements

I'D LIKE TO THANK EVERYONE WHO HAS SUPPORTED ME though the long, drawn-out process of writing this book. Whilst all the following people have helped me in all sorts of ways, I take full responsibility for the ideas contained here, many of which are controversial and highly personal. Nevertheless, I could not have written this book without the support, encouragement and practical help of all my friends and colleagues.

The source of my inspiration and learning:
Amanda Graham, Sue Sharland, Karen de Meza, Ian Graham, Roy Taylor, Simon Brown, John Byrne, Tony Hurst, Chris Kingscott, Sue Perry, Peter Robinson, Mike Selway, Christine Shea, John Edgar, Bob Foreman, Brian Burford, Amanda Smith, Paul Fowler, Shane Geddes, Ian Bryant, Wayne Platt, Dave Slaughter.

For encouraging me and helping to open doors:
Terry Gibson, David Megginson, Charles Platel, Michelle Machin Jefferies, Mike Alsop, John Hughes, Elizabeth Thomas, Karen Firbank, Elise Rasmussen, Roger Brown, Karl and Nikki Weaving, Keir Weaving.

For support, encouragement and ideas, my colleagues at Waverley Learning:
Belinda Smith, Guy Rothwell, Penny Hogan.

For helping me at the Cass Centre for Leadership Learning and Change
David Sims, Paul Dobson, Margaret Bishop.

For reading the typescript and giving me helpful feedback
David Megginson, Bob Garratt, Wesley Harry, Philip Marshall, Roger Brown.

And of course my editors and staff at Wiley
Francesca Warren, Jo Golesworthy, Viv Wickham.

For tolerating an occasionally 'absent' mother, I'd like to thank my two patient children, Grace and Eliot. And for ongoing encouragement, support, optimism, feedback, ideas, challenge, advice and help – the inspiration and effective co-author of this book, my husband, Chris.

Part One

Leaders, Blind Spots and Learning – The Issues

1

Leaders, Blind Spots and Learning

'I believe in looking reality straight in the eye and denying it.'
Garrison Keillor

We all have blind spots – they are part of the human condition. But when leaders and people in authority have blind spots, it matters. The more power a person wields, the more lives are affected by their decisions. Since blind spots seriously impair decision making, it is important that we understand what blind spots are, how they emerge and what we can do to help ourselves and our leaders overcome them. So what are they?

From a physiological perspective, a blind spot is an area on the retina lacking the receptors that respond to light. If an image falls onto this area it will not be seen. A popular experiment will allow you to notice your own blind spot.

Look at the image below and close your right eye. Hold the book about 20 inches away from you. With your left eye look at the cross. Slowly, bring the book closer towards you and as you do, you will notice the dash disappears from sight. Your blind spot prevents you from seeing the image that is printed on this page.

In psychology, the term is used metaphorically. It is based on the notion that there are parts of ourselves that we simply do not wish

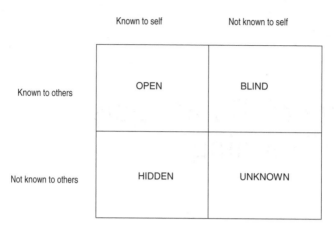

Figure 1.1   Johari's window.

to see – even though they are apparent to those who know us. A popular model of blind spots is known as *Johari's window* (Figure 1.1). Joseph Luft and Harry Ingram constructed a four-box model based upon 'what we know about ourselves' and 'what others know about us'.[1]

In this model the blind spot refers to an aspect of our personality that is not known to self but is apparent to others. For example, others may notice that I lack eye contact when talking to people. I, however, may be completely unaware of this. It is only through the process of receiving feedback that the blind spot can be addressed – I become aware of my lack of eye contact and I change my behaviour. In effect, the blind spot is reduced through learning.

In popular usage, we use the notion of a blind spot to refer to areas where people remain stubbornly fixed in their views. A person with a blind spot in a particular area will dismiss sound arguments, refute evidence and refuse to change their views in any way. The *Oxford Compact English Dictionary* definition of a blind spot is 'an area in

---

[1] Luft, J. and Ingram, H. (1955) 'The Johari window, a graphic model of interpersonal awareness', *Proceedings of the western training laboratory in group development*. Los Angeles: UCLA.

which a person lacks understanding or impartiality'.[2] The *Chambers 21st Century Dictionary* defines a blind spot as 'any subject which a person cannot understand or refuses even to try to understand'.[3] The notion of a blind spot incorporates more than a simple lack of understanding; it includes the sense that the person does not *want* to expand their understanding by listening to views or opinions that they in some way 'dislike'. The lack of impartiality and refusal to try to understand implies that we are biased towards accepting certain kinds of information and 'blind' with regards to other kinds of information.

This is not to say that we have a blind spot whenever we disagree with any idea presented to us. Blind spots only become a problem when they prevent us from adapting to changes in our environment. It is when we refuse to notice or pay attention to information and ideas coming from the world around us that blind spots become an issue, both for us and the organizations that we work for. Blind spots prevent us from learning and adapting to change.

For example, research has shown that leaders' understanding of the environment can sometimes be up to ten years out of date.[4] One academic study of a particular industry showed that many managers did not update their mental models in response to marked and obvious changes in the marketplace. This led to senior executives making decisions based on an inaccurate understanding of the competitive dynamics in their industry. It also tended to generate increased conflict, as executives with different mental models of the market perceived different challenges and promoted different solutions.[5] The research that underpins this book shows that well-intentioned, competent people do not automatically update their knowledge in response to major changes in their environment.

---

[2] www.askoxford.com/concise_oed/blindspot.

[3] www.chambersharrap.co.uk/chambers

[4] Peter's T. and Waterman, R. H. (2004) *In Search of Excellence*, 2nd edition. London: Profile Books, p. 7.

[5] Reger, R. K. and Palmer, T. B. (1996) 'Managerial Categorization of Competitors: Using Old Maps to Navigate New Environments.' *Organization Science*, 7(1), January–February.

The following definition incorporates the important links between learning, change and blind spots:

> A blind spot is a regular tendency to repress, distort, dismiss or fail to notice information, views or ideas in a particular area that results in an individual failing to learn, change or grow in response to changes in that area.

It is worth clarifying a number of aspects of this definition. First, the definition emphasizes the 'regular' tendency to miss information. Obviously, we cannot notice all information in our environment, but if we consistently fail to notice information that is relevant, either for our personal or organizational needs, we become ineffective in our leadership.

Second, a blind spot is not the same as a simple lack of knowledge. A blind spot emerges from a resistance to learning in a particular area. At the root of many of our blind spots are a number of emotions or attitudes – fear being the most obvious, but also pride, complacency and anxiety. A manager, for example, might have unsurpassed knowledge in the financial field, but her understanding of people management might be limited. Her people find her cold and aloof and want her to become more consultative and involved with the team. She, however, is resistant to feedback about her management style and refuses to change her behaviour. On closer inspection, we find that the main reason for this is that she believes that her authority could be undermined if she becomes too close to people. She fears that they will challenge her more readily if they get too comfortable with her and that she might be considered weak and even incompetent. Hence, she refuses to even consider the prospect of changing her management style. It is this refusal to consider her team's feedback, together with the emotional resistance to personal change, that indicates a blind spot.

Finally, the information we may distort, repress, dismiss or fail to notice is not simply written or codified information. It may consist of behaviours or emotions manifested by oneself or by other people. Information is embodied not simply in words but also in behaviours and emotions. Some people do not notice the 'information' embedded in their own emotional responses to events. Others do not notice the information contained in other people's behaviour; they fail to notice body language signals that indicate interest or disapproval or acceptance. Information is everywhere and is not manifested exclusively in a cognitive, declarative format.

We shall see later that blind spots are often rooted in the threat presented by certain types of information to our self concept and sense of identity. We are all subject to blind spots, and there is a tendency to assume that there is little we can do about them. For Max Planck, founder of quantum theory and one of the most important physicists of the 20th century, blind spots were so ingrained in the human mind that they presented an insurmountable block to learning:

> '*A new scientific truth does not triumph by convincing its opponents, but rather because its opponents die and a new generation grows up that is familiar with it*'.[6]

Waiting for a generation to die before accepting a new truth might be said to be a somewhat wasteful and inefficient way of adapting to change! Moreover, a lot of damage can be done in the meantime. When people in positions of leadership manifest significant blind spots, individuals, organizations and whole communities can suffer. This is best illustrated by a few simple examples. We will look at three leaders who are subject to very different blind spots which seriously affect their leadership and their organizations.

Our first example shows a leader who is confident and full of self belief. He has developed a vision for his organization and is trying to implement it. However, he is coming across resistance and he is not listening to what his people are trying to tell him. His blind spot is that he has fallen into the trap of believing that *his* understanding and vision is superior to everyone else's. Where people come up with reasons why the vision will not work, he dismisses their insights and regards them as 'resisting change'. This is a very common blind spot in organizations.

---

[6] Planck, M. (1936) *Philosophy of Physics*. New York: W.W. Norton and Company Inc.

Rick – The 'Visionary' Leader

Rick had just been made CEO of a medium sized chain of specialist home and garden retail outlets in the UK. Although he was a newcomer to the industry, having previously worked in a large food conglomerate, he was regarded as a highly competent manager – skilled technically, strategically and interpersonally. He was well liked and people warmed to his exuberant, positive and optimistic style.

He was excited by this new challenge as CEO, and soon after his new appointment set about crafting his vision for the company. He toured a number of the outlets and spent a lot of time talking to the people serving and interacting with the customers. It didn't take long before he believed he understood just what was needed in the business. There were some basic financial disciplines that were not in place consistently around the country. It was clear to Rick that increasing the profitability of their outlets was not a clear priority for staff. Nor did the outlets have a common 'look and feel' about them. They projected too much the personality of the individual managers and their staff. This was undermining the chain's brand image and leading to quality issues, particularly in areas where it was difficult to recruit staff.

Rick put together a vision for the business based upon a number of core values, emphasizing financial discipline, personal accountability, sales focus and brand consistency. However, when it came to presenting his vision to the Board of Directors, he sensed that there was some resistance to his ideas. Everyone appeared to agree but there was a distinct lack of enthusiasm.

After the meeting, Rick quizzed a few of his closest team members. It appeared that, for them, and for many in the business, quality was associated with the personal service that came from each outlet having some freedom to express the specialist interests of the local managers and their teams. Rick's emphasis on consistency and discipline seemed to be jeopardizing this autonomy and was in danger of squeezing out innovative flair.

Rick understood their discomfort. After all, they were used to having a high degree of discretion. He reassured them that people would still have the opportunity to express a degree of innovation, but continued to stress the importance of financial discipline.

He put together a number of project streams that ran across the outlets. Chief amongst these was the financial systems project, which would monitor turnover and profitability on a daily basis – outlet by outlet. However, after a period of six months, Rick started to get irritated – nothing appeared to be happening and results were not forthcoming. Projects were taking a lot longer to implement and costs were spiralling. The promised improvements were not appearing and he felt as if there was a high degree of passive resistance amongst his top team. So Rick worked closely with the HR director to bring in a new performance management system. This would ensure that everyone had personal objectives related to the change projects, and would be held directly accountable for their completion.

Staff felt increasingly pressurized. They were being held accountable for personal sales targets and their outlets' financial results. They complained that this was jeopardizing customer service, and that they felt they had to manipulate customers into buying things they did not need or want. Customers provided feedback that they felt service levels had deteriorated and that staff were no longer interested in discussing their problems or needs. Motivation levels dropped and sickness rates increased.

Soon, Rick and the board began to notice how turnover amongst staff was rising. In fact, they had lost two high-performing managers over the past six months. Rick attributed this to natural turnover resulting from the change programme. He saw it as an opportunity to recruit people who were more in tune with what he wanted to achieve. This was going to take longer than he thought, but he was not going to let a couple of setbacks and an inevitable resistance to change get in *his* way!

This is a familiar problem seen in many organizations. The business needs to improve its financial performance and Rick has crafted a vision of how this is going to be achieved. However, Rick is suffering from the classic visionary's blind spot. He is not listening. He does not have a sufficiently complex understanding of the business and he is not extracting what is valid from the inevitable complaints, natural resistances and self interest of his staff. In sum, he does not have sufficient cognitive or emotional complexity to lead change effectively and make informed decisions.

Read any textbook on leadership and you will soon be told that any leader has to have a vision. However, it is often the case that the vision is based on a personal experience that is not complex or broad enough to encompass the complexity of the situation he or she is dealing with. Everyone's experience is partial and highly personal, inevitably generating a simplistic map of what is a very complex reality. In Rick's case, his vision was based upon some important experiences in his past that helped him progress in his management career. In particular, he learned the importance of strict financial discipline.

The problem is that Rick is so focused on financial discipline that he is not able to listen to views coming from other paradigms. Rick's blind spot is around acknowledging the importance of innovation, personalized service and empowerment for the delivery of his business model. In the past, Rick has not seen these as important components of his business model, and as a result he has not developed a complex mental model of human behaviour (staff and customer) and how it interacts with the business finances. He has a sophisticated financial paradigm and an underdeveloped HR and customer paradigm. As a result, he does not recognize that his staff are attracted to working for the business precisely because of its past core values of innovation and discretion. If he ignores these values, he will find that large swathes of staff will either become demotivated or leave. The demotivated staff will affect customer service and this will impact on the bottom line. So, despite the new emphasis on financial discipline, profitability and efficiency, Rick is in danger of killing his business. This is because he is not developing a more sophisticated understanding of his business by listening to others. Nothing in his experience has led him to believe that their ideas will work, and Rick is limiting himself to his personal experience.

However, what seems impossible and irreconcilable is actually just complex. What Rick needs to do is to 'open up his construing' and allow himself to enter the zone of creative tension where he can ask the question.

> *'How can I introduce greater financial discipline into this business, guarantee a bottom line of quality and service, build a distinctive brand image and honour the innovation, flair and empowerment that has made this business successful in the past?'*

Moreover, Rick will not have the answer to this question solely in his own head. He will have to engage his staff in coming up with some of the answers to this question and, as a result, will have to go about putting his strategy together to some extent from the bottom up. This presents a challenge for Rick – he has never done this before. Even contemplating it would cause a degree of anxiety and uncertainty.

A vision is often necessary, but in a complex world, visions require a psychological sophistication that many leaders lack. Visions contain a paradox – they are not expressions of 'truth', nor are they necessarily 'right', but they must at times be treated as if they are right whilst leaving space to consider ways in which they may be inadequate, partial and simplistic. This is psychologically difficult to achieve. Leaders need confidence that they are leading the organization in the right direction, and this confidence can be undermined by a recognition that the vision might need to change or adapt. It is difficult to know when to listen to feedback that suggests you may be wrong and when to ignore it as a manifestation of the natural resistance to change.

Our next example concerns a leader who lacks self awareness. Jay Conger, Professor of Organisational Behaviour at the London Business School, explains that one reason that visions fail is that the vision reflects the needs of the leader rather than the needs of the market.[7] Self awareness is important, as this can highlight when we

---

[7] Conger, J. A. (1990) 'The Dark Side of Leadership.' *Organizational Dynamics*, Autumn, 44–55.

are making sense of the environment in a 'self-serving' manner in order to protect ourselves in some way. Jane's story shows how a lack of self awareness can lead to some difficult and damaging problems.

Jane – The Unselfaware Leader

Jane was angry. This was her first senior appointment. If she succeeded as MD of the medium-sized consumer goods business recently bought by her multinational employer, her career would thrive. She had been in place as MD now for over a year. This was going to be a major test of her ability to lead a business. But she was nervous and angry. She had spent a day with her marketing team examining their progress, finding out what they had achieved with the extra resources they had been given over the last eight months. It seemed that they had very little to show for all the additional spending. Having spent a long morning in a meeting with the senior managers, she had devoted the afternoon to mixing with the staff and watching their activities. She had felt her frustration growing and growing as the day wore on. There was no clear, consistent message emerging from the department; moreover, they seemed to be churning out old ideas but with a few new images attached – very expensive images too. And when she had spoken to two of the marketing account managers, they could not say clearly where the business was going and how the marketing strategy would be supporting the business changes. What's more, she had witnessed a huge row between the marketing manager and one of the line managers about what could be delivered by when. The two managers were in the midst of a full-blown, bloody battle before they saw Jane emerging from an office around the corner. The place seemed chaotic. She determined to challenge her directors at the next board meeting. What was going on around here? The end-of-year results did not look promising and she could see why – the marketing department was not being run effectively due to the lack of high quality staff and management. She resolved to talk to Hugh, the HR director, about their hiring and promotion practices. She wondered how on earth all these people got to such senior levels in the organization in the first place.

However, at that very same time, Hugh was sitting with two other board members discussing the very real problems with the lack of strategy – someone was going to have to approach Jane about the problem, but she just did not appear to be listening.

What is interesting about Jane's learning is not what she observes, but *how she makes sense of what she observes*. Jane has interpreted the performance problems as being due to a lack of high quality staff and management. She sees this as a recruitment and promotion issue. However, Jane does not believe that she has *interpreted* the situation (and chosen one interpretation amongst many), she believes she has distilled the *truth* of the situation. And Jane's subsequent decisions and actions are based upon the conclusions she draws from this sensemaking.

The HR director, Hugh, has drawn a different conclusion. He believes that the problem is due to the lack of a clear strategy in the business. Other directors in the business are complaining about it but do not have the courage to talk to Jane. They believe that Jane should be conducting a high level review of the business strategy in order to clarify what is happening in the marketplace and where the business should be heading over the next five years. Hugh has tried to convince Jane of this but Jane is not listening. She sticks firmly to her view that the problem is one of a lack of managerial competency at senior levels in the organization. She refuses to contemplate the alternative interpretation. She has a blind spot.

Why does she have a blind spot in this area? If we were to delve deeper into Jane's world, we would see that she would have to face a truth about herself that she would find painful – she is not a good strategic thinker. Jane's sensemaking is driven by a subconscious desire to defend her existing self concept as a good strategist and to avoid confronting her limitations in this area. In fact, if we go deeper, we can see the problem that Jane faces. Jane believes that to be a good leader you need to be a strategic thinker. Hence, if she confronts the fact that she is not a good strategic thinker, she thinks she will have failed as a leader. She has based her self esteem on her status as MD of a business, and so confronting the possibility that she might not be a good strategist will jeopardize her deepest and most important needs. The implication in her own mind is that she will have failed. As a result, she feels threatened when people like the HR director tell her that the organization lacks a strategy, and particularly when they look to her to provide it. Emotionally she cannot face this interpretation and so the problem bubbles away below the surface, though often erupting in arguments and disagreements between staff and their managers on the front line. She has constructed an explanation of the problem that protects her current knowledge and self esteem rather than facing the tough emotional work involved in renegotiating her belief systems, self concept, behavioural strategies and identity.

But blind spots are not simply defences used by the unselfaware. Let's look at another example of a blind spot arising from the effects of success.

Janet – The Complacent Leader

Janet was happy. It had taken a long time but her tireless striving to get to the top had worked. She had been determined and single-minded and as a result, she had achieved her goal – she had been appointed CEO of Harrisons, an international HR consultancy, over three years ago. The company was doing well and she had quite a high profile. After having appeared in an international business magazine only six months ago, she found that she was approached regularly to offer commentary to the media and had even been offered a regular newspaper column exploring issues around women in business. Because the business was on target and was in a relatively stable, fairly niched market, she did have time to concentrate on other things. And she really loved the lifestyle her higher profile was offering. A large part of her role involved PR, which meant attending functions and meeting powerful people from business and politics. Her network was extending considerably and she was popular.

She was warm, approachable and had a quick humour; she was able to get people to relax and laugh. She also enjoyed being a woman in a world populated largely by men – she stood out and she had always loved attention.

The only fly in the ointment was Howard. Everything seemed to be operating smoothly at work; most of her top team had been together a long time and had welcomed Janet's appointment. Her only competitor for the job had left shortly after he had failed to be appointed. But then there was Howard, the marketing director. He was always pointing out problems. He claimed that a small competitor had been successful in winning a couple of contracts against them and he accused the top team of being complacent! She knew he was sewing discord amongst the team, but she also had complete confidence in the support of the board members. Howard claimed that there had been an increase in complaints from clients – as far as she could make out, this amounted to two complaints, both of which had been handled satisfactorily. But Howard joined the two instances together and saw a trend! At one recent board meeting, Howard had claimed that the team spent too long looking at the figures and not exploring what was happening on the ground, particularly at the customer interface. It took all her patience to explain that the role of the board directors was to provide direction and to ensure policies and strategies were implemented – not to micro manage other people, who were perfectly capable of doing their own jobs.

Howard was her one 'energy drainer' and she was going to have to tackle him sooner or later. However, for now there was too much going on. She had a trip to China next week, an important business function on Wednesday and Wimbledon on Thursday. Howard would have to wait.

Our last blind spot concerns the effects of complacency. Surprisingly, there are still many leaders around who are affected by this particular blind spot – in the public, private and government sectors. Success feeds some deep needs in human beings – needs for self esteem, needs for status, power and influence, needs for autonomy and control. Once these needs are met, we can lose the fire and determination that generated our success in the first place. There is a tendency to feel 'I deserve this; I gave up a lot to get here and this is my reward'. Janet has got herself into this frame of mind. Instead of seeing herself as a leader with responsibilities to all those who have stakes in her leadership, she sees herself as Janet – successful, wealthy CEO admired by the people who matter. Of course, she ensures that the business is doing well and takes her duty as CEO very seriously. However, she is no longer hungry for the business. Gradually, without knowing it, she has moved from an offensive mentality to a defensive mentality. From being hungry for growth and financial success, she has moved towards being concerned to protect her position. This has affected what she pays attention to in the business. She now pays attention predominantly to the figures (to determine the financial health of the business) and to the stock markets and investor opinion; unconsciously she has changed her emphasis towards *monitoring* the business rather than changing and growing the business. For her, the reasoning is watertight – Harrisons is doing well and her job is simply to maintain that success; hence, she is monitoring the situation, checking that everything is carrying on as normal and that no problems are emerging. The problem with this strategy is that it is not taking account of subtle changes in the marketplace, most of which are only being discerned by the people on the ground. Big changes are emerging but are currently barely visible. Harrisons' current success formula, whilst appropriate for the past five years, will not necessarily guarantee success for the next five years, and by the time Janet finds out, it will be too late to stave off the major onslaught to her business. From being in a business that is sustaining success, she may easily find herself in a turnaround situation.

But Janet's attention is elsewhere. She is enjoying the well-deserved fruits of her success and there is nothing that is quite so sweet as the combination of wealth, status, power, influence and the admiration of others.

Leadership Blind Spots

All of our leaders are highly successful, competent and well-intentioned. And yet all of them are suffering from blind spots that are affecting both their personal and their organization's performance. In many cases, the skills and competencies of leaders by far outweigh their blind spots. However, if we could learn to master our blind spots, we could learn how to accelerate our learning and better keep up with the pace of change.

This is particularly important today. Blind spots prevent us from adapting our behaviour, our attitudes and our understanding at times when it is imperative to do so. Today, the amount of information that we are required to handle, the pace of change and the complexity of the environments in which we work place a high demand on our ability to learn continuously, and to do so in dialogue and relationship with others. The complexity of our environment is teaching us more than ever that no one person can ever have a monopoly on the truth. All of us have highly personal insights into the bigger picture. Senior managers and those on the ground see fragments of a complex reality, and any truth they may think they have captured changes daily. But psychologically this is difficult to handle. Accepting that we can never really 'know' anything in a constantly changing and complex world feels chaotic. We can feel like victims rather than powerful, competent individuals who can impact our world. To be able to handle complexity and change we need a radically different mind-set – a mind-set that is more attuned to continuous learning.

The complexity of our working environment also places demands upon our personal flexibility – we can no longer rely on *one* way of managing, influencing and communicating. We have to match the environmental complexity with a cognitive, emotional and behavioural complexity that provides us with more ways of understanding and dealing with the problems and issues facing us. A behaviour that works in one context no longer works in another. A certain management style may work in one organizational culture or business context but not in another. A change management process that works in one industry may not work at all in another. What worked in the last few years will not necessarily work in the next year.

This, of course, is all to do with how we learn. It is often taken for granted that people will automatically learn from their experience, but this book proposes that learning is often a difficult process that takes time, skill and care to negotiate successfully. It is difficult to acknowledge that what we thought was 'right' actually does not work in a different environment.

With an increased emphasis on efficiency, however, there seems to be less time to work through the emotional and cognitive challenges associated with learning. Quite simply, more learning and personal change is required of us but we rarely have the time, energy and/or the safe environment within which to do so. Moreover, we have not yet developed a deep understanding of the skills needed to manage a life of continuous learning and change. Learning is a process that can undermine our self esteem. When change engulfs us, we may be required to learn new behaviours that challenge us. Learning can threaten our sense of competence and threaten the sources of our personal identity, particularly our values. Sometimes we resist learning because we feel that we may fail and be damaged during the process. Sometimes we resist learning because it is inconvenient and gets in the way of our goals and desires. As a result of all these forces, we often cling to our old strategies and approaches when they no longer work and may even be harming us. This is why we develop blind spots – in order to protect ourselves from difficult and painful learning.

Psychologists have long known of the processes that can lead to blind spots – cognitive dissonance,[8] groupthink[9] and defensiveness[10] are all ways of explaining some of the underlying dynamics of blind spots. What perhaps is less appreciated is how these dynamics operate subconsciously minute by minute as we constantly make sense of our environment.

---

[8] Festinger, L. (1957) *A Theory of Cognitive Dissonance*. Evanstoun, IL: Row, Peterson. Also see Harmon-Jones, E. and Mills, J. (1991) *Cognitive Dissonance – progress on a pivotal theory in social psychology*. Washington: American Psychological Society.

[9] Janis, I. L. and Mann, L. (1977) *Decision Making*. New York: Free Press. Esser, J. K. (1998) 'Alive and Well after 25 Years: A Review of Groupthink Research.' *Organizational Behaviour and Human Decision Making Processes*, **73**(2/3), 116–141.

[10] Sutherland, S. (1992) *Irrationality*. London: Constable and Company Limited. Also see Goleman, D. and The Dalai Lama (2003) *Destructive Emotions*. London: Bloomsbury.

This is particularly relevant to leaders, because leaders often find it more difficult to learn! Like all of us, leaders feel the psychological forces that tempt us to learn what feels comfortable and avoid learning what is painful or difficult. But, unlike many of us, leaders have the power to shield themselves from the painful and difficult, and followers may collude with this. Leaders are therefore more prone to developing blind spots. Yet leaders daily make decisions that affect many people. It is incumbent on these leaders to overcome their blind spots for the sake of their stakeholders. Learning is both a moral and commercial duty.

If we can understand more about the dynamics of learning and blind spots, we can discover ways of significantly enhancing and accelerating our responses to the changing, complex environments in which we live today. That is the goal of this book, to prepare leaders better for the life of continual learning and change that lies ahead.

The next chapter therefore presents the findings of the research that informs this book. It examines more closely what happens when people are required to learn in response to changes in their environment. It also reveals some of the psychological forces that can generate blind spots and resistance to change. Subsequent chapters will then develop ideas and strategies for mastering these dynamics.

2

A Model of Blind Spots, Learning and Change

'While I still hate to readjust my thinking, still hate to give up old ways of perceiving and conceptualizing, yet, at some deeper level, I have, to a considerable degree, come to realize that these painful reorganizations are what is known as learning, and that though painful, they always lead to a more satisfying, because somewhat more accurate, way of seeing life.'

Carl Rogers, *On Becoming A Person*

We have seen in the last chapter that blind spots are areas where we resist learning. Blind spots cause us to interpret cues around us in ways that preserve our existing ideas and behaviours and prevent us from adapting and learning.

Before we go into detail regarding the role of *leadership* blind spots, we need a model to help us understand the dynamics of learning and blind spots more generally. The research that underpins this book provides a model that reveals some of the dynamics of learning, blind spots and change. This chapter briefly summarizes the research and the learning model. Whilst we will not go into a lot of academic detail, this chapter will be more 'theoretical' than others in the book. Nevertheless, the model does provide a practical tool that in itself will help to overcome blind spots and accelerate learning. We will see why overcoming blind spots is a difficult and painful process, and why learning to learn (or learning agility) is a skill that requires conscious effort and ongoing support.

The chapter attempts to cover some complex ground as concisely as possible. To aid clarity, it has been divided into five parts:

- part one gives a brief overview of the research and how it was structured;

- part two offers the model of learning and blind spots that forms the basis of the eight learning practices;

- part three looks at the motivational forces that can either promote learning or generate blind spots;

- part four looks at different learning states, showing how the dynamics of learning and blind spots change according to the context and our state of mind;

- part five summarizes the key messages presented in the chapter.

1. The Research

The research that informs this book was undertaken to address the question of how people learn (or resist learning) when their organizations go through change. Kolb's learning theory, although still widely used in organizations, had come under criticism[1] and the research intended to re-examine the processes involved in experiential learning, particularly in the context of rapid organizational change.

---

[1] Holman, D., Pavlica, K. and Thorpe, R. (1997) 'Rethinking Kolb's Theory of Experiential Learning in Management Education. The Contribution of Social Constructionism and Activity Theory.' *Management Learning*, **28**(2), 135–148. Kayes, D. C. (2002) 'Experiential Learning and Its Critics: Preserving the Role of Experience in Management Learning and Education.' *Academy of Management Learning and Education*, **1**(2), 137–149. Nichol, B. (1997) 'Group Analytic Training for Management Trainers: Integrating the Emotional and Cognitive Dimensions of Management Learning.' *Management Learning*, **28**(3), 351–363. Reynolds, M. (1997) 'Learning Styles: A Critique.' *Managment Learning*, **28**(2), 115–134. Sadler-Smith, E., Allinson, C. W. and Hayes, J. (2000) 'Learning Preferences and Cognitive Style: Some Implications for Continuing Professional Development.' *Management Learning*, **31**(2), 239–256. Vince, R. (1998) 'Behind and Beyond Kolb's Learning Cycle.' *Journal of Management Education*, **22**(3), 304–320.

Two organizations, both of which were going through intensive culture change programmes, participated in the study. One was a scientific organization that had recently been privatized by the government (we shall call it Scientific Solutions). Staffed by PhDs and world-renowned experts, these professionals had to learn to compete in the private sector and to 'sell' their expertise. The MD, her senior team and a number of senior scientists and managers, totalling 13 people altogether, agreed to participate in the research.

The second organization was a logistics company, which stored and transported goods for clients all over the world (we shall call them Logical Logistics). The depot that agreed to participate was focused on one client in the retail trade delivering its goods to stores all over the country. Many of the staff employed at the depot had left school at 16 or 18 and had learned through experience at work. The General Manager was introducing a more team-oriented approach to management rather than the somewhat macho and bullying style that had existed before. The GM, members of the senior management team and a few middle managers, totalling nine altogether, all agreed to participate in the study.

The first stage of the research involved defining what was meant by learning. This was difficult, as there were almost as many definitions of learning as there were writers. The definition used drew on cognitive, behavioural, psycho-dynamic and humanist traditions in learning.[2] A distinction was made between learning as an output and

---

[2] For a detailed review of the literature, see Blakeley, K. (2005) *How Managers Learn When Their Organisations Go Through Change*, unpublished PhD Thesis, Brunel University. For a selection of readings, see:

Argyris, C. (1982) *Reasoning, Learning and Action: Individual and Organizational.* San Francisco: Jossey Bass Inc. De Board, R. (1978) *The Psychoanalysis of Organizations.* London: Tavistock/Routledge. Fineman, S. (1997) 'Emotion and Management Learning.' *Management Learning,* 28(1), 13–25. Friedlander, F. (1983) 'Patterns of Individual and Organizational Learning,' in S. Srivastva and Associates (Eds) *The Executive Mind: New Insights on Managerial Thought and Action.* San Francisco: Jossey Bass. Gardner, H. (1985) *The Mind's New Science.* New York: Basic Books. Gheradi, S. *et al.* (1998) 'Toward a Social Understanding of How People Learn in Organizations: The Notion of Situated Curriculum.' *Management Learning,* 29(3), 273–297. Goldstein, A. P. and Sorcher, M. (1974) *Changing Supervisor Behaviour.* New York: Pergamon Press. Herzberg, F. (1966) *Work and the Nature of Man.* New York: World Publishing Company.

learning as a process. Learning as output was defined as the generation of:

1. New or changed beliefs, constructs or schemas (including self concept).

2. New or changed emotional orientations towards people (including self), events and phenomena.[3]

3. New or changed behaviours.

It is not intended to suggest that it is either possible or desirable to separate these elements. Nevertheless, the definition provides three different lenses and three sets of conceptual tools through which to view learning – cognitive, emotional and behavioural.[4] Having identified what we meant by learning as an *output*, attention was focused on what learning *processes* generated these outputs. A trawl through the learning literature revealed over 25 learning processes currently in use, including experiential learning (on-the-job), coaching, vicarious learning (learning by observing others), declarative learning (formal, study-based learning), reflection, double-loop learning, etc.

MacDonald, S. (1995) 'Learning to Change: An Information Perspective on Learning in the Organization.' *Organization Science*, 6(5), 557–568. McGregor, D. (1960) *The Human Side of Enterprise*. New York: McGraw Hill. Mezirow, J. and Associates (1990) *Fostering Critical Reflection in Adulthood: A Guide to Transformative and Emancipatory Learning*. San Francisco: Jossey Bass. Nichol, B. (1997) 'Group Analytic Training for Management Trainers: Integrating the Emotional and Cognitive Dimensions of Management Learning.' *Management Learning*, 28(3), 351–363. Pedlar, M., Boydell, T. and Burgoyne, J. (1989) 'Towards the Learning Company.' *Management Education and Development*, 20(1), 1–8. Revans, R. (1982) *The Origins and Growth of Action Learning*. Chartwell-Bratt. Weick, K. E. (1995) *Sensemaking in Organizations*. Thousand Oaks, CA: Sage. Wenger, E. (1991) 'Communities of Practice: Where Learning Happens,' in R. E. White *et al.* (Eds) *Learning Within Organizations*, Western Business School, University of Western Ontario, Ontario, pp. 25–41. White, R. E., Crossan, M. M. and Lane, H. W. (1994) *Learning Within Organizations*. Western Business School, London, Canada.

[3] The term *emotional orientation* was used to refer to the emotions aroused by a cue. A cue can be a person, event or other phenomenon. We do not refer to attitudes in this model, as attitudes are commonly defined as a mixture of emotional orientation *and* beliefs in relation to a cue. This research attempted to differentiate between the cognitive and emotional elements of an attitude.

[4] The separation also acknowledges that there have, in the past, been distinct sets of literature that have informed our understanding of learning, each with its own useful set of concepts and tools.

However, many of the processes were similar (e.g. learning that causes a profound change in one's beliefs and/or assumptions is variously referred to as transformational learning, double-loop learning or generative learning). To avoid this kind of repetition, a core set of 15 different processes was identified.[5]

The research itself was conducted over the period of a year. Participants were interviewed at the beginning of the year using a semi-structured interview format. They were asked about their beliefs and feelings about their roles, the organization, the people they worked with and the changes being introduced. Throughout the year, participants completed learning diaries once a month in which they wrote down their thoughts, feelings and behavioural responses to events as they occurred. Finally, participants were interviewed at the end of the year when they were asked to describe their learning over the period. They were also asked the same questions as in the first interview, in order to track any changes in their responses. In addition, participants sought feedback from their colleagues at the end of the year. This was designed to gain an insight into what changes had been noticed by colleagues, bosses and direct reports regarding their behaviour, emotions and thinking over the year.

Using the interviews, diaries and feedback, learning outcomes were identified for each participant at the end of the year. Having identified the learning outcomes, it was possible to identify the 'story' behind each participant's learning by tracking back all the relevant references in the diaries. It was also possible to note the individual's blind spots or areas where they did not learn. Using the diaries it was often possible to see where areas of potential learning came to participants' attention but were not engaged with. In fact, the diaries provided useful evidence of how we repress, distort, dismiss or fail to notice ideas and information that could potentially generate significant and much needed learning. We will see evidence of this later in this chapter.

---

[5] These were as follows: declarative learning, discursive learning, emotional learning, practical or procedural learning, learning through coaching, experimental learning, imaginative learning, learning through feedback, reflection, rehearsal, training, vicarious learning, comparative learning and tacit learning.

2. A Model of Learning

From this research came a model of learning that focused on four key processes. The first process was that of *paying attention* to a cue. It was noticeable that every diarist was paying attention to a unique set of cues. There were only two incidents in each organization that were mentioned by more than two diarists over the whole year. All the other incidents were highly personal and idiosyncratic. This prompted the question: what leads people to attend to one issue and ignore others? Why do people 'select' certain events to learn from and not others?

The role of attention was central to the learning journey, and this was supported by much of the literature in cognitive, clinical and social psychology.[6] In order to learn from an event, attention must be paid to it; blind spots emerge when we do not pay attention to information or ideas that are relevant to our concerns.

Having noted the importance of 'attention' for learning, the learning biographies were then compared in order to determine any patterns regarding the types of learning processes that generated different learning outcomes. It was found that out of all the learning outcomes examined, only two learning processes were found in ALL examples of learning. These two processes were *emotional learning* and *sensemaking*.

Emotional learning is defined as the experience of new or different emotions in relation to a cue that are processed in a way that leads to changes in behaviour, emotional orientation or belief.

Originally the term *reflection* was used rather than sensemaking. Reflection is probably the most recognized and discussed of all the learning processes. However, this did not seem to capture fully the processes of analysis and thinking that were taking place in the diaries and interviews. Reflection implies looking back and

---

[6] Eysenck, M. W. and Keane, M. T. (1990) *Cognitive Psychology, A Student's Handbook.* Hove, UK: Lawrence Erlbaum Associates. Fiske, S. T. and Taylor, S. (1991) *Social Cognition*, second edition. Singapore: McGraw Hill. Naranjo, C. (1993) *Gestalt Therapy: The Attitude and Practice of an Atheoretical Experientialism.* Bancyfelin, Wales: Crown House Publishing.

reinterpreting past events, but people's thinking was just as much focused on the future. Much of people's thinking was devoted to understanding what was happening to them now in order to guide their actions in the future. *Sensemaking* rather than 'reflection' seemed to capture better what was going on. Sensemaking was defined as: 'the process of constructing, reconstructing and deconstructing meaning around cues, their implications and consequences in a way that led to new or changed beliefs, emotional orientations or behaviours.'[7]

So far then, learning seemed to constitute *paying attention* to a cue, *experiencing an emotion* in relation to it and *making sense* of it (not necessarily in that order). As a definition of the learning process, this seemed incomplete without the inclusion of a behavioural element. However, new or changed behaviours did not take place in every example of learning. In some cases there was a conscious decision *not* to change behaviour. Nevertheless, changing behaviour is a vital part of learning, even if it does not always occur. So it was included as one of the core learning processes. In doing so, it was not intended to imply that behavioural change always took place. Behavioural change *often* took place, and whether it did or did not, the behavioural outcome of any learning was intimately linked to the other three processes. In other words, behaviour change does not emerge from nowhere, but is based on prior changes in attention, emotion and/or sensemaking.

We could represent these processes as a cycle, as shown in Figure 2.1. The arrows indicate that these processes can occur in any order – emotion can lead to attention can lead to sensemaking which leads to action which leads to emotion.

This model also raises the important question of what differentiates a cycle that leads to learning from one that does not? Just because we pay attention to something, experience an emotion, make sense of it and act on our interpretation, this does not necessarily generate learning. For example, someone might suggest that Jim's presentation skills are not as polished as they could be – he needs to be clearer in his delivery. Jim feels intense irritation at the feedback and

---

[7] The term *sensemaking* has been popularized by Karl E. Weick in his brilliant book *Sensemaking in Organizations* (1995). Thousand Oaks CA: Sage.

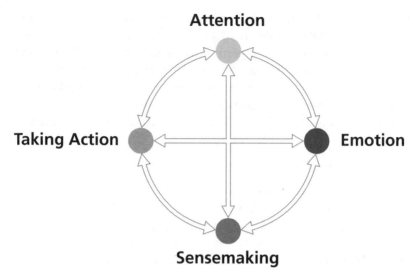

Figure 2.1   Four learning processes.

makes sense of it by using an old belief – claiming that the individual who gave the feedback knows nothing about presentation
skills and simply wants to undermine his confidence. Jim then
acts on this interpretation by carrying on as normal. As a result, he
does not learn, as there are *no learning outcomes*. If this pattern
continues, we can say that Jim has developed a blind spot in this
area.

However, if Jim pays attention to the feedback, managing his irritation, facing his feelings of vulnerability and changing his behaviour
as a result, he will have learned. His changed behaviour and more
effective delivery would be evidence of a learning outcome.

So what is different about the processes in the first example, where
blind spots block the learning, and the second, where learning is in
evidence? In the first example, Jim is simply *processing information*
based upon previous beliefs, emotional orientations and behaviours.
In other words, he is drawing on his *living knowledge*. Living knowledge is a key construct in our model of learning. It represents our
personal understanding of reality. It is what we 'know' (beliefs, ideas
and schemas), what we feel (emotional orientations towards objects,
events or people) and what we do (behaviours that we believe 'work',
enabling us to meet our needs in the world). It accumulates over time

and we develop and change it through our personal experience. Although living knowledge is a highly personal combination of beliefs, feelings and behaviours rooted in our individual experience, we tend to see it as *truth*. When we draw on our existing store of living knowledge, processing information already stored in memory, it is a relatively easy and spontaneous process.

Learning, however, is more difficult and arduous. Our second example shows Jim when he is in learning mode. He has paid attention, processed his emotions, made sense and acted in a way that has generated a learning output and grown his living knowledge. However, this process has been more painful, challenging and slow. We can contrast information processing with learning as follows.

The four processes involved in information processing are:

- *attention*: automatically attending to whatever appears in our consciousness;
- *emotions*: experiencing or noticing familiar emotions;
- *sensemaking*: making sense using existing constructs;
- *behaving*: acting automatically using our existing behavioural repertoire.

The four processes involved in learning are:

- *attention*: changing our attention patterns, noticing new or different cues;
- *emotions*: focusing on and exploring new or unprocessed/unexplained emotions;
- *sensemaking*: using new constructs or adapting existing constructs to make new meaning;
- *behaving*: experimenting with new or changed behaviours.

We can represent the activities of information processing and learning as a cycle, as shown in Figure 2.2. The diagram is intended to show the information processing cycle in the middle and the learning cycle on the outside. When we make sense of our experience using our existing living knowledge, we are processing

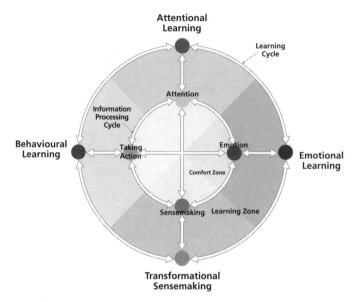

Figure 2.2   Information processing and learning.

information and no change or learning takes place. This is the tempting region known as the *comfort zone*!

Once we move outside the comfort zone, we start to learn. It is only when we step outside the comfort zone that we begin to develop new constructs, emotional orientations and behaviours, introducing the potential for more complexity and flexibility in our responses to change. This is identified on the diagram as *attentional learning, emotional learning, transformational sensemaking* and *behavioural learning*.

This notion of *dual processing* (effortful vs effortless processing) is common in the cognitive and social psychology literature.[8] It is widely recognized that using our existing living knowledge involves effortless, automatic processing that enables us to cope with many

---

[8] See, for example, Brewer, M. (1988) 'A Dual Process Model of Impression Formation', in T. Srull and R. Wyer (Eds) *Advances in Social Cognition*, Vol. 1, Hillsdale, NJ: Erlbaum and Associates. Louis, M. R. and Sutton, R. I. (1999) 'Switching Cognitive Gears: From Habits of Mind to Active Thinking.' *Human Relations*, **44**(1). Lord, R. G. and Foti, R. J. (1986) 'Schema Theories, Information Processing, and Organizational Behaviour', in H. P. Sims, D. A. Gioia and associates, *The Thinking Organization: Dynamics of Organizational Social Cognition.* San Francisco; Jossey Bass, pp. 49–74.

tasks simultaneously. Learning involves making sense of cues in a way that generates expanded living knowledge and is more difficult, slow and energy-absorbing.

Hence, our definition of the learning process would be:

> Paying attention, processing emotions, making sense and taking action so that new or changed constructs, beliefs, emotional orientations and/or behaviours are generated.

Blind spots emerge when, having been exposed to significant new information or ideas, we decide to go into *information processing mode* instead of taking the opportunity to *learn*. We interpret cues (or repress, ignore or dismiss them) in order to preserve existing constructs, emotional orientations and behaviours. This enables us to stay inside our comfort zone rather than engaging in the more difficult task of learning. As noted in the Carl Rogers quote at the beginning of the chapter, a lot of learning involves pain. Blind spots protect us from the pain of learning. We shall explore this idea further in part three.

3. The Drivers of Learning and Blind Spots

The diaries showed that learning (as opposed to information processing) often involves some psychological pain or discomfort. The greater the degree of learning, the greater the emotional intensity and, often, pain. This is particularly the case when learning involves changing our beliefs, emotional orientations or behaviours as opposed to simply adding new ones. When we go on holiday to a new country, for example, we add lots of new constructs regarding the culture and people of that country. This form of *incremental* learning is, in most cases, pleasurable. We add new constructs without challenging existing aspects of our living knowledge.

However, learning that involves change or that challenges existing beliefs, emotional orientations or behaviours is often painful. Whilst this kind of learning can involve positive emotions such as excitement, optimism and hope, there is always discomfort of some kind. Giving up old beliefs, existing values, comfortable behaviours and challenging deep-rooted feelings is anxiety-provoking. Even in the most positive of cases, when people willingly take on learning, there is always some anxiety or uncertainty.

We can see this very clearly if we look at the experiences of the diarists whose learning informed the research for this book. Even the diarists who enjoyed learning (and there weren't many!) experienced doubts and anxieties regarding their ability to come through it. The following are typical examples of how the diarists described their experience of learning:

> '*I've gone through a change process, but a painful one, because I started to doubt myself. It wasn't just "oh right," like that, it was very much . . . there were 3 or 4 weeks where I felt so low. It's like your comfort factor, you have a comfort factor which is your baseline of the way that you operate, and if you can imagine that being smashed and you're falling through, you're trying to grab hold of something, and partly it took a while to get used to where I was, and what I felt comfortable with.*'

> '*All this has resulted in me not achieving very much at work, feeling pretty unbalanced and unstable about everything in my "career" and self esteem. I've lost sight of what I'm good at, what value I can bring and going through a period of not believing it, even when I can see it.*'

> '*(doing the diaries) made me more depressed . . . because you fill it in and you think, well this is whatever I did, what have I achieved over the last month? I'm doing nothing really, I mean, OK I was occasionally finishing a job and writing a report, but I didn't feel it was very satisfying. So as a learning thing, it just makes you reflect on what you're doing and, as I say, that can be depressing.*'

Even when people were extremely positive about their learning, their diaries were full of ups and downs, frustrations and setbacks, anxieties and uncertainties.

Mike talks about the links between excitement and fear of failure:

'developing new business – quite a personal responsibility. A good deal of learning what/how to make things happen. The excitement of learning/developing something new is tempered with the small risk of failure (although this is only in the background).'

One diarist gained hugely in confidence over the period, but the experience was not always enjoyable:

'I think I'm quite pleased that I didn't bottle it really, in some ways. I think having survived the last six months, I feel much more confident in myself and that terrible situation, because that's really awful, but just sticking there, and I made one or two decisions that were OK and came out all right, but that just gave me a bit more confidence.'

As people revealed their experiences of learning and change in the diaries, it became more and more obvious that learning was not a comfortable process.[9] Information processing was altogether less effortful, less painful and less frightening than learning. When we process information in an effortless manner using our existing living knowledge, we experience anything from a mild satisfaction to an intense feeling of mastery and control. Learning entails examining difficult emotions; it involves paying attention to anxiety-provoking problems; it demands that we question our ideas and everything we have known; it necessitates experimenting with new behaviours. Learning involves losing control, accepting uncertainty and embracing risk. It is the temptation to revert to information processing, rather than engaging with learning, that leads to blind spots.

So why bother? What makes us invest our energy in learning and willingly undertake the emotional discomfort that learning entails?

---

[9] There are, of course, different types of learning. Incremental learning, for example, occurs when you add new constructs to your existing mental models in a way that does not challenge existing beliefs. This happens when you go on holiday and 'learn' new facts about a country. In this book, the pain associated with learning almost always derives from people having to *change, challenge* or *test* aspects of their existing living knowledge.

Four Drivers of Our Learning and Blind Spots

The diarists revealed some interesting answers to this question. An analysis was conducted of the main areas (or *learning domains*) in which people focused their learning, showing a remarkable degree of commonality. The analysis revealed four main drivers of people's attention and learning:

1. *Self esteem* – preserving, protecting and enhancing my self esteem.

2. *Psychological comfort* – the drive to achieve emotional wellbeing and psychological comfort. This also includes the drive to meet my underlying 'needs' such as 'being liked', 'gaining influence', 'developing my expertise', 'helping others'. It is when we are meeting our underlying needs that we feel most fulfilled and comfortable.

3. *Goals* – achieving my goals, often by understanding 'what works' in the world.

4. *Values* – affirming and protecting my values in the world.

The role of these drivers in learning has been noted by many other academics and practitioners in the area of adult experiential learning.[10] However, it is worth stressing the point that people are more likely to engage in learning if, in doing so, they see the likelihood of achieving any of the above outcomes. If learning appears to compromise any of

---

[10] Weick (1995) quotes Erez and Earley, who maintain that three needs crucially influence a person's sense of identity: (1) the need for self-enhancement (maintaining a positive cognitive and emotional orientation towards the self); (2) the self-efficacy motive (the desire to perceive oneself as competent and efficacious); and (3) the need for self-consistency (the desire to sense and experience coherence and continuity). They claim that these needs influence the nature and outcome of learning and sensemaking in organizations (see Weick, K. E. (1995) *Sensemaking in Organizations*. Thousand Oaks CA: Sage, p. 20).

Vince (1996, 'Experiential Management Education as the Practice of Change' in R. French and C. Grey (Eds), *Rethinking Management Education*. London: Sage) quotes Claxton's four personal defence systems: 'I must be *Competent*, I must be *Consistent*, I must be *In control*, I must be *Comfortable*'.

Argyris (1976) maintains that single-loop learning is governed by four variables: (1) achieve the purpose as the actor defines it; (2) win, do not lose; (3) suppress negative feelings; (4) emphasize rationality.

these areas, there is a higher likelihood that there will be a reversion to information processing and blind spots. Learning often emerged through a stop–start process driven by hope that these outcomes would be achieved and blocked by fear that these outcomes would be jeopardized. Only when the benefits seemed to outweigh the risks would it be engaged with, as we shall see in the examples below.[11]

These four drivers do not necessarily operate in alignment. Learning may involve the achievement of our goals but also risk our self esteem and our psychological comfort. Often, our learning is difficult because we have to make choices between these desired states. On the one hand, if we want to achieve our goal of career progression, we may have to take on a difficult assignment. This might jeopardize our self esteem or psychological comfort. It may also threaten our values around work/life balance. However, we weigh up the various incentives and risks and take a judgement according to the strength of our various goals, needs and desires.

There is an astonishing degree of overlap in these categories, both in terms of content but also in terms of the *number* of influencing variables that appear to be important (i.e. three or four):

This research	*Claxton*	*Erez and Earley*	*Argyris*
Goals	I must be in control	Self efficacy	Achieve the purpose as the actor defines it
Self esteem	I must be competent	Self enhancement Self efficacy	Win, don't lose
Psychological comfort	I must be comfortable	Self consistency	Suppress negative feelings
Values	I must be consistent	Self consistency	Emphasize rationality

[11] Argyris makes the following point: 'One might say that participants in organizations are encouraged to learn to perform as long as the learning does not question the fundamental design, goals and activities of their organizations. This may be called single-loop learning . . . Furthermore, most groups and organizations studied in their usual settings permit only single-loop learning. Recent research on individual adult learning suggests that human beings are also acculturated to be primarily single-loop learners in dealing with other human beings and with substantive controversial issues (Argyris and Schon, 1974)'. See Argyris, C. (1976) 'Single Loop and Double Loop Models in Research on Decision Making.' *Administrative Science Quarterly*, **21**, 363–375.

These four drivers are always operating throughout the learning process. They influence what we engage with and what we avoid – driving both our learning and our blind spots.

The effect of these drivers is best illustrated through some examples.

Self Esteem

It is well known that self esteem plays an important role in our learning.[12] So, too, does our self concept – we will tend to be more receptive to learning that boosts our self esteem and reinforces or promotes our self concept. Our self esteem is founded on at least three fundamental needs:

- the need to feel respected and valued by those around us;

- the need to feel competent and in control;

- the need to feel liked and accepted.

When information presents itself that supports these needs, we feel like we're on cloud nine! We are highly receptive, as one diarist shows:

> '*I took my CV along and I was absolutely knocked over by the response I got, because I expected to get some – "yes, we're very interested, we'll put it through the process and we'll see," but I got a very "wow, gosh we're desperate for people with these sorts of skills and these sorts of qualifications." So from feeling undervalued by Scientific Solutions, I suddenly saw the contrast between the way I seem to be valued outside and I got offered interviews for all three jobs.*'

---

[12] See, for example: Argyris, C. (1976) 'Single Loop and Double Loop Models in Research on Decision Making.' *Administrative Science Quarterly*, **21**, 363–375. Kelly, G. A. (1955) *The Psychology of Personal Constructs*. New York. Norton. Vince, R. and Saleem, T. (2004) 'The Impact of Caution and Blame on Organizational Learning.' *Management Learning*, **35**(2), 133–154. Harmon-Jones, E. and Mills, J. (1999) *Cognitive Dissonance – progress on a pivotal theory in social psychology*. New York: American Psychological Association. Brown, A. D. and Starkey, K. (2000) 'Organizational Identity and Learning: A Psychodynamic Perspective.' *Academy of Management Review*, **25**(1), 102–120.

However, when we receive information that challenges our self esteem, our blind spots tend to emerge and we are less receptive to learning, as demonstrated by the following diarists:

> '*It was implied that one of my projects was £10k overspent, but I do not believe it.*'

> '*Was slightly disappointed by the subordinates' results on the feedback. Reflected on this a little and came to the conclusion that because of the differences in the way people score, I couldn't actually read an awful lot into the results anyway.*'

An interesting example of how self esteem relates to learning came from a project manager whose project went disastrously wrong. In the immediate aftermath of the painful experience, the manager claimed:

> '*Got the report out just in time. There are lots of lessons to be learned from this but they are mostly on the contractual side. **I don't think Graham or myself could have done things much differently.** Of all the jobs I've ever worked on with SS, I've found this to be the most frustrating and probably the least enjoyable.*' (my emphasis)

So, no conscious learning has taken place at this point; the diarist has attributed the cause of the problem to extraneous factors outside himself. No new insights into how he might change as a result of this project have been derived. The diarist has reverted to information processing – making sense of the event in a way that preserves existing constructs, emotional orientations and behaviours. At this point we might observe a blind spot emerging.

However, the manager's emotions bubble away under the surface and he continues to 'fret' on his experience. Rather than burying his emotions, he tries to make sense of what happened as a way of processing and addressing the painful emotions he continues to experience. Eventually, after approximately six months, when the pain has died down, he admits:

> '*I think there is a tendency with projects to, if things start to go wrong, to sort of . . . it's almost burying your head in the sand, there*

is a tendency to try to beaver away and think "well, if I just do some extra hours on this, we'll turn it round and we'll get it right," and I think that's wrong, because one of the lessons from this is that once you start to overspend on a project, you never ever recover it. You might think you've got other tasks where you can recover the overspend on an early task, but it just doesn't work like that.'

So, his initial sensemaking around the event (there was nothing he could have done differently) was inaccurate, serving to prop up his self esteem rather than identify the 'truth' of the matter. This could only be done once the initial pain had died down. In fact, the diarist subsequently gave a presentation to his colleagues on what he should have done to avoid the project failure and the lessons he learned.

It must be said that it takes courage to learn from these kinds of painful experiences. As we saw, the immediate impulse is to make sense of the event in a way that preserves self esteem ('we couldn't have done anything differently'). There were plenty of examples where the diarists did not go beyond this kind of self-preserving sensemaking, continuing to maintain that the problems were not of their making. These examples provided important data on how blind spots emerged and were sustained.

Psychological Comfort

We all want to be happy. At a more mundane level, most of us would prefer to be comfortable than unhappy, frustrated, angry or anxious. The need to achieve psychological comfort drives both learning and blind spots. A good example of the complexity of this dynamic is given to us by a diarist:

*'I'd been feeling [unhappy] for a long time, but I suppose I eventually started thinking, well look, the original plan was always, to say, "right I'm not happy in this job, I'm going to look for another one." But once I'd left this place in the evening or for the weekend, I'm one of these people that can switch off completely. **Now if this seeming overwhelming uncomfortableness came with me when I***

***did leave in the evening, then maybe I would have done
something about it in the evening or at the weekend, but
I didn't, because once I'd left this place, I no longer had
that overwhelming motivation to do something about it,***
*and so that's why, for quite a long time, I had lots of other things on
that were higher priority in the short term.'* (my emphasis)

This diarist makes it quite clear that he was prepared to tolerate a
high degree of unhappiness at work simply because he could 'switch
off' once he got home. The motivation to make sense of the discomfort, face it and act comes from the strength, duration and *intrusion*
of the 'uncomfortableness' (does it affect life outside work? Is it
transitory? Can I live with it?). There was also a subconscious
dimension playing on this diarist's mind. Will I be even more uncomfortable if I face the problem? Will it involve more pain and more
uncertainty than simply putting up with the discomfort at work? He
decided to put up with the discomfort at work rather than face more
uncertainty by addressing it.

The drive for psychological comfort operates in many ways. When we
are experiencing high levels of pain at work, we may engage in high
levels of learning and pain in order to relieve it. However, sometimes
we may make an unconscious assessment that it is better to put up
with the current, 'known' pain to avoid the future, 'unknown' pain.
Uncertainty comprises psychological pain in and of itself.

On the other hand, if we are comfortable, we may simply dismiss
information that introduces discomfort. Beyond this, boredom comprises an excess of comfort and may well spur learning as we seek
emotional arousal and excitement.

The diarist above sensed that a lot of uncertainty would result if he
faced his pain. In fact he was correct. When he did engage with the
learning, he decided that having spent his whole career with the
organization, he would leave to consider new career paths.

What helped him to overcome his blind spot and face the learning?
He received some feedback that provided a considerable boost to
his self esteem and through some coaching, he generated a new
interpretation that enabled him to move forward. He realized that

the reason he was not enjoying his job was because it did not allow him to use his strengths – as opposed to concluding that it was because he was not good at his job (which was what he was fearful of facing).

Blind spots can perform the useful function of temporarily protecting us from difficult learning at a time when we lack the resilience to cope with it. The diarists were often able to face learning only after they had experienced a significant boost to their self esteem. This provided the resilience to overcome their blind spots and expand their living knowledge.

Goals

One of the diarists working for Scientific Solutions embraced the need to 'sell' enthusiastically. Greg's learning was fully focused on how to develop his selling skills and to develop relationships with customers. His diaries were full of minute descriptions of client meetings, business breakfasts and presentations made to clients. His learning was immense during the period, though not without its anxieties. However, during the middle of the year, he received some feedback from his team. The feedback indicated that he was not helping or managing them enough. They were finding the selling difficult and they needed his help. They felt lost and directionless.

Greg acknowledged the feedback, though made sense of it through the filter of *his own* values and goals. He claimed that they were intelligent, independent professionals and did not really need his help! This tendency to interpret new and potentially difficult information in a way that preserves existing constructs indicated a possible blind spot. However, he did make a resolution to change his behaviour.

By the end of the year he had made great strides in terms of his marketing and business development. His manager made the comment:

> '*he's grown, I think hugely, as an individual writing about this particular product, delivering conferences, articles and editorials in all the top magazines, and he's a known national figure now.*'

However, according to one member of his team:

'*I don't think Greg has changed a great deal over the year.*'

It was clear throughout the diaries that Greg's attention was focused on his expressed goal of growing his business and developing his marketing skills. Despite getting feedback that his people wanted him to manage and support them more, and despite his resolution to do this, it did not happen. This was clearly a behavioural blind spot for Greg. What did Greg say?

'*you're always juggling the balls aren't you, and thinking "am I giving this one enough attention or not?" and, I suppose there's never enough time to give them all as much attention as you'd like, so you have to make a decision as to how much really. I could probably have spent a bit more time, but it's tricky, knowing how worthwhile it is, some people don't want it.*'

Developing his team was not really a goal that Greg was deeply committed to – whether consciously or not. Greg devoted his year to his motivational goal of growing his business and developing his own selling abilities. Anything else was secondary. Greg gives us a good example of how commitment to a goal can generate profound learning. But he also shows how we will avoid learning in areas that we are not deeply committed to, regardless of how much other people need us to. Goals can generate both learning and blind spots. They can narrow our attention and may cause us to dismiss cues that do not seem relevant or helpful to their achievement.

Values

It is very common during change for people's values to be challenged. If you are a scientist and you believe that you are working for the good of society, or you are developing innovatory products that will help others, the introduction of the profit motive and the imperative to 'sell' (especially to sell services that do not meet your own high technical specifications) can undermine everything that you believe in and represent. It can also force you to adopt behaviours that you dislike and do not connect to emotionally, whilst

jettisoning behaviours that you value and are skilled in applying. If
you are a manager with strong beliefs about how people should be
treated, you may come across situations where you have to compromise your values if you want to 'get to the top' and 'keep in with
the boss'. In all these cases, uncomfortable emotions will be triggered that will either lead to a learning response or to a blind spot.
The following excerpts from the diaries show how 'values' surface
during learning:

> *'The hazard analysis in the report demonstrated a much higher risk
> than they wanted, so they've altered the results to suit themselves. I
> am disgusted . . . Quite clearly they don't give a shit about the health
> and safety of their workforce. Spoke to people here about it and it
> appears this isn't the first time this has happened. I have refused to
> work on any more of their projects. There is (to me anyway) such
> a thing as professional integrity.'*

> *'I had a stage when I first got married I looked to leave, because I
> was being made to do things I wasn't comfortable with and I find
> that difficult . . . I found that very difficult to cope with, look I'm
> sorry Karen I'm going to give you a written warning, it's not my
> decision, it's his decision, I wouldn't give you a warning at all, and
> I was in the middle there, where I was like, "I don't want to do this
> decision but they're telling me I've got to do it." . . .* **It's hard to
> take a decision I'm not happy with, it's that conscience
> thing.**' (my emphasis)

> *'Felt more as if I should be on E's side rather than F . . .* **Felt
> slightly uncomfortable (a bit disloyal to F as if I was mani-
> pulating him a bit** – *but not significant).'* (my emphasis)

> *'my initial reaction was "how," excuse my French, "how f***ing
> presumptuous" . . . what they've done is taken what their values
> are . . . to being values that I might have, without bothering to actu-
> ally question or ask what it was that made me tick and what I
> actually liked doing.'*

Whenever our values are challenged, we experience discomfort.
We then have a choice. Do we bury the discomfort and make sense

of the situation in a way that makes us feel good (generating a blind spot), or do we explore the discomfort and enter on a learning journey where the outcome is unknown and uncertain? If we choose the latter, we tend to go into a deeper sensemaking mode, asking 'is this right?', 'is this what I want?', 'why are they doing this?' When our values are challenged on an ongoing basis, we can end up by asking profound questions that can result in a rapid expansion in our living knowledge, generating deep, personal change. Values are complex and, as a result, Chapter 10 is devoted to a detailed examination of their role in promoting learning.

4. Three Learning States

This section focuses on how different moods or states of mind affect the dynamics described above. Different *learning states* influence the extent and nature of the learning that is undertaken and the types of blind spots that are experienced. Three different learning states are described: *visionary*, *adaptive* and *dissonant*. There are other learning states but these did not emerge initially from the research.

If we are in a *visionary* learning state (wanting to change the world in line with our vision), we tend to take more risks with our learning – we are excited, passionate, committed and will absorb any learning that would appear to help achieve our aim.

Leaders of change often find themselves in a visionary learning state. They have drawn up a vision for the future; they have a sense of optimism and feel that they have a personal role to play in the achievement of the vision. A lot of prior learning will have fed into the crafting of the vision – leaders will have previously challenged many assumptions and considered lots of new ideas, so the vision will embody many of their personal beliefs and passions. As a result, their self esteem, their personal goals, their psychological comfort and their values are all in alignment with their vision. Achieving their vision will enable them to meet these needs, so they are excited, motivated and driven. They are prepared to take on risks; they tolerate a lot of the discomfort and pain of learning because of the anticipated rewards (success of their goals, enhanced self esteem, the realization of their values and the meeting of needs such as status, achievement or recognition).

However, as we saw in the last chapter, visionary learning is often accompanied by visionary blind spots. Visionaries tend to narrow their attention onto those phenomena that appear relevant (and in many cases, supportive) to their visions. They can be impatient, dismissive and intolerant of information or ideas that appear to question or challenge the vision. Ideas or questions that appear to complicate the goals can be dismissed, and the people who raise them can be regarded as 'resistant to change'. We will see further examples of this in the next chapter.

If we are not leading change but having to adapt to changes being implemented around us, we may get into a slightly cautious, *adaptive* learning state. This is when we may be willing to learn but we want to be in control and limit the possibility of failure. We will experiment cautiously, carefully limiting the risk. We will learn and take risks for as long as we feel in control and as long as we feel the benefits outweigh the cost. We will be aware of the risks to our self esteem (personal failure), to our values (unsure of whether the new approaches will involve sacrificing what we believe is important), to our psychological comfort (will we be able to meet our needs for respect, liking, influence, status, etc?) and to our personal goals. Nevertheless, we will be prepared to take on the goals of the new learning as long as we are supported by our managers and colleagues, and our self esteem is not allowed to fall to unacceptable levels.

When we are in an adaptive learning state we are stepping outside the comfort zone and cautiously experimenting with new approaches and ways of seeing the world. Anxiety and confidence are evenly balanced – we feel in control, but only just. This means that our blind spots will tend to resist anything that pushes us further into the learning zone or that further challenges our sense of control. Anything that is experienced as too radical, too fast or too challenging will tend to be resisted. Control, caution and implementing small experiments to see what works are the hallmarks of the adaptive state of mind.

Sometimes, however, we can feel downright depressed and devalued by the new learning environment. Change introduces new values, new challenges and new uncertainties; it reduces our ability to take control, and suddenly we find that our living knowledge no longer works. This environment introduces intense dissonance in the learner – and dissonance is a well-documented state of learning.[13]

Cognitive dissonance theory suggests that when we encounter information that contradicts or challenges our existing beliefs, we are thrust into a tense, dissonant state of mind. This is psychologically uncomfortable and we will be motivated to reduce the dissonance by making sense of the situation in a way that reintroduces harmony in our beliefs and behaviour. We might do this by avoiding the new information or by changing our existing beliefs to support the new information. However, certain beliefs are highly resistant to change – e.g. those that appear supported by 'reality' or those that are in alignment with many of our other beliefs. Beliefs that appear core to our sense of identity are also highly resistant to change.[14] If the new information is too challenging, we have a strong tendency to distort it in order to preserve our existing, core beliefs.

Situations of intense change, particularly those introducing new values, can have a strongly dissonant effect on organizational members. Change that introduces new beliefs around what is effective, valued, competent and morally worthwhile strongly challenges existing beliefs that are highly resistant to change – beliefs around self concept, self esteem and personal values. Organizational members are thrown into turmoil as they are forced to re-examine deeply held assumptions affecting their personal identity. Their living knowledge no longer 'works' in this new environment, so, despite seeking support for their existing beliefs and behaviours, reality continuously disconfirms them. People's values and self

---

[13] Harmon-Jones, E. and Mills, J. (1999) *Cognitive Dissonance – progress on a pivotal theory in social psychology*. New York: American Psychological Association.

[14] For a detailed explanation of how and why certain constructs are more permeable and amenable to change, see Kelly, G. A. (1963) *A Theory of Personality: The Psychology of Personal Constructs*. New York: Norton.

esteem are undermined, causing many to lose confidence in themselves and their abilities. This *dissonant* learning state is full of anger, frustration, fear and anxiety. People are thrust into sensemaking mode but instinctively seek to confirm their old values and assumptions, rationalizing why the new values and beliefs are 'wrong'.

However, in order to get rid of the dissonance, the learner may eventually engage fully and deeply with the learning. This often entails quite radical change, involving the answers to questions such as 'who am I?', 'what do I want?', 'how can I achieve real happiness?', 'what's truly important to me?' At this point, when the learner fully engages with the learning, we often see radical changes in behaviour – people in the study left organizations they had been with for over 20 years, one took a year's sabbatical and one completely changed career.

Blind spots that characterize the dissonant learning state include the refusal to engage with any of the learning required – the situation is already too painful and people's self esteem is already extremely low. There is a strong tendency towards denial and withdrawal, aggression and cynicism – all being hallmarks of the dissonant learning state. This state is often characterized as being 'resistant to change'.

There are, of course, other learning states which did not emerge from the research. For example, Csikszentmihalyi[15] refers to a state of *flow*, where, after a period of intense practice and engagement, you suddenly and briefly find that your performance reaches a peak, time seems to stand still and, despite achieving extreme levels of performance, everything feels effortless. Flow situations are those in which attention is freed to achieve your goals; there is no anxiety or fear of failure. You lose awareness of time, of yourself and of anything apart from the task at hand. You are totally focused, in control and experiencing the joy that comes with a sense that you are freely expressing yourself and your talents. Flow is experienced when pursuing a challenge that is personally meaningful and completely engaging.

---

[15] Csikszentmihalyi, M. (1990) *Flow: The Psychology of Optimal Experience.* New York: HarperCollins.

Another learning state is a reflective, almost meditative, state, referred to by Senge, Scharmer, Jaworski and Flowers as *suspension*.[16] The importance of 'reflection' in learning has long been recognized, but these authors take it a step further. Suspension requires an ability to empty one's mind and 'observe' one's own assumptions. It is a state in which one aspires to 'let go' of what one thinks one knows in order to achieve a meta-awareness of one's own 'living knowledge' – its strengths and its limitations. This state of mind is promoted as a source of enlightenment by the meditative traditions of the world's great religions.

Later in the book, we refer to the *generative* learning state. This is the playful, curious, experimental and open state of mind that is conducive to creativity and innovation.

Needless to say, it is difficult to achieve these states of mind when going through profound and difficult change. Flow, meditation and creativity are often rooted in a sense of calm, peace and openness, and these qualities have to be consciously worked at and cultivated. As a result, they did not emerge as significant factors in the research. We will refer to them, however, as we go through the eight practices.

5. Summary

Learning and blind spots are two sides of the same coin. We have seen that a lot of learning, especially during periods of intense change, involves psychological discomfort and pain. We have a choice – we can either engage with the learning or we can avoid it. If we avoid the learning, we avoid any immediate risk of pain and hide comfortably behind our blind spots. If we engage with the learning, we expand our living knowledge to embrace change and complexity.

It is more likely that we will engage with learning if we see the benefits. There is a payoff to the anxiety of learning if we achieve

---

[16] Senge, P., Scharmer, C. O., Jaworski, J. and Flowers, B. (2005). *Presence – exploring profound change in people, organizations and society*. London: Nicholas Brealey.

valued goals, increase our self esteem, increase psychological comfort or affirm our values. However, if we feel that any of these outcomes will be threatened, we are more tempted to avoid learning and revert to information processing – using our existing store of living knowledge to guide our thinking and actions in the situation. Blind spots occur when we revert to information processing when learning is the more appropriate response.

Our goals, values, self esteem needs and need for psychological comfort affect all four learning processes. They affect:

1. *What we pay attention to.* We 'see' things that are relevant to our goals and values; we often miss or dismiss things that appear irrelevant to them or which impede or complicate them.

2. *How we respond emotionally to events.* We respond with an array of emotions – elation, anger, anxiety or doubt – according to how an event impacts our goals, values, self esteem or psychological comfort. These emotions need to be faced and made sense of. However, if emotions are too intense or uncomfortable, we are tempted to avoid facing them.

3. *How we make sense of events.* We will tend to make sense of things in relation to how they affect our goals, values, self esteem or psychological comfort. Constructs that are central to these four areas are often more resistant to change.

4. *How we act.* We will adapt our behaviour to achieve these four valued outcomes, but will be wary of taking action if we feel they will be jeopardized.

Our tolerance of discomfort is also affected by our mood – a learner with a vision will take more risks than a cautious learner who is slowly learning to adapt to change. A learner in a strongly dissonant state – where their self esteem is dangerously low – may limit learning in order to preserve what little self esteem they have left.

This rather long chapter has attempted to explore some of the dynamics behind our learning and the development of our living knowledge. It is a simple but useful way of understanding what is happening when we learn and when we avoid learning. It also shows how our living knowledge is in fact 'created' by us as we travel through life. We often learn in order to fulfil deep-rooted needs, stay in control and feel comfortable. Some anxiety or frustration may be tolerated if the benefits are substantial. However, if we feel we will lose control or lose our sense of competence, we may well be tempted to avoid the learning. We will tend to learn what suits our goals and may be tempted to block out information, ideas, opinions and views that get in the way. We are also more resistant to learning anything that challenges or threatens our values.

Thus, our learning is inherently biased and the living knowledge that results from it is also, partly at least, biased and egocentric. Our living knowledge is simply an expression of our personal experience and preferences – it is a unique, highly personal artifice rather than an objective expression of truth. It is also highly susceptible to blind spots.

This does not mean to say that our living knowledge is not comprised of valuable 'objective' knowledge. Amongst the beliefs, assumptions, values, emotional orientations and behaviour patterns that comprise our living knowledge, there will be 'truths' that can be objectively or relationally verified. However, the knowledge that we draw upon in our daily lives in order to guide our actions and decisions is, to a substantial degree, personally and socially constructed.

If this is the case, what are the implications for those in positions of leadership?

3

The Consequences of Leaders' Blind Spots

'All decisions are based on models, and all models are wrong.'
John D. Sterman, Standish Professor of Management
and Director of the System Dynamics Group
at the MIT Sloan School of Management

In the last chapter we saw how we construct our living knowledge by filtering experiences in order to gain a degree of control, comfort and personal efficacy in the world. Our living knowledge comprises a complex matrix of 'facts', blind spots and biases that we regard as 'true', because they have been derived from our personal experience.

John D. Sterman, Professor of Management and Director of the System Dynamics Group at MIT Sloan School of Management claims:

*'Most people are what philosophers call "naïve realists": they believe what they see **is**, that some things are just plain True – and that they know what they are. Instead, we stress that human perceptions and knowledge are limited, that we operate from the basis of mental models, that we can never place our mental models on a solid foundation of Truth because a model is a simplification, an abstraction, a selection, because our models are inevitably incomplete, incorrect – wrong.'*[1]

---

[1] Sterman, J. D. (2002) 'All models are wrong: reflections on becoming a systems scientist.' *System Dynamics Review*, **18** (4), 501–531.

Because we 'construct' our truth, people with different experiences have vastly different understandings of reality, and this leads to a high potential for conflict – particularly when they believe that their understanding is 'complete' and 'true'.

Peter Senge quotes Ted Sizer, former Dean of the Harvard School of Education:

> 'It is not hyperbole to say that the growing gap between the complexities we face and our capacity to come to a shared understanding of that complexity poses an unprecedented challenge to our future.'[2]

In order for our living knowledge to better reflect 'reality', we need to spend time in shared learning. It is only by listening to and absorbing the living knowledge that others have acquired that we expand our own understanding of reality and overcome our blind spots. This takes time and skill. As we saw in Chapter 2, people do not simply discard their beliefs. The process of changing beliefs can be painful and difficult. Moreover, in the West, we do not value time spent on reflection and we have not concentrated on developing the complex psychological skills involved in deep learning. Yet, it is the quality of our learning that will determine success in today's complex environments. Those Organizations that manage to update, enrich, share and deepen their organizational living knowledge will be those organizations that thrive in the more complex competitive world of the 21st century.[3]

---

[2] Quoted in Senge, P. M. (2004) 'Creating Desired Futures in a Global Economy.' *Reflections – The SoL Journal on Knowledge, Learning and Change*, 5.

[3] There is an extensive literature dedicated to examining the role of learning in helping organizations to adapt to changing complex environments. Examples include de Geus, A. (1988) 'Planning as Learning'. *Harvard Business Review*, March–April, 70–74. Crossan, M., Djurfeldt, L., Lane, H. W. and White, R. E. (1994) *Organizational Learning – Dimensions for a Theory*. Working Paper Series No. 94-09R. London, Canada: Western Business School, The University of Western Ontario. Crossan, M., Lane, H. W., Rush, J. C. and White, R. E. (1993) *Learning in Organizations*. Monograph from 1992 Workshop. London, Canada: Western Business School, The University of Western Ontario. Garvin, D. A. (1993) 'Building a Learning Organization'. *Harvard Business Review*, July–August, 78–91. Hayes, R. H., Wheelwright, S. C. and Clark, K. B. (1988) *Dynamic Manufacturing: Creating the Learning Organization*. New York: The Free Press. Hedberg, B. L. T. (1981) 'How Organizations Learn and Unlearn' in P. C. Nystrom

It is here that the role of leaders' learning is crucial. Leaders can choose to explore the limits of their (and their staff's) living knowledge and actively work to strengthen it; or leaders can choose to cling to the 'truth' of their living knowledge, making it easier for blind spots to infuse their decision making.

A study of over 160 companies examined what variables helped companies outperform their competitors over a period of five years. In reporting the research (known as the 'Evergreen Project'), the authors showed that CEOs directly influence a company's profitability or total return to shareholders.[4] But what was interesting about this study was that it was not the technical competencies of the leader that determined a company's success. What made the difference to organizational performance was the leader's ability to learn and to spread learning. Good leaders would:

- build relationships with people at all levels of the organization and inspire the rest of the management team to do the same;

- spot opportunities before competitors and address problems before they became 'nightmares'.

Both of these skills relate directly to a leader's learning. The leader is going straight to the front line and updating his living knowledge by talking to people who have direct experience of change. Indeed, in the same study, the authors refer to one effective CEO acting as a 'human sponge'. He spent his time regularly touring sites, talking to the people and absorbing information, ideas and new developments. He would then disseminate them throughout the company,

---

and W. H. Starbuck (Eds) *Handbook of Organizational Design*, Volume 1. New York: Oxford University Press. Huber, G. P. (1991) 'Organizational Learning: The Contributing Processes and the Literatures.' *Organization Science*, 2 (1), 88–115. Jones, A. M. and Hendry, C. (1992) *The Learning Organization: A Review of Literature and Practice*. Centre for Corporate Strategy and Change, Warwick Business School, The HRD Partnership. Kim, D. H. (1993) 'The Link Between Individual and Organizational Learning.' *Sloan Management Review*, Fall, 37–50. Lave, J. and Wenger, E. (1991) *Situated Learning – Legitimate peripheral participation*. Cambridge: Cambridge University Press. MacDonald, S. (1995) 'Learning to Change: An Information Perspective on Learning in the Organization'. *Organization Science*, 6 (5), 557–568.

[4] Nohria, N. Joyce, W. and Robinson, B. (2003) 'What Really Works.' *Harvard Business Review*, July, 42–52.

overcoming internal rivalries and divisions, spreading learning throughout the company through his extensive interpersonal network. This is a learning CEO in action, seeking out novel information and ideas, absorbing and making sense of them and then spreading them throughout the organization.

The ability to spot opportunities and address problems is also deeply relevant to a leader's ability to confront potential blind spots and learn. We shall see later that effective leaders face problems, whilst those who cannot tolerate discomfort deny them.

But maybe we are overstating the problem. Haven't leaders always winged it, got by through gut instinct? They have – but there are consequences. The following provide two examples of learning failures that occurred on an organizational level with devastating effects. Both are examples of what can happen when leaders succumb to blind spots and fail to learn.

The Collapse of Barings Bank – Blinded by Desire

In 1995 Nick Leeson became renowned as the person who single-handedly brought down Barings Bank. Leeson had gone into the Singapore money market and bought futures. Futures contracts enable you, for the cost of a 'margin' payment up front, to buy or sell shares commodities or currencies at a future date for a fixed price. If, in the meantime, the market price goes above the price you originally fixed, you are in profit; if it goes below your fixed price, you are in loss. Leeson bought futures and for a while made a profit. However, the price started to go against him and he started to make huge paper losses. Each time the loss reached a certain level, the bank had to put up a 'margin' – in effect, a percentage of the loss incurred in the future. Leeson's losses began to threaten the financial viability of the bank, but senior managers were unaware of this, as Leeson had hidden the losses in a secret account. Nevertheless, Leeson continued to ask for greater and greater 'margins' to be provided by senior management in London – this alone should have alerted some people to the fact that something unusual was occurring. In fact, some people did start to ask questions, but Leeson managed to convince his senior management that he was about to make huge profits, beyond their wildest dreams, making them all personally extremely rich. Judith Rawnsley, a journalist who wrote about the Barings events, quotes a former director of Barings, who, seeing the way events were unfolding, left the bank before its collapse. According to him, Christopher Heath, the then CEO of Barings Securities, had:

> 'lost the plot. The success of the Eighties had gone to his head. He was interested only in his Bentleys and his race horses. He hadn't a clue what was going on'.[5]

In fact there were many clues and indications regarding the massive losses concealed by Nick Leeson before they became public in 1995. A number of people amongst the Baring's management *knew* there was something terribly wrong with regards to Nick's funding requests, and others guessed that his excessive earnings were unusual and unsustainable.[6] However, whenever the problem came to light, Leeson found it incredibly easy to fob people off. Following a meeting with Peter Norris, the then CEO of Barings Bank, and Leeson's manager Ron Baker, Leeson claimed:

> 'The only good thing about hiding losses from these people was that it was so easy. They were always too busy and too self-important, and were always on the telephone. They had the attention span of a gnat. They could not make the time to work through a sheet of numbers and spot that it didn't add up'.[7]

It is interesting to see Leeson instinctively focusing on a fundamental learning disability – the inability to get managers to pay attention to the issues concerned. When the Group

---

[5] Rawnsley, J. (1995) *Going for Broke – Nick Leeson and the Collapse of Barings Bank.* London: HarperCollins, p. 88.
[6] Rawnsley, J. (1995) *Going for Broke – Nick Leeson and the Collapse of Barings Bank.* London: HarperCollins, p. 136 and p. 172. Also see Leeson, N. (1996) *Rogue Trader.* London: Little, Brown and Company, p. 185.
[7] Leeson, N. (1996) *Rogue Trader.* London: Little, Brown and Company, p. 141.

Treasurer spoke to one senior executive about a £50 million hole in Barings balance sheet, he was met with an exasperated:

> *'God . . . you're the guy who's always asking these time-consuming questions'.*[8]

Here is a clear example of another learning disability. The questions trigger annoyance and frustration. In order to get rid of the negative feelings, the senior executive dismisses the person and the questions!

Various people quizzed Nick regarding problems with the accounts. Auditors raised questions regarding unaccounted for liabilities. The Singapore financial authorities started sending letters to the bank questioning their liabilities. Whenever anyone raised these questions, Nick found it incredibly easy to dismiss them. On one occasion, Nick was quizzed by Simon Jones, the Regional Operations Manager and Director of Barings Futures Singapore. He had received a letter from the financial authorities warning him about the potential liabilities and the notorious 88888 account where all the losses were hidden. Nick found it incredibly easy to distract Simon, blaming the authorities for being overly bureaucratic. This is his account of the conversation:

> *'They're f***ing idiots', Simon agreed. 'And what's this calculation – it looks about £90 million out to me'.*
>
> *'Yeah, I know. Look, I'll draft an answer for you,' I said, holding out my hand for the letter. 'Don't worry about it'.*
>
> *'Yes, do that, will you? Get the reply on my desk by tomorrow . . . Now what are you betting on Man United?'*[9]

There are further accounts of similar conversations where Nick finds it easy to distract people's attention away from the evi-

---

[8] Leeson, N. (1996) *Rogue Trader*. London: Little, Brown and Company, p. 169.
[9] Leeson, N. (1996) *Rogue Trader*. London: Little, Brown and Company, p. 159.

dence in front of them. It seemed as if everyone was eager to believe Nick's lies. Nick concluded:

> 'As each day went on, and my requests continued to be met, the explanation dawned on me: they wanted to believe it was all true. There was a howling discrepancy which would have been obvious to a child – the money they sent to Singapore was unaccounted for – but they wanted to believe otherwise, because it made them feel richer.'[10]

This is supported by Rawnsley:

> 'Leeson's bosses were reluctant to upset their star trader . . . as Andrew Fraser commented, "in so far as one had a feeling about him [it was] for God's sake don't interfere." '[11]

This is a classic case of a blind spot that infects the whole organization. Management wanted to believe that they were going to become amazingly wealthy. They had no doubt planned their futures around their bonuses – boasted to their friends and contacts and promised their families great things. They dismissed as 'bean counters' those who were asking questions and refusing to believe Nick's obviously fraudulent figures.

Their sensemaking was driven by desire, making them blind to the truth – even though other senior people tried to draw their attention to it.

It isn't easy to spot problems, because spotting problems can be scary. All of a sudden, a future consisting of six figure bonuses is blotted out and replaced by uncertainty and fear. Nick is right, these people wanted to believe the impossible was true, because the alternative was simply too painful to face. Barings' senior management had severe

---

[10] Leeson, N. (1996) *Rogue Trader*. London: Little, Brown and Company, p. 161.
[11] Rawnsley, J. (1995) *Going for Broke – Nick Leeson and the Collapse of Barings Bank*. London: HarperCollins, p. 140.

blind spots which contributed to the downfall of an organization that, prior to that, had survived for over a century.

Learning from problems is not a rational business. It requires self discipline, courage, self awareness and painful honesty, particularly on the part of leaders. This is nowhere more obvious than in the next case – The Bristol Royal Infirmary.

The Bristol Royal Infirmary – 'Wilful Blindness, Professional Hubris and an Inappropriate Degree of Rigidity'[12]

The case of the Bristol Royal Infirmary shows how a failure to spot problems can result in truly appalling consequences – in this case, the avoidable deaths of over 30 young children.

The Bristol Royal Infirmary (BRI) had a paediatric open-heart surgery team which was found to be less competent than its peers in the rest of the UK, so that:

> 'More children died than might have been expected in a typical PCS unit. In the period from 1991 to 1995, between 30 and 35 more children under 1 died after open heart surgery in the Bristol Unit than might be expected had the Unit been typical of other PCS units in England at the time'.[13]

Once again, people both inside and outside the hospital were aware of the problems. In 1998, the government announced that a Public Inquiry would be established, investigating what had taken place at the BRI. Subsequently, the Inquiry found that:

---

[12] Quotes taken from the *Bristol Royal Infirmary Inquiry*, July 2001. Norwich: The Stationery Office Limited, pp. 163–164.
[13] *Bristol Royal Infirmary Inquiry*, July 2001. Norwich: The Stationery Office Limited, p. 2.

'Bristol was awash with data. There was enough information from the late 1980s onwards to cause questions about mortality rates to be raised both in Bristol and elsewhere had the mindset to do so existed'.[14]

Dr Stephen Bolsin, the anaesthetist, had been harbouring doubts as to the competence of the surgeons involved for a few years. He, like others, hesitated to raise his doubts as he would have been challenging two very powerful and influential surgeons. However, in 1991, a six year old boy came in for surgery. Dr Bolsin considered raising some questions before the boy went into surgery. He didn't and tragically the boy died. As a result of this case, Bolsin decided it was his duty to raise his concerns regarding the mortality rates of the surgeons, despite the risks involved. This was an opportunity to take stock, reflect and learn. What happened instead was that, over a period of time, Dr Bolsin was at first ignored, then castigated and eventually subjected to harassment. He claimed that:

'No medical or non-medical professional in the NHS should have to endure the threats and discrimination that I was subjected to'.[15]

He subsequently was unable to find work in the NHS in the UK and eventually decided to go to Australia. He is now highly respected in his field and writes and talks on the issues of ethics in medicine.

The Public Inquiry found that not only were the two surgeons implicated in the failings of the BRI, but so was the Chief Executive of the Bristol Healthcare Trust, Dr Roylance. Neither Roylance nor the Medical Director of the hospital, Mr Wisheart, did anything when presented with evidence of the problems. In other words, the two leaders denied the evidence and refused to learn, despite the fact that senior staff tried to raise concerns.

---

[14] *Bristol Royal Infirmary Inquiry*, July 2001. Norwich: The Stationery Office Limited, p. 3.

[15] Dr Bolsin is quoted as having said this on the website: www.freedomtocare.org.

How could top management refuse to consider the evidence when there were babies' lives at stake? The Inquiry attributes this behaviour to 'wilful blindness', 'professional hubris' and 'an inappropriate degree of rigidity'[16] (in other words, an inability to open oneself to learning). In effect, the two leaders wanted desperately to be seen at the leading edge of developments and accorded the status of *Supra Regional Service*. With this goal in mind, 'no question could arise of withdrawing from any activity'.[17] In addition, Dr Roylance had a strong belief in the demarcation of managerial and clinical issues and strongly discouraged staff from bringing any clinical related problems to him – 'a managerial approach (that) could be categorized as managerial blindness'.[18]

These leaders contributed towards the creation of a 'club culture' in which there was an 'imbalance of power, with too much control in the hands of a few individuals'.[19] This style of management 'had a punitive element to it' which meant that 'it was difficult to raise what were considered to be legitimate concerns'. Indeed, to bring concerns into the open was not seen as either 'safe or acceptable'.[20]

In this climate 'the needs of very sick children in the 1980s and 1990s were not given a high priority'.[21] The only priority seems to have been the goals of the senior people, their self esteem, their psychological comfort and their deep-rooted needs for control, power and influence.

---

[16] *Bristol Royal Infirmary Inquiry*, July 2001. Norwich: The Stationery Office Limited, pp. 164, 165 and 167.

[17] *Bristol Royal Infirmary Inquiry*, July 2001. Norwich: The Stationery Office Limited, p. 164.

[18] *Bristol Royal Infirmary Inquiry*, July 2001. Norwich: The Stationery Office Limited, p. 167.

[19] *Bristol Royal Infirmary Inquiry*, July 2001. Norwich: The Stationery Office Limited, p. 2.

[20] *Bristol Royal Infirmary Inquiry*, July 2001. Norwich: The Stationery Office Limited, p. 165.

[21] *Bristol Royal Infirmary Inquiry*, July 2001. Norwich: The Stationery Office Limited, p. 2.

The BRI case shows clearly how the goals, priorities, fears and desires of the leaders of an organization prevented learning from taking place, despite the fact that many other senior staff had raised concerns. As a result, the lives of at least 30 very young children were sacrificed.

Learning matters – everyone should take responsibility for what they learn and how they learn. But the learning of leaders is particularly important – the lives and wellbeing of thousands of people are affected by the judgements and decisions of leaders. Most of the time our leaders' blind spots and inability to learn do not result in death or the collapse of an organization. However, leaders' learning disabilities are common and always have deleterious effects on individuals and organizations.

Having acknowledged the significance of leaders' learning, it is probably true to say that it is even more difficult for leaders to learn than the rest of us. This is because:

- Leaders are paid to know the answers; people do not expect their leaders to admit to uncertainty or doubt and can interpret this as a sign of weakness.

- Leaders have been highly successful; it is tempting to repeat what has been successful in the past and to assume that previous strategies are 'right' whatever the context.

- Leaders' mistakes are highly visible. Learning often involves trying out untested behaviours and approaches; some mistakes are bound to occur, and when they do, the visibility can threaten a leader's credibility.

- Leaders are often surrounded by people wary of challenging their views. Leaders may encourage this by 'punishing' (often unconsciously) people who challenge them. On a more basic level, leaders often surround themselves with people who share their values and outlook on life – it is easier to communicate this way. Surrounding themselves with like-minded people means that differing views are not heard.

- Leaders are often alone and have little opportunity to discuss their concerns.

- Leaders are measured by results; they are not measured by how they deliver them, and as a result they may achieve short-term results at the expense of other valued outcomes, many of which only come to light years down the line.

- Leaders have a lot to lose if they take risks – position, power, influence, status and wealth.

- Leaders have to believe they are right in terms of their own vision; it can be very difficult for a leader to know when they are right and when they may be mistaken.

That is not to say that leaders should not have visions. Nor that they should not believe that their visions may be 'right'. But that they should hold these views with 'positive humility'. Peter Hyman, Tony Blair's advisor and strategist, who wrote many of Blair's speeches on education, gave up his political post and became a teacher in one of the most deprived inner-city comprehensives in London. He wrote a book based on his experience of what he calls his 'jolt of reality'. He writes about the challenges involved in applying a vision to the complexities of the real world:

> 'Those at the centre relish ideas and, in the main, are bored by practicalities. Those who suggest better ways of making policy work are too often dismissed as whingers or of obstructing change. Why isn't this more of a partnership? Why can't politicians acknowledge that those on the frontline might know more? Why can't they admit that good policy only works with good practice? I knew that, for my part, I was someone who loved the big vision and the symbolic policy. Now I realize that real 'delivery' is about the grind, not just the grand. It's about the combination of often small things that build over time, through individual relationships and genuine expertise and hard work'.[22]

Hyman acknowledged that the strategists write strategy because they love strategy – that's what they do and that's who they are. They dislike the boring, practical detail and have a tendency to dismiss people who see the limitations of the strategy as 'whingers' and 'obstructors of change'. From his new vantage point, however, Hyman virtually acknowledges that when leaders fail to listen, it is

---

[22] Hyman, P. (2005) *1 out of 10*. London: Vintage.

they who are the whingers and obstructors of change. Stuck in their preferred modes of seeing the world, they dismiss others who do not share that view but who have so much practical experience to offer them. The problem is that practical people too often see why strategy will not work and the strategists interpret their objections as obstructions, complicating their vision and making things too difficult.

Peter Senge addresses the 'vision' problem, showing two easy ways for leaders to avoid the problems associated with having a vision:

> 'This "bringing of vision to reality" is also the essence of great social, political or business leadership. However, because this tension between vision and reality can be uncomfortable, creative tension becomes emotional tension and we often seek ways around it. One way to lessen the emotional tension is simply to reduce our true vision, to give up our dreams and aim for only "realistic goals". Whilst this might reduce our discomfort, it also reduces creative energy. The second way is even more troubling: we do not tell the truth about current reality. Just as the dynamics of compromise – lowering our vision – are common in human affairs, so too are the dynamics of denial. But to the extent that we misrepresent current reality, we lose the capacity to change that reality. The energy of the creative process is released not just by holding true to a vision, but also by telling the truth about what is.[23]

Appreciating that none of us can be completely right about reality, Senge does not advocate giving up 'visions'. Rather, he extols us to craft a vision whilst engaging with the complexity, difficulty and emotional tension that invariably accompany its realization. Visionaries should not dismiss reality, they should not dismiss people who bring complexity as whingers and obstructors of change. Indeed, if the visions are going to succeed, leaders need to engage with the complexity, actively seeking it out and listening to alternative views and opinions.

This involves a major shift in some of the underlying assumptions regarding the management/leadership role. In the world of

---

[23] Senge, P. M. (2004) 'Creating Desired Futures in a Global Economy'. *Reflections – The SoL Journal on Knowledge, Learning and Change*, **5**.

constant adaptation, it is the job of leaders to take people on a journey of continuous learning, making sense of events as they occur and ensuring their organizations adapt accordingly. In this paradigm, all leaders are *thought leaders* – not so much visionaries and prophets but co-crafters of meaning. This means their job is not to identify personally and in isolation 'what is right', but rather to engineer the systems and processes that will generate deeper, more accurate and inclusive truths that enable effective action. It involves developing the ability of 'learning how to learn' and engaging with others in making sense of our world. It means bringing people from widely differing preferences, values and perspectives together and forging deeper, more accurate ways of seeing reality. It means being able to contain the inevitable anxiety involved in this process, reassuring people through the inevitable conflicts, confusions and ebbs and flows in trust. It means being able to spot and overcome personal blind spots and helping others to do the same.

Adam Kahane gives some examples of this type of leadership in his book *Solving Tough Problems*.[24] In one situation he describes how a diverse and fragmented group of Argentinian leaders, from all parts of a divided society, came together to address unresolved issues in the justice system. According to Kahane:

> *'They all arrived with their own perspectives and projects, disconnected and in many cases at odds with those of others'.*

The group experienced frustration, anger and despair. However, through the process of 'dialogue' that Kahane encouraged, the group managed to come together:

> *'success was achieved through a shift in the way the team members talked and listened. They came to the meeting prepared – as befitted a group of lawyers and judges – to make their arguments and to judge the arguments of others. At the beginning they were nervous and cautious, not so much listening as waiting for their turn to pontificate, to deliver their official, already-thought-through speeches. As they relaxed and got caught up in the excitement of the work and*

---

[24] Kahane, A. (2004) *Solving Tough Problems: an open way of talking, listening and creating new realities.* San Francisco: Berrett-Koehler, p. 98.

the engaging process, they started listening more openly and speaking more spontaneously and frankly'.[25]

The group started to generate new, shared insights into the problems and to create powerful new solutions. They began to expand their living knowledge of the issues by listening and opening themselves up to others who did not share their experiences, beliefs or values:

> 'That evening the participants listened intently, with empathy and wonder, and they spoke surprisingly personally and emotionally. They listened with and spoke from their hearts. Their stories were the window through which they could see two critical phenomena: each other as fellow humans and actors and, beyond the individuals, what was emerging in the situation as a whole and what it demanded of them.'[26]

This is not 'touchy-feely'; it is tough, vulnerable and creative leadership. Furthermore, it is the only type of leadership that is capable of solving the tough problems that characterize our organizations and social institutions today.

It is not easy to learn like this. But the cases of Barings Bank and the Royal Bristol Infirmary show us that it is important to try. There has been a tendency to claim that people are learning all the time; that living necessarily entails learning. This comes from a US/European 1960s, humanist viewpoint that claims that all human beings are essentially driven to learn, grow, adapt and change.[27] The same viewpoint claims that all human beings want to learn and express their creativity at work.

In the 1950s, the management theorist Douglas McGregor claimed that all managers had a theory of human nature that drove their

---

[25] Kahane, A. (2004) *Solving Tough Problems: an open way of talking, listening and creating new realities.* San Francisco: Berrett-Koehler, p. 98.

[26] Kahane, A. (2004) *Solving Tough Problems: an open way of talking, listening and creating new realities.* San Francisco: Berrett-Koehler, p. 102.

[27] Maslow, A. (1964) *Motivation and Personality.* New York: Harper and Row. McGregor, D. (1960) *The Human Side of Enterprise.* New York: McGraw Hill. Rogers, C. R. (1961) *On Becoming a Person.* Cambridge, MA: The Riverside Press.

management style. He described Theory X and Theory Y managers. Theory X managers assumed that all people were inherently selfish, lazy and would avoid work if at all possible. Theory Y managers assumed that people were motivated to learn and grow and employ creativity in their work. According to Theory Y, the desire to work and learn was as integral to the human spirit as the desire to play or rest. Since then, generations of managers have been taught that Theory Y is the 'correct' assumption and, as a result, have learned many techniques based upon that point of view.

The problem with this approach is that it is a gross oversimplification of reality (like all models!). Of course we want to learn – what suits us; we prefer to avoid what is painful and doesn't suit us. We are both self-actualizing and self-ish beings: we learn and we deny; we express creativity and we avoid risk; we are energetic and lazy. More than anything, we are happiness seekers – some seek happiness in 'freedom from pain', others seek happiness in the 'adrenalin of risk', others seek happiness in a 'retreat from reality' and others seek happiness in 'safety' and 'security'. We are all, all of these things. And, like the managers at Barings or the Bristol Royal Infirmary, we are creatures of desire and fear – and the desire and fear will determine exactly what we learn and how we learn it.

In fact, it is only when we recognize how difficult it is to 'really learn', that real leadership becomes possible.

4

Learning to Lead, Leading to Learn

'The only relevant learning in a company is the learning done by those people who have the power to act.'

Arie de Geus
Strategist, Royal Dutch Shell 1951–1980

The Arie de Geus quote above can be read in at least two ways. First, that the only relevant learning is done by the leaders in the company – those at the top of the hierarchy who can influence the company as a result of their learning. The second way is that those who are doing the relevant learning in the company (preferably everyone but certainly those people working in areas critical to the organization's success) must grasp the power to act in order to *make* their learning matter. If they do not, their companies will lose the living knowledge contained in that learning, and this will diminish the organization's ability to adapt and survive.

Leadership and learning are inextricably linked. A leader is someone who inspires others to commit to the achievement of a common purpose. By definition, the purpose is not yet achieved, and its fulfilment involves a journey into uncertainty. There will be setbacks, challenges and obstacles that have never before been encountered. Hence, there will be novel stimuli requiring novel responses. People on the journey will be paying attention to new and different things, experiencing high levels of emotion, attempting to make sense using newly emerging constructs and acting in different ways. A true journey of leadership involves a great deal of learning and, hence, potentially high levels of discomfort and uncertainty. The effectiveness of that journey is in part determined by how the leader manages that discomfort, ensuring that learning is faced and potential blind spots minimized.

So far we have looked at the responsibilities leaders have to us, their stakeholders, to learn and overcome their blind spots. Now, however, we shift the emphasis onto the responsibilities all of us have to become leaders and how our fear of learning and our blind spots often stop us from taking on those responsibilities.

Organizations are full of people who disagree with the way in which the organization is run and make that disagreement known in terms of cynicism, passive resistance and lack of commitment. Over time, these people have developed a sense of what is not working in their organizations but have not developed the will to turn those insights into action. Perhaps they feel helpless and overwhelmed by the complexity and strength of the powers ranged against them. Often they have tried in the past and failed. Often they are preoccupied and busy with their jobs and home lives and simply lack the energy to take on the system. Sometimes it boils down to the fact that people are quite simply scared to act on their insights. As one individual said once on a leadership programme 'yes, but I have a mortgage and kids to feed'. This man chose to live his life on two different planes. On one plane he articulated what he felt and believed – that the bullying in his organization was wrong – invariably this came out in the form of cynicism and anger. On the other plane of his existence, he acted in direct contravention to what he felt and believed – succumbing to and colluding with the bullying culture. He claimed that he lived like this in order to pay the mortgage and feed the kids, and, if so, maybe this was a worthy sacrifice. Or maybe he did it because he did not wish to risk making a stand. What was clear was that he had opted for security and had sacrificed his desire to live a life more in line with his values. However, he could not face the fact that this was his choice. In order to avoid the sense of personal responsibility, he blamed the leaders in his organization for his own choice and his own behaviour. He blamed 'them'. Whatever his reasons, he had made his choice – and his choice was for security rather than engaging with what his head and heart were telling him – that this way of living was wrong. Yet, there are too many intelligent, creative, passionate people living like this. They have settled into unwilling (or unwitting) compliance. Slowly, over time, they have unquestioningly conformed and eventually even colluded with their organizational cultures, enacting the values and enforcing them like everyone else. They do not interpret it like this – their blind spots protect them from facing the choices they have made, enabling them to blame others for the frustrations they feel.

After a while, people become inured to the collusion and used to the comfort and safety. For many, decades pass without ever taking personal risks with their behaviour; they become compliant; the experience of 'learning' and changing becomes a memory associated with the idealism of youth. This is one of the most common leadership blind spots in organizations – the idea that you cannot take leadership, that the system won't change and that it is all somebody else's fault. The most common leadership blind spot is the belief that 'I am not a leader and I can't do anything to change things around here'.

If our organizations are to change and adapt, we need people to take leadership at all levels. This means that people will have to start to believe in themselves again. They will have to connect their hearts and minds with their will. They will have to refuse to enact the existing culture, decide what they stand for and then step out into the unknown and start to change things – in other words, 'lead and learn'. The decision not to lead is, in part, a decision not to learn; the decision not to learn is, in part, a decision not to take leadership – not to take a stand on something close to one's heart. In other words, it is incumbent on all people who 'know' something integral to the organization's success to develop the courage to become leaders. The acquisition of relevant learning requires leadership to make it matter. Leadership is, at least in part, to do with the transition from knowing, believing and caring to taking action. The old saying that we get the leaders we deserve has a lot of merit in it. If we are not prepared to take action to make our learning matter, this leaves the arena free for a few to grasp the agenda and adapt it to their needs – consciously or unconsciously. An organization with an ample supply of leaders is less likely to fall foul of a few senior people's learning blind spots. But leaders on the ground will not emerge unless we face the blind spots that stop us from taking leadership – blind spots rooted in beliefs that we are not responsible for our own behaviour and in our fears of failure, pain and loss.

This chapter then is focused on what we have to *do* in order to expand and accelerate our own personal learning and leadership – whether we are in formal leadership roles or not. The assumption behind this is that the main blind spot in organizations is the fear we have of taking up leadership and of instigating both personal and organizational change.

Let's look at an example.

Ruth

Ruth had been with a large government department for over ten years. She had joined at 25 after leaving her first job in corporate banking, which she had found unpleasantly competitive and materialistic. She had succeeded in getting through a rigorous selection process and was proud to be offered a responsible role helping to write government policy in an important strategic area.

Over time, however, her enthusiasm had dwindled. Whilst the people on the ground were clearly engaged and committed to helping address some of society's most difficult and perplexing problems, those in higher echelons seemed only interested in pursuing their careers. And doing well in the job did not appear connected to doing well in terms of your career. There were a group of like-minded people who always seemed to get promoted – you could spot them very easily. They tended to stay in post for no longer than two years. They regarded their tenure as an opportunity to tick off measurable achievements – so they put in place achievable targets that did not address the underlying complexities of the problems they faced. This would often result in skewing the system by pulling people off long-term delicate projects and putting them on short-term task forces to address relatively minor issues.

They would also make decisions which portrayed a lack of understanding of the issues. Obviously, being in the post for a relatively short period of time, they would not have the depth of knowledge and experience necessary to understand the intricate complexities and political sensitivities of the problems. Sometimes they would make decisions that would undermine years spent in building trust with external partners. When anything did go wrong, they would not take personal responsibility, but would often blame junior staff unjustifiably.

Sometimes, detailed reports would be commissioned that clearly highlighted the issues and made excellent recommendations. It would be no surprise to find these reports sent back to the authors with instructions to 'change the conclusions' in order to make them personally and politically acceptable. She herself had authored one of these reports and sat in on a briefing meeting with a Minister. She had not been allowed to speak during the meeting, even whilst her manager was talking to the Minister and clearly giving him an inaccurate and partial account of the findings.

People on the ground, with real experience and knowledge of the problems, were not listened to. The whole system, it seemed to Ruth, was used by people to fulfil their personal ambitions. The unspoken assumptions were: 'look good; avoid bad press; cover yourself; blame others'. Over time, Ruth became disillusioned and cynical. She found herself complying with the culture. She, too, covered herself whenever she made a decision – sending out e-mails and notes in order to show she had consulted with everyone before even a minor decision was made. Reports were sent to be checked by direct reports, so if anything went wrong they could be blamed. She half-censored her research reports, knowing what would be politically acceptable and what would be sent back. As a result, she did not even believe in her own reports. She did the minimum to get by and put all her energies into her interests outside work. Whenever she talked to anyone about working for the department, she was scathing and cynical; but she never did anything to change it. She complied with the culture simply because she was comfortable and secure and did not want to take any personal risks.

However, recently she had been asked to attend a leadership course with a well-known business school. There she had been confronted with the choices she had made and with her passivity in relation to the organization's culture. Whilst she hadn't liked it very much, she had been forced to acknowledge her own complicity in this culture. She had been challenged to make small changes in her behaviour in order to change the landscape and take small steps of leadership. She had been reminded that she was still young and had a lot to offer the organization.

Since then, Ruth had begun to change things in small but significant ways. She started to build her own network of like-minded people who regularly got together to share their experiences of implementing change. She had stopped censoring her own reports and submissions. On one occasion, when she had been challenged by her boss for being 'negative', she defended her stance by claiming that she wanted to address the deeper issues rather than pretending the problems did not exist or were easy to manage. This took courage and her manager was not pleased with her approach. However, she did notice that he had taken account of her views and she recently overheard him using her arguments when talking to a senior government official. She started to take a greater interest in her direct reports and found that this interest was rewarded by greater efficiencies, more cooperation and a more pleasant working environment. The relationships she built via her ever-increasing network provided her with more intelligence regarding what was going on in other parts of the organization. People started to come to her for information and for introductions to people in other departments. Strangely, Ruth began to enjoy her work again and feel a new sense of empowerment. In fact, for the first time in many years, she began to think about applying for promotion. She was beginning to feel she could make a difference to this organization.

Ruth's journey has been one of both learning and leadership; she would not have been able to take leadership had she not learned and changed. She had to overcome her protective blind spot, which helped her avoid taking responsibility for her own behaviour. This was not a pleasant experience. However, she was courageous enough to turn that learning into small steps of leadership. This, in turn, led to further learning, which encouraged her to take even bigger steps of leadership. Like anyone who starts this journey of learning and leadership, you discover that it never stops, making life interesting, challenging and exciting once again.

It is easier for us to develop our leadership and learning capabilities if we are constantly taking small steps rather than spending ten years in the comfort zone rationalizing our passivity via blind spots and defensive thinking. In fact, people often continue in the comfort zone for ages – doing things they have always done and thinking things they have always thought. Instead of growing and expanding their living knowledge over ten years, they end up mining their existing living knowledge until its relevance is all but exhausted. Eventually, reality intrudes in the form of a crisis. For too many, the learning that ensues is painful and bitter, leaving scars that never heal.

In times of change we have to 'learn to learn' continuously – constantly taking small steps outside our comfort zone, constantly addressing blind spots and constantly growing and expanding the complexity of our living knowledge.

But what does it mean to expand the complexity of our living knowledge? In essence it means increasing the complexity of our thinking, the subtlety of our emotional responses and the range and flexibility of our behavioural repertoire. Ruth increased her cognitive complexity when she changed the constructs she held about herself – recognizing that she had been avoiding personal responsibility because of her fears and need for security. She increased her emotional complexity when she changed her dominant cynical stance and became more hopeful and positive about her future and her desire to change things. She expanded her behavioural complexity when she returned to the job and started to implement new and changed behaviours.

Let's explore these notions in more detail.

Cognitive Complexity

Cognitive complexity refers to the range, extent and connectedness of the constructs, ideas and beliefs that we employ to understand reality:

'Cognitively complex individuals are able to look at people or situations from a number of different viewpoints, whereas cognitively simple individuals use few viewpoints, or dimensions, when describing people and events.'[1]

Constructs are simply the 'notions' or concepts we develop to map the world around us. For example, we have a construct of a chair – what it looks like and what its function is. We also have a construct of 'democracy' – what it is and how it works. Constructs can reflect tangible 'things' in the world or they may reflect more abstract ideas.

Our schemas are the systems of interconnected constructs we use to understand a phenomenon. For example, we have a schema of 'furniture', into which our construct of 'chair' fits. The furniture schema may be defined as 'movable objects within a building designed to make it suitable for living or working in'. We then have a number of categories within this schema – e.g. bedroom furniture, living room furniture. Within these categories we will store our concept of 'chair'. We extend our cognitive complexity when we develop new constructs or schemas, or change our constructs or schemas so that they more accurately reflect the world in which we live.

The easiest way of developing our cognitive complexity is by listening and talking to people from different cultures, experiences, values and professional backgrounds.

Behavioural Complexity

We also need to develop a more intricate and complex web of behavioural strategies to cope with the complexities and uncertainties

---

[1] Goodwin, V. L. and Ziegler, L. (1998) 'A test of relationships in a model of organizational cognitive complexity.' *Journal of Organizational Behaviour*, **19**, 371–386. See also Kelly, G. A. (1955) *The Psychology of Personal Constructs*. New York: Norton. Driver, M. J. and Streufert, S. (1969) 'Integrative Complexity: An Approach to Individuals and Groups as Information-processing Systems'. *Administrative Science Quarterly*, **14**, 272.

inherent in our interactions with people. Behavioural complexity refers to the range of behaviours and strategies that people develop in order to achieve their goals. A senior executive might be blunt and direct with an American colleague, for example, but he might be more subtle and indirect with a Japanese colleague – reflecting different behavioural norms in those countries. Whilst a strategy of 'driving through change' might work in one context, in another context, a more consensual and gradual approach needs to be adopted. Behaviourally complex individuals develop a variety of styles to deal with the wide range of contexts they deal with.[2]

Emotional Complexity

Emotional complexity refers to the depth and range of sensitivities and psychological strategies that an individual develops to help notice, appreciate and manage their own emotions and the emotions of others. We are constantly developing our emotional complexity throughout our childhood and into early adulthood, but there is often less incentive to develop emotional complexity throughout our adult life. For example, a child who has just lost a tennis match might fling down his racquet and burst into tears. The adults around him may sympathize and accept that this response is part of childhood. However, it is clearly not an appropriate response for an adult. Hence, the coach or parents of the child will gently and insistently teach the child to change his emotional and behavioural response to losing. Eventually, the child learns that it is not 'sporting' to sulk or be rude to his opponent. He learns to control his emotions, congratulate his opponent and 'act' a sporting resignation. But he also learns to channel the emotional tension that flows from the disappointment into a greater determination to practise and perfect his game.

The child has a loving and supportive community to direct him in his emotional development, but once into adulthood we often lose this community. We do not have people around us to tell us quite

---

[2] Goleman, D. (2000) 'Leadership That Gets Results'. *Harvard Business Review*, March–April.

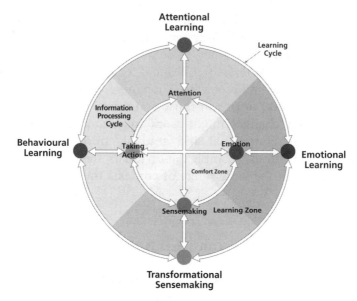

Figure 4.1   Information processing and learning.

directly that it is not appropriate to shout at our direct reports, that it is unacceptable to sulk, withdraw, become sarcastic and negative when things don't go our way. Once into adulthood, our emotional development often slows down. It depends on us receiving good quality feedback and being totally honest with ourselves.

So how do we expand our cognitive, emotional and behavioural complexity? If we go back to our learning cycle, we can see that as we move outside of the comfort zone, so the space taken up by attention, emotion, sensemaking and action expands. In other words, our attention span increases, we start to notice and respond more to our emotions, we make sense of events in deeper, more collaborative, more complex ways and we expand our behavioural repertoire – increasing the range of skills and behaviours in everyday use.

The eight learning practices that follow are based upon these principles. Developing the complexity of our living knowledge involves putting these practices into action day by day, minute by minute. It involves us forcing ourselves outside our comfort zone, confronting blind spots and moving more and more into the learning zone. And as we do this, we begin to notice that we are having an impact on the people around us. We start to exercise leadership. No longer moaning by the coffee machine, complaining that the world is not like we want it to be, we are out there making a difference!

Hence, the learning cycle described above is perhaps more accurately described as *the leadership learning cycle*. And the eight practices below are characteristic both of leaders who learn and of learners who lead – translating their emotional and cognitive learning into action.

The Eight Learning Practices

1. *Direct attention* – This practice encourages you to broaden attention to include cues you would normally miss and to focus your attention on what is truly important to you and the stakeholders in your learning.

2. *Harness emotions* – This involves noticing your emotions and interpreting them effectively in order to increase the quality of your decisions. It entails managing the impact that emotions have on your sensemaking and behaviour.

3. *Overcome defensiveness* – This practice enables you to become aware of your defensive patterns and overcome them in order to face difficult truths.

4. *Deepen sensemaking* – This involves making sense of events in ways that are more inclusive, more complex, more systemic and more comprehensive.

5. *Engage creativity* – Creativity is about daring to be different, taking risks, seeing the world in different ways, questioning taboos and making new connections.

6. *Reality check* – This ensures that we check our beliefs against external measures of reality in order to avoid the temptations of denial and fantasy.

7. *Change behaviour* – This is the ultimate 'leadership' practice. It encourages people to take action and expand the range of

behaviours and skills that they are able to employ and feel comfortable with.

8. *Nurture integrity* – Integrity entails tuning into the different forces that are driving your behaviour and making decisions that are 'right' as opposed to 'convenient'. It ensures that your behaviour, values and deepest beliefs are in alignment.

When we act on these practices we begin to overcome our blind spots and start to develop the complexity of our living knowledge. This, in turn, helps us to cope with and manage the increased levels of complexity in the environment. Our minds, bodies and emotions 'mature' to cope with the additional demands placed upon them by our increasingly complex social and organizational context.

Problems with the Learning Practices

Considering these advantages of undertaking the learning practices, one might have thought them easy to implement. However, they are deeply counter-intuitive. It can appear a waste of time focusing our attention on seemingly irrelevant issues. It is often regarded as 'touchy-feely' to concentrate on emotions. Too much time spent in sensemaking can be frustrating, leading to 'analysis paralysis'. Listening to others with different views and values is frustrating and uncomfortable. Venturing outside the comfort zone is seen as too risky. Learning different ways of approaching tasks can feel uncomfortable and ineffective.

There is no point reading about the practices unless we are prepared to face the fact that implementing them will not be easy. More than anything it will involve personal discipline. We have been told for too long that we have to instil leadership in organizations, inspire innovation and creativity, empower people, trust them, encourage teamwork, build a learning organization, listen to people, consult and involve them, but . . . it doesn't happen! And it doesn't happen because of old learning (self-defeating beliefs and attitudes) and a fear of completing the learning cycle – i.e. taking action based on what we know is right. We rationalize this lack of learning and leadership by telling ourselves:

- we tried before and it did not work;
- there is too much to do already;
- it's too risky to challenge the status quo;
- there's too much at stake – I have a career to protect;
- I'm not a leader;
- this organization will never change;
- I'm too busy.

But let's be clear, not only are we are fooling ourselves, we are letting others down! Our organizations and our communities need people of influence and insight to take leadership – now more than ever. We can no longer rationalize our collusion with outdated organizational cultures by telling ourselves that taking action will be too difficult and will not help us achieve our goals.

We all have three choices in life:

- we can learn but refuse to complete the learning cycle by not acting on our learning;
- we can avoid learning and leading altogether until 'reality' comes crashing down on us like a massive tidal wave;
- we can learn and ensure we complete our learning cycles by making our learning matter – taking action and leadership.

This is why leadership and learning cannot be separated. No-one likes living their lives according to a set of values and practices they do not agree with – whether it's for mortgage and kids or not. Everyone wants to live their lives holistically – doing what they believe in and believing in what they do. It's just that it often requires leadership to say what everyone is thinking and to be prepared to cope with the consequences and the complexity!

The rest of this book will examine the learning practices in more detail, providing thoughts and suggestions as to how to apply them. This is inevitably only a start, and our hope is that the book will stimulate further ideas and tools. The last chapter offers a range of practical exercises which can easily be applied in the workplace.

The eight practices outlined in the following chapters are aimed at different people:

- leaders who want to leave a legacy and make a difference;

- people who care but who maybe don't quite know how to turn their caring into action (budding leaders);

- all of us who feel that we have capacities and talents that are underutilized and who would like to live our lives more holistically – believing in what we do, and doing what we believe in.

In essence, these practices are for learning leaders who want to make their learning matter.

Part Two

How to Overcome Blind Spots and Accelerate Leaders' Learning

5

The First Practice –
Direct Attention

'Choice of attention – to pay attention to this and ignore that – is to the inner life what choice of action is to the outer. In both cases, a man is responsible for his choice and must accept the consequences, whatever they may be.'

W. H. Auden

We can think of attention as a form of choice. Over time, out of the plethora of events, people and phenomena that bombard our senses, we develop a pattern of choice – paying attention to some cues and ignoring others. This pattern of choice may be conscious or it may be unconscious, but it exists. It is simply not possible to pay attention to every single phenomenon that sweeps fleetingly across our senses. Developing patterned choices saves a lot of time and effort, avoiding the need to consciously analyse the significance of every cue we perceive.[1]

Once our choices are made, they have an immediate impact. As soon as we choose to pay attention to one area we begin to develop our cognitive, emotional and behavioural complexity in that area. However, this is often at the cost of other areas where the complexity of our living knowledge fails to develop as quickly. For example, a CEO may be worried about profitability and may focus her full

---

[1] See, for example, Louis, M. R. and Sutton, R. I. (1999) 'Switching Cognitive Gears: From Habits of Mind to Active Thinking'. *Human Relations*, **44**(1). Lord, R. G. and Foti, R. J. (1986) 'Schema Theories, Information Processing and Organizational Behaviour' in H. P. Sims and D. A. Gioia (Eds) *The Thinking Organization: Dynamics of Organizational Social Cognition*. San Francisco: Jossey-Bass, pp. 49–74.

attention on the company's cost base. She works tirelessly to bring the costs down, making staff redundant, putting financial monitoring systems in place and even closing down operations. Those who are worried about staff morale and its effect on customer service find that whilst the CEO acknowledges their concerns, she does not do anything about them. Her attention is not really focused on this area. As a result, these people do not feel they have been listened to. The CEO in this case is focusing her attention on one paradigm (costs) and as a result, is learning a lot about how the company's cost base operates. However, she is marginalizing other important areas (or paradigms) – the customer service paradigm and the people (or staff) paradigm. So, whilst her cognitive complexity in the area of cost control is growing, it is stagnating in the areas of staff, customers and the future strategic needs of the company. This limits her understanding of how these areas are all interconnected as part of a complex system. As a result, her cognitive complexity does not reflect the systemic complexity of the organization or problems she is dealing with. This is one reason that leaders are sometimes highly adept at dealing with certain situations (e.g. crisis, downsizing or cost control), but are unable to adapt to situations that require an entirely different kind of living knowledge.

It may be that our attentional choices seem sensible at the time. It seems sensible to focus on costs when they are spiralling out of control. But what really drives the choice to pay attention to A as opposed to B – is it a rational judgement or is it more emotional and personal? Do we have attentional blind spots that channel our attention towards some areas and away from others? Furthermore, is it possible to expand our attention capacity – for example, is it possible to pay attention to cost-cutting, staff morale, customer service *and* strategic growth?

Many would argue that this is exactly what is required of those in leadership positions – the more senior the role, the more it is necessary to expand one's attentional scope and complexity.[2] This is because the leader's attention patterns strongly influence the goals

---

[2] Charan, R., Drotter, S. and Noel, J. (2001) *The Leadership Pipeline – How to Build the Leadership-Powered Company*. San Francisco: Jossey-Bass.

and priorities of the whole organization. A good example of this can be seen in the recent history of Marks and Spencer, once one of the UK's leading retailers. Judi Bevan's account of the company's rise and fall demonstrates how the leader's pattern of attention and blind spots hindered the organization's ability to identify and respond to external threats.

Marks and Spencer's biggest rise and its subsequent fall from grace occurred under the CEO and Chairman, Sir Richard Greenbury. Greenbury had been very successful during the 1980s and had led the organization to new heights in terms of its market and financial standing. Greenbury was courted by the City elite and increasingly began to narrow his attention, focusing almost exclusively on the company's financial results and share price. He set himself a personal goal. He was determined to become the first British retailer to reach the magic £1bn profit figure and, hence, go down in British corporate history. This goal became an obsession, and Greenbury, having been highly successful during the 1980s, believed he knew exactly how to achieve it.

However, the world of retailing was changing rapidly and whilst his formula may have worked in the 1980s it was not appropriate for the more competitive and fast moving 1990s. Greenbury developed a blind spot with regards to these changes in his market. The question that all M&S chairmen used to ask of their staff was 'what's new?'.[3] This question symbolized a culturally embedded recognition that financial success relied on being in touch with changes in customer and market trends. According to Bevan, Greenbury stopped asking the question. He narrowed his attention on the paradigms that were truly important to him – the City and the financials.

In 1997, the non-executive directors identified problems:

'The company had become too big to be ruled by one man, and the directors could see they were not addressing the outside world. "We

---

[3] Bevan, J. (2002) *The Rise and Fall of Marks and Spencer*. London: Profile Books Ltd.

don't spend enough time with investors", "We don't take the press seriously", "We do not meet our international partners often enough" were frequent comments'.[4]

But although his fellow board executives

'grumbled about him behind his back, none . . . tried to stop him; on the contrary, they aided and abetted him every step of the way. Whatever criticisms they had, the traditional sycophancy was so ingrained that none would ever reach the Chairman's ears.'[5]

A survey of customer attitudes was commissioned, showing a number of serious problems. Customers were increasingly dissatisfied with M&S and were shopping elsewhere:

'Greenbury was not impressed. He thanked Norgrove (the author of the survey) *for his work, but found its conclusions hard to stomach. He refused to let him present the report at a full board meeting . . . When any of the non-executive directors tackled Greenbury privately on the matter – backed up as ever by complaints from their wives about how M&S was slipping – the answer was always "Look at the profits"'.* (my unitalicized comments)[6]

Before his downfall, Bevan notes:

'To some, Greenbury's refusal to embrace technology for his own use may have seemed an endearing eccentricity. To others, it signalled that here was a man no longer open to the changes in the modern world. He had long since ceased to ask his young managers what was new; perhaps he didn't want to know. And he continued to pour scorn on the competition, be it in food or clothing. One friend recalled almost pulling him round a new Tesco (M&S's closest rival) *to*

[4] Bevan, J. (2002) *The Rise and Fall of Marks and Spencer.* London: Profile Books Ltd, p. 165.

[5] Bevan, J. (2002) *The Rise and Fall of Marks and Spencer.* London: Profile Books Ltd, p. 178.

[6] Bevan, J. (2002) *The Rise and Fall of Marks and Spencer.* London: Profile Books Ltd, p. 179.

make him aware of what it was doing. But Greenbury refused to show any interest. [7]

Here we see how a highly intelligent and successful man suddenly decides to stop paying attention to the changes going on in his environment. He was focused on one goal ('Look at the profits'), and any other measures of success (customer attitudes and buying patterns, investors' opinions, competitive positioning) were ignored.

Paying attention is not always a rational business. Psychologists have long known that there are many non-rational factors that affect our attention patterns.[8] We are subject to confirmatory biases, where we pay attention to anything that confirms what we already believe; self-serving biases, where we focus our attention on anything that boosts our sense of self esteem; and decisional biases, where we pay attention to information that supports recent decisions we may have made.[9] But much of the writing and research in this area has been restricted to the worlds of academia or clinical psychology. These distortions are often regarded as interesting areas of academic study, as manifestations of psychological illness or sources of entertainment and amusement. However, these attentional and sensemaking biases suffuse our learning, impact our day-to-day decision making and affect the workings of our organizations. In the case of the Bristol Royal Infirmary, the attention patterns of the leaders affected people's lives.

So, what can we do to ensure that we pay attention to what our stakeholders need us to pay attention to, as opposed to what makes us feel comfortable and secure? How can we pay attention to a wider range of paradigms and issues? How can leaders ensure that they pay attention to what is important, avoiding the temptation to focus on the familiar and what has worked in the past? Our

---

[7] Bevan, J. (2002) *The Rise and Fall of Marks and Spencer.* London: Profile Books Ltd, p.180. My comments in brackets.

[8] Fiske, S. T. and Taylor, S. (1991) *Social Cognition,* second edition. Singapore: McGraw Hill. Engel, A. K., Debener, S. and Kranczioch, C. (2006) Coming to Attention. *Scientific American Mind,* August/September, p. 46.

[9] Sutherland, S. (1992) *Irrationality – The Enemy Within.* London: Constable.

first learning practice introduces us to some of the ways of developing the effectiveness of our attention patterns. We have divided this practice into two areas: broadening attention and focusing attention.

Broadening Attention

In many respects we see what we already know. For example, if we have a well-developed political paradigm in organizations, we recognize the signs of political manoeuvring. We become more alert to certain behaviours and notice things that other people might miss. However, if we are more trusting, we may not have developed a sophisticated understanding of organizational politics. We will not 'see' certain behaviours and signs of hidden agendas. Having a political paradigm offers another way of interpreting information. If we do not have a strong political paradigm, we will neither 'see' certain phenomena nor will we generate certain interpretations. The more paradigms you use to interpret the world, the more information you will notice and the more varied the interpretations available to you. In other words, the more paradigms you use, the more you will develop cognitive complexity.

Let's look at a true example.

Icon Inc.

A number of people in the sales division of a major IT company were interviewed regarding their views of their company's performance. They were all asked some fairly broad-ranging and simple questions concerning their markets, their strategy and the organizational capacity to respond to the market demands. What was most noticeable about the responses was the number of paradigms used by people to answer the question.

One man responded very powerfully, with an intricate knowledge of the market, the competitors and the customers. However, he rather woefully explained that nobody listened to him! Another person described the internal organizational politics in great detail, linking key strategic decisions to a variety of competing interest groups and prominent players in the hierarchy. His description was linked, in a fairly general and vague way, to market demands and the organization's ability to respond to them. The HR person described the people side of the business, relating the skills, competencies and training needs of the people to the demands of the strategy and the finances.

The senior manager, on the other hand, talked with ease about the strategy, the competitors, the customers, the organizational processes and politics, the staff and financial constraints – effortlessly moving from one paradigm to another and describing the links between them. She had mastered the use of more than seven interlocking paradigms, whereas her staff mostly used two or three. The aforementioned strategist failed to understand organizational politics and the importance of networking. As a result, he could not communicate his insights to people and was marginalized in what was primarily a sales-led, present-focused company. The person who focused on the internal politics noticeably did not appear overly interested in the product or the customers or the market. He was focused on his own career and networks. It was not surprising when, shortly after the interview, he left to go to a competitor! However, the HR person was a trusted colleague of the senior manager, because he was able to talk not just about the people needs, but was able to relate them to the strategic needs of the whole business.

We naturally, effortlessly pay attention to those events or phenomena that are comfortable and easy for us. Our natural preferences, values, skills and strengths channel our attention patterns in certain directions. When this happens we develop detailed mental models in certain preferred paradigms, which we rely on in order to understand the world around us. Other paradigms, usually less preferred, languish – they are relatively undeveloped and hence have less explanatory power and are less used. This self-fulfilling prophecy effect reinforces our belief that our preferred paradigms 'work' whilst our less preferred paradigms do not. This is an important source of blind spots.

The following tables represent just a few of the paradigms used in business – the higher you go in an organization, the more you need to employ.

Commercial Paradigms	
Clients	Do you know your clients as real people with their own needs, hopes and aspirations? Do you know their strategies, business plans, issues and concerns, what's really important to them?
Strategy	Do you stay in touch with changes in your markets? Do you think about different strategies for dealing with them? How are you doing in the implementation of your strategy? What is the latest thinking/practice about strategy and how to implement it?
Competitors	Can you list your competitors, key individuals who work for them, their strengths, weaknesses, current concerns and activities, what's going well for them and what isn't, their strategies and plans? Do you know what their competitive advantages and disadvantages are?
Commercial	What current opportunities and risks are you dealing with? What major deals is your organization pursuing? How are they going? How do you manage risk? What attention do you pay to business development? Do you have a culture that supports people who respond to commercial opportunities?
Suppliers	What changes are taking place in your suppliers' worlds? How do you treat them? How are you viewed by your suppliers? What changes are taking place which affect your relationship with your suppliers?
Global	What social, political, environmental and economic forces may impact your organization, both now and in the future? What about rising generations and countries and stakeholders – how will their changing expectations affect your organization?

Human Paradigms

Power	What are the main sources of power in your organization? What type of people 'get on' in your organization? What are your sources of power? Do you have access to lots of sources of information and networks of people? Are you generally known, trusted and liked by people?
Staff	What are the needs, drives, emotions, aspirations, hopes and dreams of your staff? What problems and issues are they facing right now? Do you have the right staff in the right roles? How do you feel about your key staff? How are you managing succession issues? How are you developing the talent of the future?
Self	Are you happy, content, fulfilled, valued? Are you aware of your strengths and the unique contribution you bring to your organization? To what extent do you take note of your feelings and respond appropriately to them? Do you consider the impact you have on others? Do you adapt your behaviour in order to meet the differing needs of those around you? Do you regularly review your performance, thinking about what is working and what you might need to change? What values do you role model in the organisation?
Climate	What is the emotional climate like in your organization? What does this say about the performance of the organization? In your view, how does emotional climate relate to organizational performance?
Leadership	What do you think makes a good leader? How do you develop followership? What do you want to be different as a result of your leadership? How do you influence your peers and those more senior to you? How are you personally developing the leaders below you? How is the leadership in your organization regarded? How do you know? Are you listening to the right people, paying attention to all the stakeholders in your leadership, regardless of whether they agree with you or not?
Relationships	Who do you have close relationships with? Where are your relationships more distant? How do you identify which relationships are important? How do you improve your relationships with different parts of the business? Which relationships do you value? What relationships do you ignore?

Organizational Paradigms

Structure	Does the structure meet the needs of your strategy? What is the latest thinking/practice on structure in your industry/field? What structures characterize the leaders and the up and coming leaders in your field?
Marketing	How efficient, creative, effective and useful is the contribution made by your marketing? How often do you speak to your marketing people? Do they have the right input into key strategic decisions?
HR	What is the role of HR in your organization? Do you know the key players well? What are they doing to support the organizational strategy? Are you aware of how HR could help implement the business strategy? What are the views from those in HR as to how the business could improve?
Processes	Are you aware of the latest business process tools? Do you know what is available in the market to help you align your processes? What are your competitors doing? Where are your processes efficient and where are they not? How do you know?
Culture	How well is your culture aligned to your strategy? Are your organizational values aligned? What are the espoused values of the senior team and what are the lived values? What messages does this send out to staff, clients and other stakeholders?
Corporate governance and business ethics	How much attention have you paid to this area? Who is working in this area? How often do you talk to them? What are their concerns and issues? What is your ethical role in the world – how do you behave in the countries where you have interests? Are you a positive force for good in your markets or do you just grab and run? What about the example set by your senior leaders?
Technological	How often do you talk to your IT people? Are you up to date with changes in IT and what your suppliers, customers and competitors are doing in this area? How is technology changing in your industry? How will changes in technology affect your markets in the future? What is your attitude towards technology – are you an innovator, an early adopter or do you lag behind your competitors?

Financial Paradigms

The stock market	Who are the main investors, how well do you know them and what they need of you? Are your people aware of how stock markets work and how their work feeds into the share price performance? How do you communicate with your institutional investors? How do they view you and why?
Management accounting	What are your systems like for recording costs, revenues, projected forecasts, monthly budgets and financial performance? How accurate and timely are they? How accessible? Are people aware of how their decisions affect budgets? Do they have the right information in order to make timely, informed financial decisions?
Financial accounting	How well do your staff understand balance sheets and profit and loss accounts? Do relevant staff analyse clients' accounts and competitors' accounts?

Our personal training and preferences will mean that we naturally develop some paradigms more than others. It can be difficult to pay attention to things that you do not like, that you do not feel comfortable with, that you are not good at or which go against your values! You say to yourself 'this is irrelevant'. We all have ways of dismissing approaches that do not suit us. The 'caring professions' attract people who have values around helping other people and promoting their wellbeing. Pressures to operate efficiently can be dismissed angrily as attempts to reduce everything to money. There may be a tendency to dismiss those who are trying to drive through efficiency as 'bean counters', 'heartless bureaucrats' or 'incompetent managers who don't understand anything about the organization or profession'. In certain organizations where people are driven primarily by financial reward, the opposite often occurs. HR professionals can be dismissed as 'overheads', 'wishy washy' or 'irrelevant'. In both cases, people are dismissing complex and valid ways of looking at the world but making themselves feel good by rationalizing their blind spots with reference to their personal value set.

Nevertheless, in an increasingly complex world, it is incumbent on us to acknowledge a wide variety of paradigms – enabling us to see and interpret phenomena we would otherwise miss. This is the only way in which we can develop the requisite cognitive complexity to deal with our increasingly complex world. It also has the added advantage of enabling conversation across paradigms, as people can share common observations and interpretations.

The important point about broadening attention is to understand just where your attentional preferences lie and make sure you expand your attention beyond those preferences in order to better support your and your stakeholders' priorities. One quick way of broadening your attention is to identify a weak paradigm on the paradigm list and find someone who is strong in this area. You could take them out for lunch or simply invite them in for a chat. Ask them about their goals and priorities for the organization; what they think is done well and what not so well. Listen for the constructs, ideas, beliefs and schemas they use. Listen for the names of the people they refer to. Use the opportunity to listen and learn from the conversation. The more senior you become in an organization, the more important it is to have people around you that can cover all these paradigms; and the more important it is that you develop your understanding of their language and constructs.

Broadening attention is actually quite easy – it's about people. Sir Terry Leahy, CEO of Tesco, the UK's most successful retailer and, in terms of profitability, second in the world, spends at least one day a month on the shop floor – talking to customers and staff. This enables him to understand the concerns and issues of those who are key to the effective delivery of the business model. By entering the world of different people, you expand your own world by absorbing their paradigms and perspectives. The easiest way to broaden attention is to speak to people you do not normally speak to. And the most important people to speak to are your customers and the people dealing with them. As a leader, people will try and skew your attention in ways that suit them, so it is particularly important that you regularly get to the direct data.

Another way of broadening attention is to listen to people that you instinctively dismiss or dislike. They may be encapsulating a view that you find difficult or threatening. All the more reason to listen to it! This is not just about knowing your opposition; it is about understanding your own resistances and intolerances.

Once you start to broaden your attention and begin learning, you will find that you are on an exciting journey. The more you listen to people, the more you will gain access to ideas and perspectives that help you see things that you would have missed and understand things that you would have misinterpreted.

It will not always be easy. It is frustrating and annoying to listen to some people. It is deeply challenging to listen to people who have paradigms that we instinctively dismiss or do not understand. We will look at how to handle some of the difficult emotions associated with learning in the next chapter.

Focusing Attention

In July 2005, the UK Prime Minister, Tony Blair, was about to host the G8 summit at Gleneagles in Scotland. Bob Geldof, a world-renowned leader in the world of popular music and lobbyist for the poor in Africa, had organized a concert that was being broadcast worldwide in order to focus attention on what the G8 summit would deliver for Africa. The world's attention was on Tony Blair and his leadership of the G8. However, just three days before the summit began, Tony Blair flew out to Singapore. He wanted to provide support for London's bid for the 2012 Olympics. London was not in the running; Paris was the favourite. Very few people believed that London stood any chance of winning. So there was both shock and elation in the UK when London's winning bid was announced. People in London (and Paris) could not believe it. In the aftermath, the media commentators concluded that Blair's presence in Singapore just before the final vote probably swung it.

This is a great example of well-focused attention. Despite chairing an extremely important summit, with the eyes of the world upon him, Tony Blair decided to focus his attention for a brief period of time on Singapore and the Olympic Games, and, as a result, helped to win the games for London.

Having a wide range of paradigms to access gives you the ability to broaden your attention. It also gives you the ability to choose where best to focus your attention at any one time. Aware of what is going on in a number of different areas, you are able to choose – what area will most benefit if I pay it some personal attention? What is really important right now and where should I focus my attention to bring about the greatest benefit for the organization? These are the questions that effective leaders ask when they seek to focus their attention.

So, the first step in focusing attention is to be very clear about what you want. You will have to go through a process of defining your values, being clear about what is important to you (and why) and elaborating in some way what legacy you would like to leave behind you. This involves listening to yourself; finding your own authentic voice. As Steve Jobs puts it:

> 'The only way to do great work is to love what you do . . . Your time is limited, so don't waste it living someone else's life . . . Don't let the noise of others' opinions drown out your own inner voice.'[10]

This is perhaps the most difficult challenge of leadership – tuning into and staying in touch with your own voice whilst also tuning into the voices of others. Whilst it is important never to lose touch with your inner voice, it is also important to listen to others. This is all part of developing cognitive, emotional and behavioural complexity – recognizing that surviving in a complex world is about reconciling tensions and managing dilemmas. What do your stakeholders want you to pay attention to? Who are your stakeholders (the list of business paradigms can help here)? What are their values, goals and

---

[10] Steve Jobs, 114th Commencement Address at Stanford University on 12th June 2005. You can access a transcript of the speech at http://news-service. stanford.edu/news/2005/june15/jobs-061505.html.

desires? Where do they collide? What seems really important in all of this? And what do you have passion, energy and commitment for? It is no good pursuing a goal that does not fire you with passion – you will need the passion to get you through the journey that is leadership.

It is not possible to focus attention unless you have a clear idea of what is truly important – what are the issues *you* feel a passion for; what do your stakeholders need you to address; what are the most important questions that need to be answered; where do we need to get to and why?

It is not unusual for people in top positions to find themselves in a leadership role without any idea of what questions they would like to address or where they want to lead their organizations to. In the absence of a focus 'out there' in the form of a challenging but motivating goal or target, we all know where the natural focus of attention will default to – '*self*'! Am I doing all right? What do people think of me? Did I make a good presentation? Did they notice that mistake? If I get this then my options will be worth £1/2m. If I can clinch this deal I might be up for promotion. I wonder if I'm doing OK. I'm not quite sure what's expected of me. . . . The value of having a shared direction and focus is that it liberates us from the clutches of our exhausting self-preoccupation. It enables people to put their energies into something that matters more than their personal self-doubts and insecurities. We all want to get outside our own haunting and debilitating thoughts, and a common goal enables us to do just that. When leaders focus their attention, it is empowering and liberating for others.

However, it is, of course, not quite as simple as that. If those in leadership positions do have a clear idea of where they want to go, they are sometimes overwhelmed by the sheer complexity and uncertainty of it all. This can leave leaders unsure as to whether their views are correct, what the right strategy should be, how to interpret events and trends, 'how' to go about getting everyone aligned – people in leadership positions often find themselves both anxious and uncertain.

They also find themselves having to respond to events and crises, and hence end up fire-fighting (the opposite of focusing attention).

This is why it is important to take regular 'time out' and, like American Presidents and other world leaders, go on retreat. This is a time to reconnect with your original purpose, to evaluate how it's going and reflect on what is helping and hindering in its achievement. It is a time when you can look at what you are paying attention to and assess how useful this is. You can decide what to delegate and how to drop attention stealers. You can face the fact that you may be avoiding paying attention to some difficult issues, whilst at the same time paying attention to activities inside your comfort zone. Having done this work, you are then refreshed with a new focus, determination and clarity. These kinds of leadership retreats are remarkably powerful.[11]

The challenge is to combine the focusing of attention with regular opportunities to broaden attention. The broadening of attention enables the organization to learn and adjust the focus accordingly. The focusing of attention helps provide the direction and psychological climate for people to take leadership throughout the organization. Our focus may or may not be 'right', but as long as we are continually feeding and updating our mental models by broadening our attention and listening to other voices, we can make changes in our focus, as necessary. Remember Greenbury's story – he had a very clear focus for his attention (achieving a profit figure of £1bn), but ironically the extreme narrowness of this focus almost brought the organization down.

---

[11] At Waverley Learning, we regularly run retreats for leaders that address these issues. It is remarkable how many people leave with a refreshed clarity of purpose and a renewed sense of confidence and conviction that enables them to take leadership in an area where previously they would have felt disempowered.

6

The Second Practice –
Harness Emotions

EMOTIONS AFFECT WHAT WE PAY ATTENTION TO, HOW WE make sense of cues and how we act. They affect our decision-making processes, our judgement and our propensity to take risks.[1] Damasio, one of the world's leading experts on the neurophysiology of emotions, claims:

> 'emotion is integral to the processes of reasoning and decision making, for worse and for better . . . selective reduction of emotion is at least as prejudicial for rationality as excessive emotion. It certainly does not seem true that reason stands to gain from operating without the leverage of emotion. On the contrary, emotion probably assists reasoning, especially when it comes to personal and social matters involving risk and conflict'.[2]

Research has shown that patients who have experienced damage to parts of the brain associated with emotions find it difficult to make decisions.[3] We know that when we process cues and store them in long-term memory, we access both the emotional and logical parts of our brains. As a result, many of our belief structures are charged with emotion, and this emotion is activated whenever our beliefs

[1] Goleman, D. (1996) *Emotional Intelligence*. London: Bloomsbury.
[2] Damasio, A. (1999) *The Feeling of What Happens – Body and Emotion in the Making of Consciousness*. London: Heinemann.
[3] LeDoux, J. (1998) *The Emotional Brain*. London: Weidenfeld and Nicholson.

are recalled from memory.[4] However cold, logical and objective a decision you appear to make, emotion has had a hand in it somewhere.

The role that emotions play in our sensemaking and our decision making is particularly relevant when it comes to blind spots. We have already seen that blind spots often arise from our desire to avoid the difficult and painful emotions experienced whilst thinking and learning. However, we do this at our cost: emotions convey complex meanings. If learning is going to take place, it is important to surface the emotions and interpret the meanings effectively.

The challenge here is that the heightened emotional intensity experienced whilst learning (for example, fear and anger) can confuse and misguide us. Blind spots often result from a mishandling of our emotions. Sometimes we let our emotions rule our thinking – we believe what we feel. When we feel despair, we believe there is no hope; when we feel angry, we believe others wish us harm. Allowing emotions to infuse our thinking like this causes us to make poor decisions. On other occasions we suppress our emotions and refuse to make sense of them. When we do this, our emotions make their impact at a subconscious level and we make decisions influenced by emotions we are not aware of. Managing our emotions during learning is a complex skill; we need to be able to tune into sometimes difficult emotions, interpret them clearly and then manage our reaction to them.

The ability to harness your emotions and learn from them is particularly relevant to leadership. Taking leadership is an emotional business. When you take leadership you make public commitments and arouse expectations. Leaders are exposed. As well as feeling excited and hopeful, at times they feel vulnerable and lonely, frustrated and anxious. These emotions can affect their judgement. For example, feelings of insecurity may drive leaders to surround themselves with friends and 'yes men', sealing themselves from criticism and alterna-

---

[4] Lodge, M. and Taber, C. S. (2005) 'The Automaticity of Affect for Political Leaders, Groups and Issues: An Experimental Test of the Hot Cognition Hypothesis.' *Political Psychology*, **26**(3), 455–482. David, D. and Szentagotai, A. (2006) 'Cognitions in cognitive-behavioural psychotherapies: toward an integrated model'. *Clinical Psychology Review*, **26**, 284–298.

tive views. These strategies may increase confidence and security, but do so at the cost of effective sensemaking and decision making.

The area of emotional intelligence is a huge subject and has been covered extensively in other books.[5] In this chapter, therefore, we will focus on three areas where handling emotions is critical for effective sensemaking – *hot cognition, cold cognition* and *tacit emotional processing*. The following chapter will address the phenomenon of defensiveness, probably the most important source of blind spots and underperformance in organizations today.

Hot Cognition

Hot cognition is 'thinking that is infused with strong emotion'.[6] This strong emotion affects how we make sense and how we make decisions. This may be beneficial. A leader who is passionately committed to a strong vision may make sense of a difficult situation more optimistically, and hence persevere, where others may give up. When our thinking is infused with hope, love or empathy, it can generate powerful learning and change. However, hot cognition can lead to blind spots. This is because we may refuse to make sense of information in a way that contradicts or challenges the way we feel.

We have already seen examples of hot cognition in relation to goals, values, self esteem and psychological comfort. When we process a

---

[5] For example, see Goleman, D. (1996) *Emotional Intelligence*. London: Bloomsbury.
[6] Abelson first proposed the notion of *hot cognition* to describe concepts and cognition that are affect-laden (see Abelson, R. (1963) 'Computer simulation of "hot" cognition', in S. Tomkins and D. Messick (Eds) *Computer Simulation of Personality*. New York: Wiley). Since then it has been tested and refined by psychologists in cognitive, social and political psychology. See, for example, Lodge, M. and Taber, C. S. (2005) 'The Automaticity of Affect for Political Leaders, Groups and Issues: An Experimental Test of the Hot Cognition Hypothesis.' *Political Psycholgy*, **26**(3), 455–482.

cue that is relevant to any of these areas, it is more likely that we will be using hot cognition. In addition, we all have areas of sensitivity, personal *hot buttons*, that can trigger hot cognition.

When in the grip of hot cognition we can:

- believe what we feel – for example, we *feel* angry because people are challenging us, and therefore *believe* that people want to obstruct our plans. We *feel* sad at a significant setback, and therefore *believe* that we will never achieve our goals.

- refuse to listen – our minds shut down their receptive faculties. We refuse to consider any other argument – we stop learning.

- attack and judge other people and/or their positions – instead of considering what others are saying, we look for ways of attacking both them and their arguments.

- defend our positions – any thinking we do is done to support our existing arguments.

- revert to simplistic and highly emotional sensemaking – instead of considering elements of opposing arguments that may make sense, we simplify the issues, reverting to black/white thinking (if you are not with me you are against me).

We often see simplistic sensemaking in political discourse where many of the issues are highly complex but often hinge on differences in values. For example:

- If anyone attempts to *understand* the opposite point of view (e.g. the views of 'terrorists'), they are dismissed as excusing, agreeing with and supporting that point of view. When it comes to clashes of interests and values, we see an instinctive flight to oversimplification and a rigid intolerance of complexity. There is often a genuine fear that if we *understand* the other's point of view, we may indeed come to support it and weaken our own position.

- Ridicule of the opposition's point of view, generating hatred and derision of the opponent (who may nevertheless expound an intelligent and convincing argument). This is seen when one side labels the other side with a concept that is extremely emotional, ridiculous or verging on the taboo, and hence is difficult to argue with (e.g. the opposition are 'terrorists', 'racists', 'thought police', 'traitors' or, less extreme but just as dysfunctional, 'geeks', 'bleeding heart Liberals', 'bean counters').

Of course, these ploys are all part of the 'game' of debate and argument. However, people fall into the trap of *genuinely* making sense of reality in this way, and they do so when they are in the grip of strong emotions. People do genuinely feel that one side of a debate is 'right' and the other is 'wrong'. This can cause us to view highly intelligent people who have a genuine living knowledge of the subject as wrong, misguided or even stupid.

In complex areas, it is rare that people are wrong. They may be wrong about 'facts' of course, but their point of view is rarely wrong – there will ALWAYS be an element of truth in most people's arguments. This is because their arguments will be based upon their own living knowledge – *their* interpretation of *their* personal experience. However, it is depressingly familiar to hear each side in a conflict (and their supporters) vilify and simplify the other side's views. As a result, people's mental models of the complex systems they are dealing with (e.g. education, health, energy, law and order) are partial, skewed and biased. This means that the answers they generate to fix the problems simply will not work – they are not complex enough to take account of the complexity of the systems they are intended to manage.

These distortions in our thinking have long been recognized by psychologists, who call them *cognitive biases*. The following is a list of common cognitive biases:

1. *Confirmation bias* – only paying attention to and believing data that confirm what you already believe; dismissing evidence that contradicts what you already believe.

2. *Black/white thinking* – seeing the world in terms of a few extremes – if it is not black then it must be white. Refusing to take on board the complexity of a situation.

3. *Mind reading* – assuming you know the motivations, thoughts and feelings of others.

4. *Flooding* – if emotion is felt strongly enough, it must be justifiable; allowing strong emotions to 'flood' our reason; the belief that strong emotions are always 'right'.

5. *Overgeneralization* – taking one event or piece of evidence and making general rules based upon it.

6. *Personalization* – believing that the motives for other people's behaviour concern how they affect you: 'I know he said that to hurt me'.

7. *Stereotyping* – classifying people in crude and often negative ways that deny their individuality. Blaming these groups for problems as a way of denying personal responsibility.

8. *Self-serving bias* – the tendency to take credit for events that are successful and to deny responsibility when events are less successful.

9. *Mood bias* – evaluating a situation more optimistically when one is feeling happy and less optimistically when one is feeling sad.

10. *Recency bias* – paying more attention to data that was most recently brought to your attention.

In sum, hot cognition can, if we are not careful, lead to an oversimplification in our sensemaking. Strong emotions drive us to rationalize what we feel and dismiss any 'fact' or opinion that may suggest our feelings are not accurate. Sometimes we have to pause before we think and examine our feelings, recognizing that making sense using 'hot cognition' tends to generate poor decisions in complex environments.

But, *how* do we harness these feelings and manage their effects on our sensemaking? As always, the first stage is recognizing when you are in the grips of hot cognition and acknowledging how it is affecting you. Once you recognize that you are exhibiting, say, confirmation bias, you can decide to stop it! Like all of these practices, much depends on an element of self awareness and self discipline!

It is also important to recognize that learning requires a different state of mind. When we decide to learn, we enter a different kind of mental state – a state of quietness, calm and receptivity. We will explore this in more detail later on, but for now it is important to recognize that it is much harder to 'learn' when one is subject to feelings of anger, frustration or despair. In order to learn, we need to take a conscious decision to step back and reflect. Learning requires an investment of both time and energy.

Cold Cognition

Cold cognition is defined as 'thinking that suppresses emotions, particularly those associated with compassion for and moral obligation towards others'. Compassion for and moral obligation towards others are commonly associated with empathy and guilt. The diaries show that both empathy and guilt can be profound catalysts for learning if handled correctly. Let's start by taking an example based on one of the diarists' experience.

Bill Harris – Guilt and Learning: A True Story

Bill was a senior manager in a logistics company that was introducing a culture change. He was responsible for driving the culture change through the company, where traditionally the values were based on nepotism, not questioning the hierarchy and divide and rule tactics. Bill, however, had strong values around teamwork, involving people in decision making, integrity, fairness and honesty and was strongly committed to the changes that involved introducing a more professional set of values.

Bill soon became absorbed in the culture change process. He was fascinated with the dynamics of change and spent a lot of time talking to the consultant that had been brought in to help. He became very close to the General Manager during the change process, as they both shared an interest in organizational change. They spent many an early evening chatting about the changes being introduced. Other people soon began talking about a senior management clique. The senior team split into two camps, with the out-group feeling excluded and marginalized.

As the changes evolved further, it became clear that the senior management team had to be reduced. Bill, knowing that this would be a painful process, nevertheless knew it was necessary for the business. He identified what the new team would look like, how this would be communicated to the rest of the team and how it would be implemented.

Feeling a little nervous about the forthcoming announcement, Bill decided to devote more time to the rest of the senior management team. As he relaxed with them over coffee, he was overwhelmed by the depth of feeling he encountered. The team expressed their anger at being excluded from the decision making, and at being relegated to an out-group, leaving Bill feeling increasingly uncomfortable.

That evening Bill reflected on his experience. The overwhelming feeling he was experiencing was that of guilt. Whilst the changes were correct, he began to realize that *how* he had gone about implementing them directly contravened his own values. He hadn't involved the people in teamwork; he hadn't consulted them; he hadn't been entirely open and honest with them. In fact, he had pretended to consult them, when in reality the decisions had been made behind closed doors between him and the GM.

Bill realized that people did not feel that they had been consulted in the changes, and that as a result they felt devalued and had lost confidence in themselves. He felt personally responsible for the difficulties they experienced. He felt concern and sympathy for the recipients of change, and this made him realize he needed to show more patience and tolerance. He concluded you cannot always consult everyone on everything. He could not truly have consulted the team about the strategic reorganization of the team itself. However, what was wrong was saying you were consulting (to yourself and others) when clearly you were not – Bill was not being honest with himself or with others. Furthermore, he could have been more sympathetic, more supportive and less impatient. This was a profound learning experience for Bill.

Bill learned a lot through this incident, but only because he was prepared to face rather painful truths about his behaviour. The depth of feeling from the others stimulated the realization that he had contravened his own values. This, in turn, prompted the guilt that caused him to reflect. And, rather than bury the guilt, he was courageous enough to face it and analyse it. From this reflection came a great deal of learning, which led to significant changes in his beliefs, emotional orientation and behaviour – changes in his living knowledge.

However, for every diarist that responded to guilt in this way, three more rationalized it away. The problem with emotions such as guilt and compassion is that they are not comfortable or convenient. Both compassion and guilt tend to get in the way of one's goals. Guilt can be horribly corrosive, leading to a drop in self esteem. However, if handled correctly, both compassion and guilt can generate profound mind shifts.

An example of the role of compassion and guilt in learning is provided by Adam Kahane, again in his book *Solving Tough Problems*.[7] Kahane facilitated a group of leading figures from Guatemala – a country with a terrible human rights record. The group consisted of 'academics, business and non-governmental organization leaders, former guerrillas and military officers, government officials, human rights activists, journalists, national and local politicians, clergy, trade unionists and young people'.[8] All of these people came from different sides in the conflict that had ravaged the country for many decades. At one point in the proceedings, a man named Ronalth Ochaeta, the director of the Guatemalan Archdiocesan Human Rights Office, told a story:

'Ochaeta had gone to a Mayan village to witness the exhumation of a mass grave – one of many – from a massacre. When the earth had been removed, he noticed a number of small bones. He asked the forensics team if people had their bones broken during the

---

[7] Kahane, A. (2004) *Solving Tough Problems*. San Francisco: Berrett-Koehler.
[8] Kahane, A. (2004) *Solving Tough Problems*. San Francisco: Berrett-Koehler, p. 114.

massacre. No, the grave contained the corpses of women who had been pregnant. The small bones belonged to their fetuses.

When Ochaeta finished telling his story, the team was completely silent . . . The silence lasted a long time, perhaps five minutes. Then it ended, and we took a break.

This silence had an enormous impact on the group. In interviews years later, many members of the team referred to it.'

Kahane quotes some of the group members' recollections:

'In the end, and particularly after listening to Ochaeta's story, I understood and felt in my heart all that had happened. And there was a feeling that we must struggle to prevent this from happening again . . .'

'What happened in this country was brutal . . . But we were aware of it!. . . the workshops helped me to understand this in all its human dimension. A tremendous brutality! I was aware of it but had not experienced it. It is one thing to know about something and keep it as statistical data, and another to actually feel it . . . after understanding this, everyone was committed to preventing it from happening again.'

'His testimony was sincere, calm and serene, without a trace of hate in his voice. This gave way to the moment of silence that, I would say, lasted at least one minute. It was horrible! A very moving experience for all . . . If you ask any of us, we would say that this moment was like a large communion. No one dared break the silence.'

This is the opposite of cold cognition. It is cognition suffused by compassion; it is mature, holistic and enlightened. This type of mature, compassionate cognition moves people. And this is the problem – many people do not want to be moved; they want to continue pursuing their goals. Goals 'harden' us. One of the insights revealed by the Ochaeta story is how most cognition is cold, most of the time. Cold cognition protects us from responsibility, from guilt and from the need to take action. It is reminiscent of the philosopher Hannah Arendt's term – 'the banality of evil' – used when reporting on the Eichmann trial to describe the events of Nazi Germany.[9] Arendt uses the term to show how one of the greatest evils in history could be perpetrated by people just pursuing their own small goals, obeying, conforming and doing their jobs without asking too many questions regarding the outcomes of their actions or their responsibility to others. The banality of evil is made possible by means of cold cognition in its most extreme form.

In organizations, we need to challenge cold cognition and encourage more rounded, balanced and mature cognition. Balanced cognition does not mean adopting a 'touchy-feely' approach to management or leadership. Difficult decisions that cause hardship to others *have* to be made all the time in business, government and in the not-for-profit sectors. Balanced cognition simply means allowing yourself to feel the pain that others will feel when they experience the consequences of your difficult decisions. Balanced cognition feels the pain and attempts to ameliorate it without avoiding the tough decisions that need to be made. Quite simply, balanced cognition is not afraid to embrace the fact that we are all fully thinking, fully emotional human beings and that emotions are a legitimate and important part of organizational life. The Greeks have a word for balanced cognition: it is known as *sophrosyne*. Sophrosyne means reaching wisdom through a balance between reason and emotion. This is a quality that our leaders increasingly need to develop.

Tacit Emotional Processing

According to LeDoux, most of our emotional processing takes place unconsciously. We learn to love, hate, fear, like and dislike largely through our unconscious brain. If this is the case, this tacit emotional processing is not always functional, effective or conducive to healthy relationships.[10]

Let's take an example from the diaries. Rob is a senior manager with Scientific Solutions. Having come out of a session looking at

---

[9] Arendt, H. (1994 edition) *Eichmann in Jerusalem: A Report on the Banality of Evil.* London: Penguin Books.
[10] LeDoux, J. (1998) *The Emotional Brain.* London: Weidenfeld and Nicholson.

personality types and how they influence teams, Rob is sensitized to individual differences. He writes in his diary:

> *'Reflected on how my behaviour towards Jack (supportive, under-standing) is different to my behaviour to Tim. Both are product champions – but I'm fairly negative with Tim. Because I think him lazy?'*

This simple insight has a profound effect on Rob. As he begins to reflect about Tim, probably for the first time, he begins to see that he has somehow picked up an unwarranted prejudice about him. He describes his learning in an interview:

> *'And that changed me completely. Strange, really strange. Because I don't know where I picked up this issue with Tim – obviously by something I picked up from other people because I don't interact with him. I was on a training course with him and . . . I quite liked Tim, and yet we came to the same business years later, and I had this bias and I couldn't tell you where I got it, I mean I obviously picked it up from other people. And things weren't going well with the interaction with Tim, and it exactly matched the bias and it just, it was just reinforced.'*

By reflecting on his attitude to Tim, Rob realized that he had unconsciously picked up an unfounded prejudice, the realization of which profoundly shocked him. This insight forced him to reflect further on Tim and to evaluate how he had come to pick up this prejudice. As he reflects he begins to empathize with Tim:

> *'Before I had been to see him I thought he was a lousy bastard and that's why it wasn't working, and afterwards I thought about what I can learn about this, I was thinking, it must be a very lonely existence being a one person team here, because the rest of his team are spread out, and I looked at him much more sympathetically and my interaction with him then was much better, much better.'*

So, whereas a year ago, Rob might have dismissed Tim as someone not worth bothering with, a year later he realizes that there is more to this colleague than he had realized. As a result, he changes his attitude to Tim and suddenly starts to put a lot of effort into helping and supporting him:

> '*I mean after that, Dave and I did a one-day workshop with him . . . to help him with business planning. If I hadn't spotted my prejudices . . . I'd have just said sod him, I really would. So we went out of our way to set something up . . . and Tim put together a reasonable plan, had a good response from the board. Now, none of that would have happened if we hadn't undone my prejudice.*'

Rob never knew where his dislike of Tim had come from – a chance conversation, gossip, a fleeting impression? Yet this dislike was affecting all his interactions with Tim. As soon as he became aware of and challenged his own prejudice, he was able to help Tim put together a business plan which was accepted by the board.

Emotions are subtle things. Rob's case shows how emotional orientations build up over a period of time, quite unconsciously, and affect how we make sense of things – events, other people, ourselves. In Rob's case, he has picked up an emotional orientation and rationalized it according to his values – dismissing Tim as 'lazy' (something that Rob disliked intensely).

If we do not attempt to tune into our emotions, they will constantly affect our sensemaking, without our being aware of it leading to significant blind spots. Having tuned into them, we have to explore and, indeed, challenge them. We pick up emotional orientations that are unfounded and biased. We need to learn when our emotions are imparting important information and when they represent prejudices that have never been examined rationally.

One diarist describes the slow build up of emotion that affects people subconsciously over a period of time as an organization goes through change:

> **Karen:** *So, do you sometimes take these negative events and sit down and really think about what are the implications of these, what should I do, or do you just let it rest?*

Sally: *No, I don't even know I consciously register them at the time, it's just that at some other point in the reckoning that it suddenly comes to your mind, but it's registered with you. I think as a here and now thing nothing happens, you take it on board but don't do a lot about it at the time. I think it's lots of things that slowly add up . . . everything you do affects you one way or another, you get the job right, it affects you, if your boss is shitty, it affects you, so it all affects your emotions one way or another. I can't sort of say that there's one thing or other that affects me more emotionally, because everything does positively and negatively.*

Here, Sally very graphically describes the slow build up of emotions that takes place day by day, affecting feelings, self confidence and how you interpret things around you. Every day, some little thing happens that makes you doubt yourself – nothing much to worry about, some small slight, but one that stays. And a few days later, something similar happens. Before you know it, a year down the line, Sally has lost a great deal of confidence in herself – and she can't put her finger on how precisely this has happened to her. The events that have served to undermine self esteem have not seemed particularly memorable. Many of them have been to do with new company policies and decisions. Many of them relate to how she has been treated by management and colleagues. They all accumulate to create an emotional climate that affects everyone. Other diarists, mostly in middle management positions, described similar changes in emotional orientation and self esteem that took place over the year.

It is particularly important in difficult times that we challenge these emotional orientations. You do not have to believe what you feel. Like Othello, we so often believe something is true because we feel it. In situations of change, it is common for people to feel threatened; they focus on their own survival and on their own feelings of anxiety and frustration. They no longer have the energy to think about others, so, quite inadvertently, they become less supportive and interested in their colleagues. This sends out signals that people are no longer valued. Everyone becomes inward looking and anxious; the support and help and social glue that enables work interaction to take place, breaks down. This is all picked up and made sense of unconsciously, though there is a sense that everyone is out for him or herself. This, of course, tends to drive more selfish behaviour and the organization gets caught in a downward spiral, without even noticing it.

This all happens at a time when leadership is needed from people at all levels. But, instead of feeling confident and energized, people feel undervalued and lacking in self esteem. This is a perfectly normal response – but it is not helpful. Time out is needed to tune into the emotions, make sense of them and start to challenge them. Time out can be taken in the form of leadership retreats or change management workshops. During this time it is important to surface all these emotions, to acknowledge fears and hurts and to reconnect with one's vision of what is both desirable and possible. It is important to remember that the future has not yet been enacted, and that, working together, with renewed energy, clarity and confidence, the future is entirely open – to be enacted in whatever way people see fit.

In all of the above examples we have seen that learning requires a different mindset. Learning in the midst of activity and the flow of day-to-day emotions is difficult. We all suffer from hot cognition, cold cognition and tacit emotional processing (another way of putting it might be we all suffer from simplistic sensemaking, selfishness and prejudice). In order to learn effectively, we need to enter a calm, reflective and receptive state of mind where we are prepared to listen to both ourselves and others.

Adam Kahane quotes a colleague, Otto Scharmer, who talks about four kinds of listening.[11] The first is *downloading*, when we listen by evaluating and judging from within our own story (or from within our own living knowledge). We listen for what resonates with our own living knowledge and fail to hear what does not. In essence, we are listening for confirmation of our own beliefs and experiences. This is the opposite of learning.

The second form of listening is *debating*. This is when we listen and try to judge the objective 'correctness' or coherence of what is being said – either by others or by ourselves.

---

[11] Kahane, A. (2004) *Solving Tough Problems*. San Francisco: Berrett-Koehler.

The third form of listening is *reflective dialogue*. We no longer assume that we are stating truth, but recognize that we are sharing our own limited, but personally 'true', living knowledge. We also listen for the background story that is generating the contributions that others are making. We listen with empathy to their contributions and we challenge our own contributions more critically.

The fourth kind of listening is *generative dialogue*. This is more complex. Essentially, instead of simply listening for the individual truths inherent in each person's living knowledge, you also listen from the vantage point of the whole system, sensing what it requires of everyone. This, partly, is a matter of integrity. It entails the ability to envisage and empathize with all the participants in the system, their needs and the needs of the whole. An example might be trying to listen to the individual stories of a German oil executive, a member of OPEC, an oil worker from Nigeria, an 'environmentalist' from the United States and an automotive worker from China, all within in the context and demands of the planet as a whole!

It is difficult to engage in generative dialogue during everyday activity. If we are to learn deeply and profoundly in a way that will make a difference to our societies and organizations, we need to invest time in learning 'off-line' – spending time on retreats and awaydays and learning to discipline ourselves to do what many of us find most difficult – really listening to people! It is only when we really listen to people, however, that we begin to learn.

7

The Third Practice – Overcome Defensiveness

'Humankind cannot stand very much reality'.

T. S. Eliot

In *Good to Great*, Jim Collins sets out what it is that differentiates great from mediocre companies. His research identified 11 companies that had gone from being mediocre to excellent, outperforming the stock market by between 4 and 18 times over a period of 15 years. He then compared them to companies in the same industry that started in similar positions but failed to manage the breakthrough. One of the six qualities he mentions that differentiates the great companies is the ability to 'confront the brutal facts'.

It appears then, that confronting the brutal facts differentiates the great from the mediocre. But why should it be so unusual to confront facts? Why do people shy away from confronting facts? Is this not self-defeating? Is not confronting facts one of those logical and rational things that businesses and organizations do best?

Collins quotes Fred Purdue, an executive interviewed from Pitney Bowes, one of the 11 'great' companies:

> *'When you turn over rocks and look at all the squiggly things underneath, you can either put the rock down, or you can say, "My job is to turn over rocks and look at the squiggly things", even if what you see can scare the hell out of you.'*[1]

---

[1] Collins, J. (2001) *Good to Great*. London: Random House, p. 72.

And here is the nub of the issue. Facts can be like the squiggly things underneath rocks – unpleasant and scary. And, generally speaking, we do not like to feel uncomfortable emotions, so, in order to regain our equanimity, we put the rock down and pretend we never saw the squiggly things in the first place.

We have seen this on innumerable occasions already. We saw it with Barings and the Bristol Royal Infirmary. We saw it with our diarists, who avoided painful evidence and denied that 'facts' were true. This fear of the 'squiggly things' is a powerful source of blind spots in leaders and their organizations.

Collins focuses particularly on the problems that *visionary* leaders have in confronting facts. Writing of one of the comparison companies that failed to achieve breakthrough performance (in fact it filed for bankruptcy), Collins refers to the role played by its visionary leader, Roy Ash. Whilst he acknowledges that Ash was a visionary who tried to inspire his company to achieve great things, he points to the fact that Ash refused to acknowledge mounting and compelling evidence that indicated his vision was going to fail.[2]

It is difficult for visionary leaders to spot when resistance to their vision derives from unjustified pessimism, simple discomfort with change or from a balanced and sympathetic examination of the facts. The danger for visionary leaders is that they can become 'happiness junkies' – people who only want to hear good news. These types of leaders generate 'good news' cultures, where people feel it is only acceptable to present information that confirms senior executives' 'visions' and makes them feel good. To dwell on problems is considered negative and unacceptable; as a result, problems are avoided until it is too late to do anything about them.

Of course, this avoidance of difficult facts is the exception rather than the rule – otherwise we would not have the thriving, successful organizations that we do. But these defensive blind spots can creep into organizational cultures like a virus, undermining the organization's effectiveness and inhibiting its ability to recover. Once the virus sets in, the more things go wrong, the more difficult it is to

---

[2] Collins, J. (2001) *Good to Great*. London: Random House, p. 72.

summon the courage to face them. The more we avoid the squiggly things, the bigger and scarier they get. Then it is highly tempting to focus one's attention elsewhere, pretend the problems don't exist or rationalize them away – it was just a one-off, it will go better next time. Moreover, there is some sense in responding in this way.

First, it is very difficult to make sense of a situation in the presence of high levels of negative emotion. When in the grips of 'hot cognition', we are likely to catastrophize the situation – that was a disaster – rather than learn rationally from it.

Second, one of the problems with handling setbacks is that we fail to put them in perspective. We dwell on them, blaming ourselves, rubbing the wounds of our embarrassment and failure. Before you know it, we become depressed, our thinking becomes distorted (I'll never make it, I'm no good) and we sink into learned helplessness (there's nothing I can do to change my life or situation, I'm useless . . .).

Both of these are problems of interpretation. We fail to interpret our setbacks effectively. We overpersonalize them, attributing them to our personal weaknesses and failures of character, rather than seeing them simply for what they are – steps on the journey of learning. These problems of interpretation can lead to emotional disorders, phobias and obsessions. More commonly, they lead to stress, heightened anxiety and poor self esteem.

This is why it is so important to 'learn' how to handle setbacks and frustrations effectively, particularly if you are in a leadership position. Leaders often battle with the challenge of facing difficult information and interpreting it correctly. As Collins puts it:

> *'There is nothing wrong with pursuing a vision for greatness. After all, the good-to-great companies also set out to create greatness. But, unlike the comparison companies, the good-to-great companies continually refined the* **path** *to greatness with the brutal facts of reality.'*[3]

---

[3] Collins, J. (2001) *Good to Great*. London: Random House.

And, of course, refining the path to greatness with the brutal facts of reality is simply another way of saying 'they continually learned'. It is also another way of saying that learning is painful. But in the 'great' companies, leaders managed their emotions so that their fear of the squiggly things did not overcome their duty to look at them, think of them, analyse them, interpret them and act on them.

If leaders do not do this, the anxiety never goes away, it just pervades the organization, creating a defensive, anti-learning culture. People are aware of problems but know that it is not acceptable to refer to them. In defensive organizations, people do not question anything. Unrealistic budgets are put together – no-one questions them. Expensive projects fail but success is claimed and behaviour justified. At all costs avoid talk of failure. Never criticize, never evaluate or suggest that results are disappointing. If something goes wrong, find a powerless individual low down in the hierarchy and blame her.

Defensive cultures are characterized by fear. And fear triggers the well-known fight/flight response. This consists of a collection of physiological and behavioural reactions intended to protect us from physical danger. These reactions have their origins deep in our evolutionary past. In the presence of a physical threat, such as a wild animal, our bodies need to be prepared for action – either fighting off the threat or fleeing from it. Hence, the body automatically prepares itself so that:

- the pupils dilate and the mouth goes dry;

- the muscles tense and sweat is produced;

- the lungs breathe faster;

- the heart beats faster;

- our blood pressure rises as blood moves from our internal organs to our muscles;

- adrenalin and noradrenalin are released.

In effect, the body is readying itself for the physical exertion of defending itself. Once the threat is fought off, the energy is released and the body returns to its normal state.

The problem is that the fight/flight response is triggered whenever we experience a threat to our more intangible, existential needs at work. Moreover, the perception of threat does not even have to be conscious:

'the system operates independently of consciousness – it is part of what we called the emotional unconscious . . . Interactions between the defence system and consciousness underlie feelings of fear, but the defence system's function in life, or at least the function it evolved to achieve, is survival in the face of danger'.[4]

Anxiety not only triggers a physiological response but also a range of behavioural, cognitive and emotional responses. These are commonly known as *defence mechanisms*. These defence mechanisms are also generated in the presence of a threat to our existential needs – goals, values, self esteem, psychological comfort, etc. We saw in the last chapter the cognitive distortions that often result when we experience a threat to our needs. The following list describes further defence mechanisms that are commonly found in organizations.

1. *Denial* – refusing to perceive or face unpleasant realities. Denying that unfavourable situations/facts exist. This can involve reverting to alcohol or drugs in order to dull the pain rather than deal with it.

2. *Blaming* – refusing to take responsibility for one's actions; blaming others for outcomes for which you have some responsibility.

3. *Verbal aggression* – criticizing, belittling, mocking and ridiculing others. Arguing and not listening to others. Dismissive and hostile. Shouting, threatening, bullying and intimidating others.

4. *Flippancy* – becoming childish; being flippant and facetious. Using humour to deflect criticism and avoid serious discussion.

5. *Conformity and Self censorship* – absorbing the values and beliefs imposed by others. Suppressing doubts about the group's ideas

---

[4] LeDoux, J. (1998) *The Emotional Brain*. London: Weidenfeld and Nicholson, p. 129.

or beliefs. Deferring to others, particularly more senior people, in order to protect oneself.

6. *Rationalization* – denying the emotional drivers of your actions by supplying logical reasons for your behaviour.

7. *Withdrawal* – going into your shell. Reducing involvement and withdrawing in order to protect oneself from hurt. Aloof, closed to others; refusing to show one's emotions.

8. *Playing victim* – not taking any responsibility for anything that happens to you. Seeing yourself as a victim of circumstance and helpless to respond.

9. *Dependency* – being self critical to elicit pity or reassurance from others. Sending out dependency signals in order to elicit protection from someone else.

10. *Illusion of invulnerability* – exaggerated belief in one's abilities. Believing that nothing could go wrong or that you could never make a mistake. Belief that you are always right.

11. *Cynicism* – channelling one's anger, bitterness or disappointment into overly negative assessments of the situation or people around you. Ridiculing more positive interpretations of the situation.

12. *Excuses* – denying personal responsibility for events. 'Yes butting'.

13. *Harmonizing* – suppressing conflict by soothing people's feelings; asserting that people's interests are in complete accordance. Denying that conflict exists.

14. *Avoidance* – avoiding disagreements or conflict, avoiding risk, being passive.

All of these forms of defensiveness corrode organizational performance by inhibiting dialogue and eroding trust. The role of leadership is crucial in exacerbating or preventing this. Leadership plays a number of important roles with regards to defensiveness – leaders can:

• spread it by being unable or unwilling to control their own defensiveness;

- enable it to flourish, either by not recognizing it or by fearing to confront the individuals that spread it;

- prevent it by encouraging a culture of openness and by being ruthlessly disciplined with their own behaviour and confronting those who spread defensiveness.

The following two case studies show just what can happen when defensiveness takes root in a person and/or organization. The first case shows how a leader becomes defensive with regards to a particular issue over which he feels vulnerable. This then becomes a blind spot for the whole team, and indeed the whole organization. In this case, people recognize the blind spot but cannot do anything about it, because the leader vetoes further discussion.

In the second case, we have an individual in a leadership position who has developed a 'defensive personality'. Defensive leaders can do terrible damage. The main reason that they are able to do such damage is because everyone – from the Chairman down – is petrified of them.

Andy – Defensiveness and Self Awareness

Andy has worked for ACI, a European food retailer, for over 15 years. He joined having graduated from university with a first class degree in Business and European Languages, and rose rapidly through the hierarchy. With a phenomenal facility for understanding complex systems, he has an enviable knack of knowing just what to do in order to deliver the required goals and outcomes – often gaining the respect of others by doing some of the most complex work himself. He is fascinated by business systems and has spoken at a number of industry conferences in this area. His last post was Head of Operations, where he had been involved in a comprehensive business re-engineering project that had saved the company millions of pounds.

It was no surprise when Andy was promoted to head up a large division over 2½ years ago. However, what has surprised some people is the difficulty that Andy has had establishing his control and leadership. Recently, he received some feedback via the 360° process that suggested his direct reports were unhappy with his refusal to delegate and his tendency to get involved in too much detailed implementation. The feedback implied that he was not leading the division as effectively as he could.

Andy was not expecting this feedback and became furious with his direct reports. He felt angry and betrayed. He made it clear that he would not tolerate criticism of his management style, particularly in an area where he was considered an industry expert. His direct reports were both surprised by his outburst and intimidated. No-one said anything and the issue of Andy getting too involved in implementation was never raised again. The functional heads withdrew to their functions, and what had once been a good team began to weaken. The functional heads competed to 'please' Andy and a sense of insecurity and distrust invaded the team. There was a sense that Andy favoured operations over and above any of the other functions; those outside operations felt that he neither understood nor valued what they did.

Andy began to feel increasingly out of control. Suddenly, he had to rely for implementation on other people – people who, he felt, were not as good as him. People did not understand as clearly, act as quickly or implement as decisively as he did. He often lost patience with them and did not care to hide it. He started to blame his people for being incompetent.

However, nothing he did would get rid of this background feeling of anxiety that continued to gnaw away at him. And the more he felt this anxiety, the more snappy, impatient and intolerant he became. The division was yielding acceptable results, yet, at some deep level, he felt uneasy and it would not go away. Andy found himself drinking more heavily and, for the first time in his life, found it difficult to sleep.

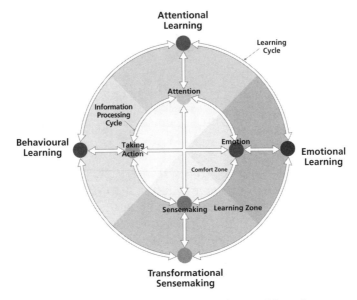

Figure 7.1   Information processing and learning.

It is easy to see exactly where Andy's learning falls down. Andy's 360° feedback provides him with some new information about himself that contradicts his existing self concept and challenges his high self esteem. This generates strong emotions – as he moves from the comfort zone into the learning zone. The emotions are painful and intense, consisting of anger, disappointment, self pity, fear and a sense of betrayal. Looking at our learning cycle, his attention has been grabbed by the 360° and he is experiencing new emotions.

At this point, he has a choice. He can continue round to the sense-making phase to try and make sense of what is happening using new constructs and beliefs. If he does this, he will have generated new insights about himself, his direct reports and his situation. However, the pain of the emotions he is experiencing, and particularly the fear that he might, for the first time in his life, fail in a job, drives him back toward the comfort zone. He does not want to engage in this painful sensemaking as he does not know what he might find out. He is drawn back to the comfort zone, and the primary aim of his sensemaking and actions is to maintain his existing beliefs, behaviours and to maintain his self esteem. His learning journey stops at this point, and he makes sense of his situation using his current constructs. But, whilst he successfully defends himself against uncomfortable learning and change, the knowledge that all is not right remains in his subconscious, waiting to be let out. It is this knowledge that continues to nag him in the form of a background anxiety, drawing his attention to important information he needs in order to survive. In order to suppress this voice, Andy turns to drink.

This is how defensiveness operates. It interrupts the potential learning journey in order to preserve emotional comfort, existing beliefs and current behaviours. It draws people back to the comfort zone. But, despite the denial, the knowledge will not go away. Andy's subconscious mind is picking up the signals – it knows something is wrong, but Andy won't focus on his emotions to allow the insights to bubble to the surface. As a result, the anxiety stays and Andy has to develop strategies to cope with it.

This example shows leaders manifesting defensiveness with regards to a particular event, relationship or decision. But it can happen that leaders live their whole lives defensively – they become defensive personalities. They focus their attention on one or two deep-rooted needs or fears, and have learned methods that appear to get them what they most want. In effect, these people learn that their defensiveness 'works'. Of course, it is questionable that these defensive personalities are 'leaders'. They are more likely to be senior managers occupying leadership positions. The next example shows us what can happen when defensive people get into senior, 'leadership' positions.

Claire – The Defensive Personality

Claire was recently appointed as the head of a local government department responsible for providing services for disadvantaged young people in the area. Rumours suggested that she had a forceful, no-nonsense management style and could be quite intimidating. When Claire came into the department, she found that, on the whole, it was functioning fairly efficiently. However, there were some elements that, according to Claire, needed to be changed. First, she found that the department had developed a fairly cosy relationship with the schools in the area. She found that numerous informal decisions were being made, which, whilst not against the rules in any way, meant it was difficult to control what was happening. Second, she found that her staff were working with the schools and not recording their costs properly. This meant that schools were gaining access to all sorts of informal services that they were not paying for.

Claire immediately put a stop to the provision of uncosted services. From now on, she announced, all contacts with schools were to be monitored and accounted for. She also decided that notes of all relevant meetings should be taken and sent to her. She had already decided that one decision should be vetoed, as it was not in the interests of the department.

The staff were outraged at this intrusion into their working practices, but when a case worker called Jo complained, everyone discovered what lay at the root of Claire's reputation. She erupted. She shouted at and criticized Jo. She asked Jo what right she had to question her decisions and accused her of looking after her own vested interests at the expense of the department. She made it clear to Jo that she would be watching her with great interest over the next few months. Jo left the encounter with Claire and promptly burst into tears. Soon, the story of Claire's outburst had spread throughout the department.

The individual officers were petrified of Claire. They never quite knew when she would start screaming and shouting at them. Claire's decisions were erratic and often could not be anticipated. Individual officers were placed in highly embarrassing positions, unable to operate or deliver their promises to clients until Claire had deigned to give them her attention.

Whilst those reporting to Claire were sometimes astonished at the decisions she made, they felt they could do nothing about it. Claire's boss was preoccupied with putting together a strategic plan for the region, and they rarely saw him. If he had heard about the goings on within the department, he did not seem to show any concern, and certainly was not doing anything to manage Claire. Claire seemed to be completely in charge. She made all the most important decisions and no-one dared challenge her.

All attention was focused on personal survival, and the officers knew that the people who were suffering were the disadvantaged children themselves. Before Claire, everything ran smoothly and activity was focused on the children's needs, even if it was all rather informal. Now, however, all attention seemed to be focused on Claire and the insecurities, fears and anger that she bred around her.

In the meantime, Claire's boss, the head of the department, had heard some rumours regarding Claire's behaviour and management style. But the work was being done and no deadlines had been missed. As far as he was concerned, it was up to her how she ran her department; he had to focus on more important, strategic aspects of his job.

In this case, then, we have two leadership blind spots – Claire's blind spots about herself, her motivations and the inappropriateness of her behaviour, and her boss's blind spots regarding his need to performance manage and confront Claire.

Claire's manager is not in control of the situation. There may be a number of reasons for this, but two common reasons are:

- senior managers are too interested in promoting their careers upwards to take a real interest in what is going on below them;

- many managers are frightened of confronting unacceptable behaviour – the Claires of this world are adept at intimidating not only direct reports and peers, but also those senior to them, including their own bosses.

This is an important source of blind spots in organizations and a reason why many 'values statements' are derided and ignored. Many leaders are not prepared to defend the company's values (or even their own) by confronting behaviour that undermines them. Many leaders are wary of and dislike performance managing people. Yet, performance management is a vital tool for delivering values, especially in situations where defensiveness is rooted within an organization. The outlining of objectives, the clarifying of priorities, the communication of values and the provision of feedback are all vital parts of the leader's toolkit. It is surprising how many leaders are nervous of using them. They are wary of facing an employee's defensiveness and potentially difficult emotions. They may be frightened of hurting a person's feelings or of undermining their confidence.

Some leaders are wary of adopting a 'directive' style with their people. They have learned that it is not acceptable to 'command and control' people. They have to persuade and influence. With managers like Claire, however, the command and control style is necessary. In fact, a directive style of management is always appropriate if used to defend the values against those who would undermine them.

Nor is Claire's case so unusual. It is surprising how many defensive managers gain positions of significant responsibility. Like Claire, they usually manage through fear, which can be a highly effective management tool – certainly in gaining compliance. In our example, Claire has excessive needs for control and has developed a style which gets her what she wants – total control and compliance.

The question is what do you do about a 'Claire'? It is clear that Claire is not going to change herself. The key to this situation is the director of the department – he needs to recognize the implications of his own blind spots and accept that now is the time to overcome them. He has to confront Claire with the inappropriateness of her behaviour. He needs to learn how to performance manage his people.

However, in the absence of a proactive and skilled boss, what can her direct reports do? They have a limited number of choices:

- reason with her;

- reassure her and gain her trust;

- comply and keep a low profile;

- be assertive – show that her methods do not work;

- collectively bring Claire's behaviour to the attention of her boss or other relevant individuals.

Reason With Her

This is the preferred option taken by many. Many people simply feel that this is a complete misunderstanding on Claire's part, and that if she only realized that she was jeopardizing the department's goals, she would desist. In every case I have come across, this never works. This is because the defensive person develops their own logic. First, they rationalize their behaviour, claiming to be acting in the best interests of the organization. Second, whether consciously or not, they are highly attuned to meeting their needs and extremely sensitive to any perceived threat to these. Also, they have learned over time that their methods work for them. Claire has learned that her methods help to meet her control needs, they get the work done (according to her criteria – notice she focuses on costs, she is not interested in outcomes for the children) and what's more, they appear to get her promoted. She has learned that her methods are highly effective – for her. And no-one is going to tell her anything different. You will also notice that the defensive personality lives in their own hermetically sealed world – they do not listen. Defensive personalities are trying very hard to make the world fit their needs – they want to make the world what they want it to be – in this case, completely controllable.

They are immune to reason, because your reason does not resonate with their reason. They are asking themselves different questions, such as 'how can I meet my needs for control in the current environment?' If you start to talk about meeting other stakeholders' needs, Claire will always find a way of explaining how she is meeting those needs by adopting her preferred strategies.

Reassure and Gain Trust by Meeting the Underlying Need

Defensive people are driven by fear. If you can gain an insight into what is feared, then it is sometimes possible to reassure them that you will not do anything that will give them any cause to fear your actions. In Claire's case, she has excessive needs for control. In order to reassure her, you could give her what she wants – minutes of meetings, e-mails and voicemails keeping her updated on what you are doing and any decisions that need to be made. In effect, you help her meet her control needs and in time she learns to trust you. If everyone does this, eventually Claire may learn to 'relax'. Of course, there are disadvantages to this approach – it reinforces and colludes with her behaviour. With some defensive people, who have high power and status needs in addition to control needs, they may glory in the extra power that this gives them and may misuse it further.

However, in some circumstances, this can work. Particularly when a manager first comes into position, they can be very nervous about being successful. In these early days they can be quite defensive and on guard, unsure who to trust. The placating strategy works well in these types of circumstances, when the defensiveness is more context or even relationship specific. In the case of specific relationships, where you find that individuals are being defensive to you, the placating, trust-building approach works well. In effect, you are showing that you are not a threat; in fact, by going out of the way to help someone who is wary of you, you can eventually build a relationship of trust and mutual respect.

Comply and Keep a Low Profile

This is effectively what is happening in our example. It has the advantages that no risks are taken – you can be sure that you will not be fired. However, this approach has a number of disadvantages:

- it reinforces Claire's behaviour – she is learning that, once more, her particular strategies are working for her;

- the clients (in this case the schools and the disadvantaged children) continue to suffer;

- the stress that her behaviour is causing in the department will continue to build, causing people to leave and to be more susceptible to illness;

- the long-term relationships that the department relies on for its effective operation will be damaged.

However, when a manager like Claire gets into position, attention tends to narrow down to one thing – personal survival. People tend not to worry so much about other stakeholders in their work. This tends to be the preferred option of many.

Be Assertive – Show That Her Methods Do Not Work

The only reason people like Claire operate like they do is because it works 'for them' – not others, but for them! We have seen that, in this case, the main tool is fear. The people in her department have to learn to overcome their fear and begin to stand up for themselves. All they need to do is make a simple, uncontroversial statement, in a calm tone of voice, such as: 'do not shout at me Claire' or 'I will not be sworn at, Claire'. The statement must be focused on particular behaviours. Accusing Claire of being 'aggressive' will not work – she will simply deny it. You have to focus on something they cannot deny – e.g. 'raising their voice', 'shouting', 'swearing'. Her direct reports can take this further and refuse to talk to Claire until she speaks in a reasonable tone of voice: 'I will not be shouted at Claire. I will come back and talk to you when you are polite to me'.

The reason that people do not stand up for themselves is that they are scared – exactly as Claire wants. But what are they scared of? This is an interesting question. In Claire's case, the last thing she wants is to draw her senior's attention to her operation by sacking someone. The reason she is getting away with her behaviour is that no-one is monitoring it. If she were to sack someone, her boss would be involved and there would have to be some type of enquiry where all sorts of allegations might be made. What's more, Claire would start to lose control – her nightmare scenario. So, people like Claire operate by the inculcation of a non-specific climate of fear – through the tacit suggestion of threat rather than by carrying the threat out. The direct reports need to sit down and think – what precisely am I scared of? If I were to stand up for myself in a calm, rational manner, what would happen? As soon as they start to confront their fears, they start to realize that many of them are unfounded. Of course, this is best done collectively in a group, where mutual help and support can be given. This brings us to the next point.

Do Not Get Hooked!

It is easy to get hooked by the defensive person, because they always seem to know just what to say to trigger people's personal fears and insecurities. If someone is insecure about their looks, the defensive person will mention their appearance. If someone is new and insecure about their performance, the defensive individual will imply that someone made a comment about their poor performance. Once an individual is hooked, it is easy to lose control of the situation.

In dealing with defensive individuals, the first step is to acknowledge one's own feelings and insecurities. In particular, it is important to face your fears and examine them rationally. Provide rational responses in your own mind if the individual mentions your weak spot. For example, if someone criticizes your performance, provide a rational response in your own mind:

> 'She is saying that simply to make me feel bad. I **am** finding it tough, but this is entirely normal as I am new. I will go and speak to my boss about this tomorrow to get some support. In no way, however, does this justify her behaviour to me'.

It is sometimes helpful to recognize the process that is taking place. If you are feeling fear, then it may be that the defensive individual is feeling fear. Fear is what she wants you to feel (consciously or not). Simply acknowledging this, pausing and taking a deep breath

and then saying to yourself something along the following lines can
help:

> *'if I am feeling fear, so is she. I will not allow her to manipulate me
> through my fears. I am strong and powerful and I will not be
> manipulated.'*

You can then voice what you are feeling:

> *'you know, I feel as if I am being criticized'.*

Defensive people often work through the manipulation of emotions
that exert their influence secretly, below the surface. The articulation
of these emotions reduces the power they are trying to exert. You
can then deliver the message you want to get across – e.g.,
your refusal to tolerate a certain kind of behaviour.

Another way of getting hooked is by 'arguing' or debating with her.
Never do this; you will not win, as there is no rational answer that
will satisfy her. Simply focus on your core message and repeat it,
using typical assertiveness skills such as the broken record technique
(the repetition of a simple message over and over again).

Collectively Bring Claire's Behaviour to the Attention of her Boss

This is a more risky decision. By going above Claire's head, the
direct reports are simultaneously jeopardizing Claire's control needs
and potentially threatening the senior manager. In effect, their
actions imply that the senior manager has not been doing his job,
and might, if they came to anyone else's attention, jeopardize his
standing in the organization. In defensive organizations, where
everyone is out for themselves, there is a tendency for the senior
managers to look after their collective interests – clubbing together
in an alliance which says effectively, 'it's a dangerous, lonely world
at the top; you look after my interests and I'll look after yours'.

This is what we saw in the Bristol Royal Infirmary case. Stephen
Bolsin found that not only was he 'frozen out' when he questioned

the competence of the surgeons at the Bristol Royal, he was criticized, his competence was brought into question and, most significantly, he could not find another job in the NHS in the UK. This is not uncommon in professionally led organizations. In a professional culture, there is often a tacit agreement not to question or challenge senior professionals; in fact, challenging a senior professional can be one of the deepest, darkest, most tacit taboos. In a defensive organization, once you put patients'/clients'/users' interests *above* the interests of the most powerful people in the organization, you have broken a taboo and you will be punished.

Going back to Claire's case, whilst it is risky going above her head, it might, of course, work. The senior manager's lack of attention might be inadvertent – perhaps caused by an inordinate amount of pressure on him in his role. However, if the inattention signals something else – a lack of interest in what is going on at 'lower' levels in the organization – this action could well provoke a defensive response.

We also have to hope that Claire's boss is prepared to handle her behaviour. As we have mentioned previously, many senior managers are wary of confronting difficult behaviour in the workplace and do not know how to do it in a skilful manner.

The alternative, safer, option is, of course, to talk to HR, either in an informal chat over coffee or ultimately to have a more formal conversation.

★ ★ ★

Claire's case is both instructive and important. It shows that once a defensive person gets into a leadership position, it is very difficult to do anything about it. It also demonstrates how a defensive 'leader' tends to generate a defensive culture. This leads to massive blind spots, as everyone's attention is focused on one thing – their own survival. Patients' interests, clients' interests, users' interests and a whole range of stakeholders are ignored in the struggle for survival.

This is why it is critical that all managers learn the skills of performance management, are able to recognize defensive behaviour (in themselves and others) and learn how to handle it at all levels.

8

The Fourth, Fifth and Sixth Practices – Deepen Sensemaking, Engage Creativity and Reality Check

'Even though we can never know reality directly, to survive and flourish we must always strive to make interpretations that are as close to reality as possible.'

Dorothy Rowe, *A Guide To Life*

One of the greatest sources of blind spots lies in our limited capacity to map and understand the full complexity of the problems facing us. Complexity challenges one of our most primal needs – the need for control. If we cannot see or understand the causal links between events, we do not know what we need to do in order to control them. If we cannot control something, it has the potential to control us.

In our rationalist, activist culture, we are used to defining problems, allocating resources to them and solving them. We want our leaders to define problems in ways we agree with and then solve them in ways that relieve us of the need to worry about them. Leaders who present us with the problems and all the complexities associated with them – leaders who make us think and worry – are rarely tolerated. Von Foerster, scientist, philosopher and key figure in the field of cybernetics, recognized people's intolerance of complexity:

'The more complex the problem that is being ignored, the greater are the chances for fame and success.'[1]

In other words, leaders who ignore the complex are those who are most rewarded. Many politicians know that the biggest problems facing our society are highly complex and simply not resolvable by one party sitting through one or even two terms of government. Many complex problems require a timetable of decades to sort out. However, it is taboo to say this. Politicians are not encouraged to talk about the intricacy and complexity of the problems facing us. When being interviewed in the media, they are given little time to present their answers, they are interrupted and any inconsistency, paradox or dilemma is exploited ruthlessly. As a result, politicians themselves feel pressurized to come up with a solution rather than spending time understanding the complexity of the problem. This has ramifications throughout the system. Civil servants working with politicians often complain that politicians are not interested in the complexities of the issues they are dealing with, they just want solutions. Complexity implies that solutions will be difficult, long term, painful to implement and uncertain in their outcomes. But, often, politicians do not want to hear this. Attempts to draw attention to the difficulties involved with policy are regarded as attempts to hinder progress, and individuals are dismissed as obstacles and troublemakers. In the end, it is not unusual for civil servants to agree to implement a policy that they know will not work.

This traditional, 'just do it' approach to problem solving no longer works. Our societies, communities and organizations have become *extremely* complex. In a *Fortune* magazine article, CEO of Hewlett Packard, Mark Hurd, refers to the global span of control generating huge complexity in his job.[2] Lowell Bryan, a top partner at McKinsey and Co. is quoted in another *Fortune* article claiming that we simply do not know how to work in the new complex reality of the

---

[1] Von Foerster, H. (1972) 'Responsibilities of Competence'. *Journal of Cybernetics*, **2**, 1–6 (quoted in Mitroff, I. I. and Linstone, H. A. (1993) *The Unbounded Mind: breaking the chains of traditional business thinking*. New York: Oxford University Press.

[2] 'Mark Hurd Takes His First Swing at HP'. *Fortune*, August 8th, 2005, p. 19.

21st Century.[3] The article quotes him as saying that the scope and complexity of business have grown tremendously. He claims that jobs have been created that are literally impossible to manage. The costs in terms of organizational effectiveness, personal wellbeing and social cohesiveness are profound.

There is a growing trend for companies to recruit two senior executives for one role. NewsCorp appointed two Presidents of 20th Century Fox Television. *LA Times* editor, Dean Baquet, split his previous Managing Editor job into three, Baquet cites the growing complexity of major newspapers, claiming that the job was too big for one person. With such 'gigantic' jobs, it was inevitable that important issues would simply be ignored.[4]

In Australia, Mattel appointed two CEOs to replace their previous one.

It is becoming increasingly difficult for one person to lead some of the massive, multinational corporations that span the globe. Nor is this simply a commercial problem. In individual countries, health, education, environmental and energy problems are intertwined with complex social, political, technical and international economic systems. As a result, our actions have unintended, often chaotic, consequences.

In a complex world, the role of decision making is vital. Perhaps the most important function that leaders play is to make decisions, though this function is rarely analysed in great depth. The quality of our decisions is influenced by many factors. We have already seen how emotional factors affect our decisions. Another important influence lies in the fit between our living knowledge and the reality it represents. We all have a notion of how the 'world out there' works, and our decisions reflect those views. Of course, whilst acknowledging Sterman's warning that 'all decisions are based on models and all models are wrong', most people would recognize that some mental models *are* more effective at reflecting reality than others. If our living

---

[3] 'Get A Life!' *Fortune*, November 28th, 2005, p. 42.
[4] 'Get A Life!' *Fortune*, November 28th, 2005, p. 42.

knowledge is seriously outdated or full of blind spots, our decisions will be flawed. We will be making decisions based on a faulty understanding of reality. The outcomes we anticipate will not emerge; others will. Complex systems will interact, generating a series of seemingly chaotic events. Decision makers will not be able to understand what is happening, because they will not have the right mental models in place to see the links between cause and effect. Hence, they feel powerless to effect any control. But as their role *is* to exercise control, they attempt to control the chaos in the grip of anxiety, anger or frustration. So now their decision making is affected by blind spots caused by negative emotions as well as impoverished living knowledge! The only hope they have is to continually and rapidly update and reorganize their living knowledge based on the feedback they collect from the outcomes of their decisions. And, as we have seen, this requires discipline, self control and a little humility.

An example of leaders attempting to exercise control employing inadequate mental models is found in the UK. In the year 2000, the UK government announced a ten-year strategy for modernizing the country's National Health Service, supported with an initial £20 bn of government money. The UK's National Health Service is a highly complex system where the budget is equivalent in size to the GDP of a small country. There was some success in controlling the system – many waiting lists were reduced according to targets set by government. However, many more problems ensued, leaving political commentators and journalists questioning whether anything had been achieved with the money. Frank Blackler, Professor of Organizational Behaviour at Lancaster University's Management School, conducted research into what went on during the period. He claims that the government, naturally concerned about efficiency and return on investment, attempted to exert control over a highly complex system by imposing targets and robbing Chief Executives and front line staff of discretion. However, this simply distorted the system, skewed local priorities, wasted resources and prevented people from responding to patient and hospital needs. He states:

> '*current approaches to managing complex institutions from the centre provide no more than an illusion of control; what is*

needed . . . is an approach based on the notion of continuous learning.[5]

However, it is easy to criticize. We have to recognize complexity is also embodied in the dilemma facing the government. In effect, the government *has* to attempt to exercise some control, because demand for health services is limitless and resources are not. The question is – what kind of control can the government effectively exercise, and how should it do it?

These attempts to centralize the control of complex systems remind us of Hyman's description of the government's attempts to manage education from the centre. He described visionary, but blinkered, politicians and advisors dreaming up policy, dismissing those with knowledge and experience as 'whingers' and 'blockers of change', and he pleaded for more of a partnership between those on the ground and those at the centre.

In both situations, the attempts to manage a complex system from the centre provided heads of government with 'an illusion of control' – so they continued, despite the fact that their living knowledge was not, and never could be, up to the job. Their mental models were impoverished and inadequate reflections of the reality they were trying to control.

In an increasingly complex world, this is an important source of blind spots in leaders. When leaders oversimplify complex situations (in order to rationalize their desire to act), others suffer. It is well known that both Bush and Blair dismissed those who warned them about the complexities associated with managing the aftermath of the Iraq war. There were many people around to inform both leaders of the potential consequences of their actions, but neither wanted their goals to be hindered by complexity – so the arguments were ignored.

Our need for psychological comfort, our need to feel in control, tempts us to dismiss, deny or devalue complexity. This is under-

---

[5] Blackler, F. (2006) 'Chief Executives and the Modernization of the English National Health Service'. *Leadership*, 2(1), 5–30.

standable. If we acknowledge complexity, we have to engage in dialogue with different and potentially conflicting communities. We have to acknowledge that *human and organizational change will not comply with our deadlines*, and, worst of all, we have to acknowledge that we might not be *right*.

The temptation to deny complexity is at direct odds with our need to understand the increasingly complex world in which we live, in order to make high quality decisions. Since psychological comfort is one of the great drivers of our learning, this is an important tension. As soon as a problem begins to get so complex that it is (a) difficult to understand and (b) difficult to resolve (especially in political, moral and psychological terms), blind spots are triggered and problems are simplified. Of course, different people will reach this complexity barrier at different stages of the problem appreciation. Some people have a low tolerance of complexity and ambiguity, others have a much higher tolerance. Some people will simply not have the understanding or skills necessary to cope with the complexity, and those that do are often not listened to.

There are many reasons why those with a greater understanding of complexity are dismissed. We have already explored some of the emotional issues – complexity gets in the way of us achieving our goals, so, when it is evoked, it generates anxiety and frustration, which, in turn, causes us to dismiss it. Another reason why we ignore complexity is that those with a less complex mental model of the world do not 'see' what those with more complex models 'see'. Hence, they think those with more complex mental models are wrong. This is a problem recognized by one-time Shell strategist and scenario planner, Arie de Geus. He talks about the problems involved in transmitting all the learning that they, as strategists, had acquired over a considerable period of time:

> '*we had spent nearly 15 man-years preparing a set of scenarios which we then transmitted in a condensed version in 2½ hours. Could we really have believed that our audience would understand all we were talking about?*'[6]

---

[6] De Geus, A. (1988) 'Planning as Learning'. *Harvard Business Review*, March–April.

Clearly, they did not, and this was a problem for the planners and strategists at Shell – how could they 'change the microcosm, the mental models that these decision makers carry in their heads'?

A similar problem was faced by Bush's and Blair's expert advisors almost 20 years later – how to get the key decision makers to understand the huge complexity of managing the aftermath of an Iraq war. Those without the complex mental models don't see or understand the complexities, hence they have a strong tendency to dismiss advisors as being overly pessimistic or difficult.

So, how do we ensure that our mental models are the most effective they can be? How can we develop a cognitive map that more accurately reflects the complexity inherent in the environment?

It would appear that it is easier to develop more complex living knowledge if our cognitive maps are:[7]

- highly differentiated and integrated;
- flexible and responsive to change;
- capable of spanning many paradigms;
- open to new constructs and beliefs.

We can see what this might look like if we take a look at the mental models of the owners of two small, independent food retailers in a medium-sized town.

George's mental model of the food retailing market is shown in Figure 8.1. George is quite happy with the state of things as they are. He feels that there is plenty of room in the market and that his business is doing well.

---

[7] Much of this thinking is taken from Kelly, G. A. (1955) *The Psychology of Personal Constructs.* New York: Norton.

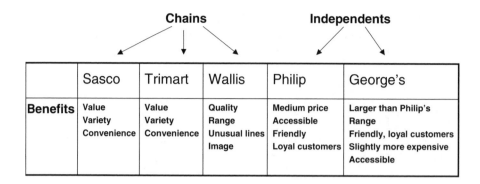

	Sasco	Trimart	Wallis	Philip	George's
Benefits	Value Variety Convenience	Value Variety Convenience	Quality Range Unusual lines Image	Medium price Accessible Friendly Loyal customers	Larger than Philip's Range Friendly, loyal customers Slightly more expensive Accessible

Figure 8.1   The market: George's mental model.

Alice's mental model of the market is shown in Figure 8.2. To Alice, the market does not look at all settled. She knows from her conversations with Will at Trimart that they are planning to set up a new metro store which will supplement their big, out-of town site. She also knows that the petrol retailers plan to expand their retail operations. Looking at her depiction of the market, Alice's store does not look as if it's in a strong position. She is relying on the convenience of her site and the friendliness of her staff to attract custom. However, there is a large contingent of buyers who simply do not have time to have a chat, who do not care about friendliness and who simply want to get in and out as quickly as they can. Alice sees that her store looks increasingly out of date and out of step with the market. She has to make a decision as to what to do next. Although she recognizes that her business is not as profitable as she would like, she knows it is more profitable than her local competitors in the sector. This she senses by going round and visiting their stores, observing their prices and staffing levels. She also owns her property freehold and so is not so subject to large hikes in rent. She decides to introduce a loyalty card of her own, and even thinks about talking to some of the niche stores to see if they are interested in sharing a loyalty scheme. She decides that she is going to spend some money on smartening the store up, and wonders, too, whether the bakery in the next village would be interested in selling some of its produce in her store.

This is a highly simplified example of course, but we can see how Alice's mental model of her market is more complex than George's,

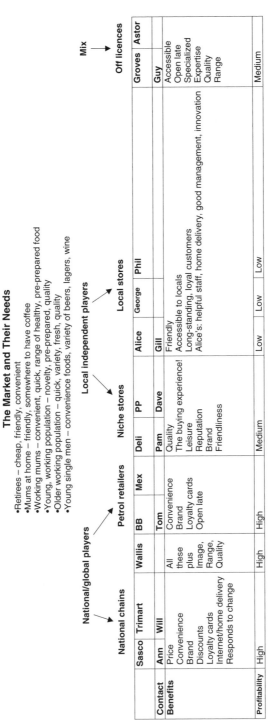

Figure 8.2 The market: Alice's mental model.

and this affects how she thinks about her business. In fact, what is noticeable about Alice's mental model is that it:

- Is more integrated – all her constructs flow from her concept of 'the market'. All of these constructs – the market and all the individual categories within the market – are connected and are part of a system. Hence, she realizes that changes in one part of the system imply changes in other parts, many of which will affect her.

- Is more differentiated – she has more constructs, categories and levels in relation to how she sees her competition. This makes her able to notice small changes in parts of the system and understand their implications for the whole. It also means that she can adjust small parts of her mental model without having to reorganize the whole system. This means she can adjust her mental model (or 'learn') without having to re-think everything she believes, which is something that we are highly resistant to doing.[8]

- Includes people – the source of her information about what is happening in each category.

- Is more dynamic and responsive to change – people are a source of dynamism and change in her mental models, because they bring in goals, plans and aspirations for the future. Because she knows the plans of some of her competitors, she has a sense of the trends. She understands that this picture is simply a reflection of a particular time and a particular place; tomorrow things may change.

- Has more constructs, such as 'the buying experience' at the delicatessen. Alice realizes that, for many people, shopping is not only a functional activity, it is also a leisure activity. She has also included 'loyalty' cards and 'brand' as important constructs in determining buyer behaviour.

- Contains more 'abstract' constructs than George's. Abstract constructs tend to have more explanatory power. For example, her notion of 'the market' incorporates a wide array of potential

---

[8] Kelly, G. A. (1955) *The Psychology of Personal Constructs*. New York: Norton.

buyers, classified according to their lifestyles and ages. This enables her to distinguish more sources of competitive advantage than George (e.g. 'the buying experience'; 'innovation'). George does not really have an explicit notion of the market as such; he has a construct called 'buyers,' which is a description of the people he actually sees and knows about – the people who come into his shop. His construct is concrete, based on his experience. Alice's is more abstract, based on a combination of experience and theory.

- Is more receptive to new constructs, as she has more categories than George. So, when Trimart open a new metro store, Alice already has a category within which to fit that event. George probably won't even notice it, because he doesn't have a category in his mind into which it will fit.

- Reflects more paradigms. Alice is consciously aware of her customers and what motivates them (customer paradigm); she is aware of the competition and knows some of them personally (competition paradigm); she also considers the financial structures of the market (financial paradigm); and she is very focused on her staff – how to motivate them and generate a positive buying experience (staff paradigm).

Alice's living knowledge is far more comprehensive, complex, flexible and powerful than George's. Alice may not be feeling quite as complacent and comfortable as George, but she is in touch, learning, growing, developing her living knowledge and, in two years' time, will still be in business. George's discomfort will come later – when it is too late to do anything about it.

Developing cognitive complexity is a discipline, and one that is easy to let slip. It involves always seeking out the new, listening to others, never assuming one has the final picture of reality. Most of all, we have to realize that just because we don't 'see' something, that doesn't mean that it does not exist! Often, our inability to see something says more about the comprehensiveness, flexibility and complexity of our own mental models than it does about the truth of any 'reality' out there.

The temptation to dismiss other versions of reality is great once you get to the top. This is a trap that seems to have ensnared Carly

Fiorina, ex CEO of HP. Carly engaged in a highly risky strategy of buying Compaq. In doing so, she fought a battle with Walter Hewlett (son of HP founder, Bill Hewlett), who resisted the move into the 'achingly competitive, heavily commoditized computer world'.[9] There is nothing wrong with this, of course. Business leaders stand up and fight for their strategies all the time. However, perhaps one of Carly's failings was to dismiss her rival's claims and doubts. She became certain that she was right and that her rival's view was 'wrong'. She seems to have suffered from the attitude that often entraps the unwary visionary leader. She shut out the voices of intelligent people with views that were rooted in a valid 'take' on reality. In a *Fortune* magazine article exploring the problems at HP, one of her colleagues says that she cannot admit to her mistakes and learn from them.[10] In fact, Fiorina is depicted as someone trapped in her own denial, rationalizing the profit disappointments and setbacks and claiming to be greatly satisfied with the performance of the company.[11] What's more, the article noted that there was a huge 'brain drain' under Fiorina, whilst at the same time observing that the CEO's job at HP is so complex that is it perhaps beyond the ability of any one person to handle well.[12]

Many leaders find it difficult to tolerate other great minds with diverse views. This appears to have happened at HP. The brain drain was in part initiated by Carly (through firings and redundancies), and in part the brains departed of their own initiative – going to where they were better utilized.

Whilst acknowledging that we know little of what *really* happened at HP, we might hazard a guess that perhaps Carly would have done better to beat her rivals by absorbing and filtering their views and, hence, developing a more complex mental model of her environment. Every time we dismiss someone, we dismiss the potential to add richness to our living knowledge. In the past, it

---

[9] 'Why Carly's Big Bet is Failing'. *Fortune*, February 7th, 2005, pp. 40–51.
[10] 'Why Carly's Big Bet is Failing'. *Fortune*, February 7th, 2005, pp. 40–51.
[11] 'Why Carly's Big Bet is Failing'. *Fortune*, February 7th, 2005, pp. 40–51.
[12] 'Why Carly's Big Bet is Failing'. *Fortune*, February 7th, 2005, pp. 40–51.

might have been possible to dismiss rivals' views; now it is wiser to absorb them.

Psychologically it is difficult to absorb the views of people whom you dislike, fear, mistrust, scorn and dismiss. The problem is that we often 'judge' others according to criteria that have nothing to do with the problem. We dismiss the 'geeky' computer guy, because he's not financially savvy; we scorn the HR department, because they are 'touchy-feely'; we fear and mistrust our peer in marketing, because we feel threatened by them. So, we end up dismissing the views, insights, ideas and living knowledge of people who are clever, switched on and who know something that we could learn from. Why? Because it makes us feel good!

So how do we go about developing our living knowledge? How do we give ourselves time to think? How do we filter and absorb important perspectives, even if we don't agree with them? How do we manage the conflict between the need to achieve our goals quickly and the need to embrace complexity?

This is where our three cognitive disciplines come in: deepen sensemaking; engage creativity; reality check.

Deepen Sensemaking

This discipline entails creating more integrated, differentiated and flexible mental models of our environment, rather like Alice's version of the marketplace as opposed to George's. However, Alice's mental model was a static representation of the world out there. We also develop what psychologists call *scripts* of how we can best operate, both on and in that world. Much of our sensemaking is driven by the need to understand what works out there. This comprises two sets of understandings – what does 'out there' consist of? How do I act in it in order to meet my needs – 'what works?' Obviously, as we all have different needs, we will all develop different ideas of what works. A person who has strong needs for harmony and prefers to avoid conflict will develop a different strategy for operating in the world to someone who has strong needs for achievement. Both will have an idea of 'what works' in the world and both will be quite different.

Hence, our mental models and scripts will be infused with our personal needs, as well as our subjective and objective experience.

So, how do you develop more integrated, differentiated and flexible mental models? Quite simply by listening to a huge variety of other people and opening yourself to their constructs and their understanding of 'what works'.

This is where something that appears to be quite dry and 'intellectual' becomes quite challenging and emotional, because in order to do this properly, we need to venture outside our comfort zones. We have to talk to, mix with, listen to, tolerate and respect people who are different from us, and who our instincts may tell us to dismiss. We have talked about the emotional dynamics of this in previous chapters. Here, what we will do is look at *how* to listen to others.

Let's imagine an MD is trying to convince his senior manager to move a member of her team to another unit. Their discussion goes as follows:

Brad: *You've got to get rid of her. She's not up to the task. If we don't get this completed by December we're in real trouble.*

Gill: *She **is** up to the task. She's worked with me for over six months, I know what she can do. She's just been a victim of circumstances recently. It wasn't her fault that they missed that last deadline – they were affected by computer problems, which were nothing to do with her.*

Brad: *You're always defending her, Gill. You know it doesn't look good with other members of the board. You can be seen as being too soft on staff. It's absolutely vital we deliver to the customer on time – you know that we start incurring penalties if we don't.*

Gill: *Yes, I know, I know. But it's just not fair to start blaming people when its much more complicated than that. You always do that, Brad. It's just easier to do that than to look at the real problems, which, if you'd listen to me, you'd realize were more to do with how our work is evaluated and the whole measurement system. It means that people don't take responsibility for problems if they are not directly affected by them and . . .*

Brad: *You keep on going on about this Gill, but there's nothing we can do about it and it doesn't address the problem about*

> *getting this all done by December. Look, what are you going*
> *to do about Anna – are you going to put your own reputation*
> *on the line here?*
>
> **Gill:** *Brad, you're not being fair. How do I respond to that?*
> **Brad:** *You've got to decide Gill. You've got to decide whether*
> *you're tough enough to lead at this level.*

This conversation is absolutely packed with constructs, values, goals, mental models and scripts/strategies. But neither speaker is learning or listening to the other. Let's look at the basic building blocks of their mental models – their constructs (or concepts):

	Brad	Gill
Main constructs	1. 'Up to the task' 2. (Anna is not) competent 3. (Gill is) soft on staff 4. Perceptions of board 5. (Gill is) too soft 6. Board critical of Gill 7. Client deadline 8. Penalties 9. Powerless (to change) 10. Laying reputation on line 11. Tough enough to lead	1. 'Up to the task' 2. (Anna is) a victim of circumstance 3. (Anna is) competent 4. Computer problems not her fault 5. Blaming people vs understanding complexities 6. (Brad is) a blamer 7. (Brad) avoids complexities 8. Real problems 9. Measurement system 10. Taking responsibility for problems 11. Fairness
Minor constructs – those that are not valued or given much weight	1. Measurement system 2. Junior staff	1. Client deadline 2. The board
Values	1. Tough decision making 2. Client first 3. Managing perceptions upwards	1. Fairness 2. Looking at the complete picture 3. Taking responsibility

Brad and Gill are communicating, but they are not communicating and learning, they are communicating and fighting. They are trying to impose their own versions of reality onto each other. What is also clear is that they both have different values, and these values are leading them to concentrate on different paradigms. Brad's main paradigms are the client, commercial and power paradigms. Gill's are the staff, psychology and systems paradigms. This is a recipe for deeply flawed communication – because they do not value each other's paradigms. Moreover, by not valuing these paradigms (all of which are valid and have something to add), their cognitive maps are oversimplified and they cannot appreciate the full complexity of the situation they are dealing with.

In a learning dialogue, each of them would take time to unravel each other's constructs, really attempt to incorporate them into their own understanding and, as a result, increase the complexity of their own map of reality. This would take time and commitment to achieve. An example of a learning conversation might look as follows (though in reality it would take a lot longer). The text in square brackets beneath the dialogue comments on the thinking and technique involved in developing the learning element of the conversation:

Brad: *You've got to get rid of her. She's not up to the task. If we don't get this completed by December we're in real trouble.*

Gill: *She **is** up to the task. She's worked with me for over six months, I know what she can do. She's just been a victim of circumstances recently. It wasn't her fault that they missed that last deadline – they were affected by computer problems, which were nothing to do with her.*

Brad: *OK, look, we're not communicating here. We clearly have different understandings of the situation. Why don't we take turns explaining our views of the situation?*

[Instead of carrying on arguing, Brad recognizes that they need to have a learning conversation. He disciplines himself, managing his frustration and makes the first move.]

Gill: *OK. You go first then.*

Brad: *This is a **really important** client. This job is a sort of test to see whether we're up to doing something bigger. If we can get this job done to their satisfaction, they will probably give us something much bigger. If we do this well, the future of* *the company will be much more secure. I feel frustrated when other people don't seem to appreciate the urgency of this task. It seems to me sometimes that the staff feel as if the company is here to serve them!*

[Brad expresses his feelings in an assertive way – using 'I' language and explaining what he feels and why he feels it. This enables people to talk about their feelings in a calm and constructive way. He elaborates his mental model more, showing why he thinks as he does.]

Gill: *Well, I didn't realize quite how important the job was, I'll admit that. But what I see is that we are always getting ourselves into a mess around client deadlines, because we don't plan things properly and we seem to thrive as a company on deadlines and last minute panics. Our systems are not being used as efficiently as they could be, but no-one seems to have the time or inclination to sort them out. It's almost as if everyone loves the stress and the chaos. It's also easier to blame individuals than to spend time understanding the underlying systems that generate the damaging behaviour in the first place.*

[Gill acknowledges the limitations in her own living knowledge. In doing this, she acknowledges that she has absorbed Brad's constructs.]

Brad: *Well, I don't really know what you're talking about Gill, I'll admit that, too. It sounds a bit woolly to me, but maybe we need to sit down and explore this in more detail. But it also seems to me that we have different priorities – mine is the customer and yours is staff and systems.*

[Brad reciprocates. Although he doesn't see Gill's point, he is ready to credit her with a valid take on reality. He agrees to suspend his disbelief and make an effort to understand her view. Brad grasps the important fact that they are prioritizing different paradigms.]

Gill: *Well, I care about the customer too Brad, but I get a bit fed up when everyone and everything is sacrificed in the name of the customer. We use the concept of customer to justify a lot of unacceptable work practices. But that's not relevant now. What I'm hearing is that we have a bit of a crisis on our hands – the December deadline.*

[Gill is now expressing her feelings. However, she is sensitive to the time element of the conversation. She acknowledges Brad's mental model and agrees to incorporate it into her living knowledge.]

Brad: *Yes, we have. If you can sort this out for me, I promise we will sit down and get to grips with these system issues, Gill. I'm still not sure about Anna though . . .*

[Brad reciprocates – even though he still doesn't understand or even agree with Gill.]

Gill: *Well, you're right, Anna doesn't have the same level of experience that some of the others have, so she is a bit slower – but that's because she's younger. It's not through lack of competence. I'll put someone else on the job to help Anna, and I'll promise you to meet the December deadline. But you've got to trust me.*

[Gill now brings in her more complex mental model of Anna – one that did not get aired before, as Gill felt the need to defend Anna.]

Brad: *Fine Gill, but I do need to be kept informed. The board is prioritizing this – all eyes are on your operation you know!*

Gill: *Really? I didn't think about the board being so involved.*

[Gill's lack of power paradigm is manifesting itself. She is beginning to understand its importance.]

Brad: *Well, if this goes well, we might get your systems stuff on the board agenda too. Anyway, we'll think about it after December.*

[Brad links the power paradigm to Gill's system paradigm – showing her the importance and relevance of the power paradigm to her own agenda.]

Gill: *OK, thanks Brad.*

It is important to note that 'listening' like this – i.e. in a way that leads to greater cognitive complexity for both participants – is *not* just a skills issue. It stems from a philosophy, an attitude of mind and a discipline.

The *philosophy* concerns your assumptions around the nature of knowledge – what scientists refer to as *epistemology*. We all have an epistemology – whether we realize it or not! The epistemology we are promoting here maintains that, in many areas of life (particularly when it comes to organizations) it is not possible to 'know' anything for certain. In other words, our knowledge is socially constructed or co-created – each community constructs its own truth. 'Truth' reflects the biases, values, experiences, priorities and needs of the community that constructed it. Our personal 'truths' are also constructions – reflecting our personal values, needs, experience, goals, culture, background, etc. If this is the case, my truth will always be incomplete, and in order to gain a more valid picture of 'reality', I need to supplement my truth constantly with insights from other people's truths. If this is your epistemology, you will find it much easier and more natural to listen to people. However, if your epistemology is based upon the assumption that it is possible to know the truth of reality out there, and you believe that your take on truth is always better than other people's, you will not be able to listen easily to the views and opinions of other people.

The *attitude of mind* is best summed up with one word – 'humility'. Jim Collins refers to 'level 5 leaders' who can transform their good or mediocre organizations into outstanding leaders in their field. These level 5 leaders have two qualities – absolute determination and humility. But, in our culture, humility has connotations of weakness, deference, yielding to others and powerlessness. Why? Because in a culture that values winning, power, fame, opinions and conspicuous consumption, humility has no place. It is seen as the opposite of everything that is valuable. We tend to prefer arrogance to humility – and arrogance is the enemy of learning. Humility, on the other hand, is a virtue that helps us recognize our limitations as well as our strengths; it helps us acknowledge that we do not and cannot know everything, and that others, with different values, have something to offer. Those with humility are ready to listen, to learn, to grow, to experiment and to observe what works, rather than dismiss ideas from the perspective of their own limited mental models. Those with humility find it easy and natural to listen; those with a more arrogant attitude find it impossible.

Finally, there is *discipline*. This refers to the behavioural element of listening. We tend to be a society of immediate gratification; we experience desire and we want to satiate it – immediately. We experience anger, frustration, fear and we respond by noticing those emotions and either expressing them externally or focusing on them internally. What we do not tend to do is learn to discipline them. But if we are going to learn from our conversations, we will have to get used to handling a wide array of emotions and not responding to them as soon as we feel them. As soon as someone says something we disagree with, the natural response is either to challenge them or simply to dismiss what they are saying in our heads – turning off and not listening. However, if we are really to engage in a learning conversation, we have to learn to discipline this natural response – to open ourselves up to what the other person is saying, when instinctively we want to close ourselves off.

This is just an introduction to how we can deepen our sensemaking. Fundamentally, it is all about constantly updating our living knowledge, primarily by listening to others – particularly those who we might prefer to ignore. But it is also based upon a particular epistemology concerning truth and knowledge – greater humility and greater personal discipline.

Engage Creativity

Much has already been said about creativity, and it is not the intention of this book to explore this huge subject area. However, we will explore the notion of creativity from the vantage point of how we can use creativity to expand our cognitive, emotional and behavioural complexity (and vice versa). We see an example in the following conversation:

Mark: *Look, the opportunity is there right now. We have got to grasp it. We can work out the details later, but this is a time for action – not your typical 'analysis-paralysis'.*

Richard: *I can see the opportunity is there right now – and it's an opportunity that could kill us if we're not careful. If we go into partnership with a relatively unknown company, in a part of the world that is not overly stable, we could be jeopardizing our reputation for financial prudence. It's highly risky, and I am not happy about the level of research that has been done to evaluate and assess the risk.*

Mark: *If we wait and do a full risk analysis, the opportunity will have been handed on a plate to our competitors.*

> *We'll then be on a back foot in Asia. This is a fantastic*
> *opportunity Richard. We'd be mad to turn it down.*
>
> **Richard:** *Sorry, Mark, I can't support you on this.*

This conversation is, in effect, a clash of values – often in itself a rich source of creativity and insight. However, instead of 'fighting', the two colleagues need to recognize the creative tension involved in the opposition of their two ideas.

The point about creativity is that it is often bypassed due to the desire to resolve (or avoid) the emotional stress or tension associated with the need for a decision or action. If, in a management meeting, it is discovered that there is a conflict between two ideas, there is often a desire to resolve the conflict as quickly as possible, make the decision and move on. It is this desire to settle and close down issues that is so inimical to creativity.

However, there are many simple creativity techniques that can help trigger creative responses in situations like this. Recognizing that the emerging conflict concerns values is a good start. We can then express affirmation of both sets of values – 'entrepreneurialism' and 'risk management'. We can then ask a simple 'both . . . and' question.

Helen: *Look guys, you both seem to have a point. The question is, then, how can we take advantage of the opportunity whilst at the same time minimizing the risks?*

Richard: *Yes, that's a good way of looking at it.*

Mark: *I agree with that, except that we have to act fast. Sometimes you just have to take risks; you can't avoid them.*

Helen: *But if you could take advantage of the opportunity at a lesser risk, would you be happy?*

Mark: *Of course I would.*

Helen: *So, how can we minimize the risk without losing the opportunity?*

Richard: *I know people I could call. There's a load of work already done in this area. I also know someone who's working out there in our field. It wouldn't take long – perhaps two days – to put together a report highlighting top level (not detailed) risks. We have been doing some work on this ourselves – in anticipation of this request.*

Mark: *You never told me that!*
Richard: *I was not going to encourage you! Look, it won't be enough to do a full risk analysis but what it will do is pinpoint the main areas of risk that we could go into further detail with if necessary. The question is, would this be too long for you Mark?*
Mark: *Well, if I can get back to them today just to say we are actively considering the opportunity, I'm sure I can hold them for a while. It's better than a blanket 'no', which is where I thought we were heading.*

This is a simple example, but purposely so. The point is that creativity is a state of mind – one which feels open, generative and positive rather than closed and combative. It is a state of mind where people become open to expanding their constructs (e.g. absorbing the other person's point), expanding their emotional complexity (restraining frustration, disciplining oneself not to judge) and expanding their behavioural complexity (cooperating rather than competing and undermining when one's values are under threat). It is a state of mind we can choose to be in at any moment in time. It is also a state of mind that we can help others to engage in by asking simple 'both . . . and' questions. As soon as Helen asked her 'both . . . and' question, the atmosphere changed and people became more cooperative as they felt their ideas being given serious consideration. In fact, creativity is another kind of learning state. Unlike the visionary, adaptive or dissonant learning states, the creative learning state is relaxed, playful and fun-loving. The type of learning that emerges from this state of mind does not arise when people are highly focused on meeting deadlines and completing tasks. The creative frame of mind – open, playful, curious, experimental and receptive to possibilities – is referred to as the *generative* learning state.

Asking the right questions is vital to creative thinking. Examples include:

- How can we build *both* commercialism into the culture *and*, at the same time, respect values around risk avoidance?
- How are problems a, b and c connected?
- How many ways can we find to . . . ?
- How many options can we generate . . . ?

- What would happen if (we did the opposite of what we were thinking or if we didn't do anything right now)?

- If I had the power to change anything I liked, what would I change?

Creativity arises from exploring connections, possibilities and options and riding the tension associated with that. Creativity is often associated with complex problems but can be stifled by the frustration that builds in the desire for a quick solution. The key is to stay with the frustration for a bit, without feeling the need to resolve it by making a hasty decision.

We spend too much time in organizations closing issues down rather than exploring them and truly understanding them. It is not too much to ask that, occasionally, people are asked to explore issues with no expectation that they will have to come to a conclusion if they do not feel ready. It is possible to run creativity sessions around key issues in the business or organization without pressuring people to come up with premature solutions. Regular creativity exercises operate as 'learning workouts' – they loosen up our thinking patterns, opening us up to new patterns of thought and feeling and behaving. They help team building, boost morale and stimulate creative problem-solving throughout the organization. If people go into the session curious and wondering whether anything of interest will emerge, they are far more likely to learn and develop useful ideas than if they adopt a critical evaluative frame of mind, judging the session according to how many effective ideas are generated.

Whilst it may feel like 'wasting time', all learning involves taking steps back and out of the chaos. Sometimes this entails deep reflection, but sometimes it entails quite simply having fun. Both are important ways of accelerating our learning. Companies such as Google seem to embrace fun, creativity and chaos as integral parts of their business models. According to *Fortune* magazine,[13] it appears that these more 'chaotic' business models are proving to be the most successful in today's business environment. The

---

[13] *Fortune*, September 2006.

companies that truly embrace creativity appear to be the business role models of the 21st century.

Reality Check

Our last practice involves 'reality checking'. There is nothing much to say about this practice other than – 'do it'. Everything we have said so far stresses the impossibility of accurately mapping reality. At the same time, we have stressed the importance of constantly striving to do so. Reality checking is the practice that unites this paradox. You can never map reality accurately, so you have to check your maps to ensure they are as accurate as you can make them. The importance of this practice cannot be overestimated. The following are some examples of what happens when it is not taken seriously enough:

> *A senior manager took on a regional role responsible for four local offices. When she started, everything seemed to be functioning smoothly and the offices were in great shape. She saw her role as supportive and let the individual office managers run their own shows. However, 12 months into the role, one of her office heads resigned and went to a competitor. When she visited the office, the staff informed her that they had been worried about how various items and sales were being accounted for. When she looked into the matter in detail, she discovered that widespread fraud had been taking place, and the office was going to have to suffer a huge blow to its bottom line in order to recover.*

> *A senior politician took over a government department. All seemed fine and he got on well with the civil servant running the department. She seemed intelligent, efficient and friendly. However, 18 months into his office, an embarrassing scandal emerged from the department. As the politician in charge, he was blamed for it, despite the fact that he only knew of the problem when it emerged in the press. Nevertheless, the press discovered that it had been bubbling away inside the department for years. Many civil servants knew about the problem and had raised it with their managers – but apparently the culture was characterized by bullying and denial. The senior civil servant in charge was arrogant and intimidating. Many of her direct reports did not dare to raise their concerns, and those that did were ignored.*

A middle manager applied for a promotion. He was pretty sure he would get the job and was dismayed to find that he was not even considered. This was due to his people management skills. He protested, saying he had excellent people management skills, that his team was in good shape and everyone worked well together. His department had achieved profits above target and his team had performed extremely well. However, in a subsequent session with a coach, he discovered that his team was terrified of him. His regular outbreaks of anger, his moodiness and his direct way of talking about problems intimidated others. He had no idea, and was astonished to learn that the team that he had believed was so cohesive and happy was, in fact, terribly unhappy with his leadership.

Most organizational reality exists inside people's heads. Perception is everything – especially as you get further up the hierarchy. In an organization, you are nothing more than the combination of people's perceptions of you, so it is important to check how you are perceived.

However, there are also 'real', as opposed to merely 'perceived', problems. These real problems or 'landmines' lie under the surface waiting to explode. Whilst they may be difficult to spot, people working in the area will know about them, and there will always be some indications of their existence. The challenge is to find these problems out before they explode publicly. This means mixing with people on the ground and actively expanding one's living knowledge by talking to a range of people at all levels in the organization, constantly probing for facts.

One way of doing this is to ask certain types of questions.

Sensing Problems

- Where are problems likely to emerge from?

- What's the worst that could happen?

- What scenarios could develop that could threaten the organization and/or my leadership?

- Where is there conflict or tension in the organization?

- What must go right for me to succeed in this post? How much do I know about what is going on in these areas?

- What signs should I look for that might indicate problems or areas of concern?

- How do I know that my answers to these questions are accurate?

Sensing Opportunities

- Where are opportunities likely to develop?

- What's the best that could happen?

- What scenarios could develop that could boost my organization and/or my leadership?

- Where is there excitement in the organization?

- What is going on in these areas on the ground?

- Do I have some bright people who have a lot to offer but who are ignored?

- Can we develop a process that spots and focuses attention on potential opportunities?

- How do I know that my answers to these questions are accurate?

The answers to these questions lie in the heads of the people all around you. Therefore:

- Host regular informal lunches/breakfasts/meetings with client-facing staff or people on the ground.

- Tour sites and have regular sessions where people can gather and talk openly.

- Conduct regular problem/opportunity sensing surveys.

- Host web pages where people can log their ideas and/or feedback.

- Build an informal network throughout the organization.

- Use systems and measures to gather 'hard' data, against which to test your perceptions.

Some people are sensitive about talking to people on the ground for fear of alienating the direct managers – going through them to get to their staff as it were. Often, the direct manager can feel exposed by a senior manager talking to his or her staff. This can be handled sensitively but it must *never* get in the way of the intelligence gathering that is part of a leader's job. You can make it clear that you see your role as one of intelligence gathering, mixing with staff at all levels and problem/opportunity sensing. Whilst you do this, constantly check your perceptions – of yourself, your team, your organization, your key performance indicators (how are those figures compiled?) and your competitors, and encourage your direct reports to do likewise.

The one area we have not stressed as much as we might have is the importance of spending time off the job to make sense of all the data you gather. If you spend time constantly gathering data but not taking time to make sense of it, you will end up overloaded – stressed and out of control. It takes time to put all the pieces together and evaluate them. There are two good ways of taking time out – hiring a coach or going on a leadership retreat.

President Roosevelt was responsible for the first modern-day retreat. In 1942, just as America entered World War II, he had his own retreat built for him just outside Washington. It was here that he took time to reflect, relax and explore complex issues, both with his staff and other world leaders, in an environment of natural beauty and peace. This retreat is now known as Camp David.

A leadership retreat is a venue, normally in the country, which is simple, not occupied by other business people or conferences, and where the main commodity on offer is peace. Retreats can be taken alone or alongside a coach or mentor, who is there to help you clarify your thoughts. It is also possible to go on guided retreats, where people provide you with structured exercises to help clarify your thinking in a particular area.

The important point about retreats is that they should be places of beauty and calm. The environment of a retreat nurtures a reflective and generative state of mind that is highly receptive to learning. Hence, retreats are not taken within plush but busy hotels with easily accessible business centres and multiple means of contact with the outside world. Some people take their retreats in monasteries or convents, where there are no distractions and there may be someone to talk to who has no stake at all in the issues you are engaging with. Retreats are places to reflect, wonder, play around with ideas and come to considered conclusions. Leadership retreats are becoming increasingly popular, and should probably be considered a critical part of any 21st century manager's toolbox.

★ ★ ★

This chapter started by describing the complexity of the world we live in today, and stressing the importance of developing greater cognitive complexity in order to better survive in that world. The three practices outlined here – *deepen sensemaking, engage creativity* and *reality check* – will help in this process. But we also showed that even more important than these were the underlying philosophy, attitude of mind and personal discipline required to take full advantage of the practices. We outlined an epistemology that stresses how we 'construct' our living knowledge from personal values, experience and preferences. Our own living knowledge is simply a personal construction that will always benefit from further development and refinement. We described an attitude of mind that stresses humility – the discipline of listening to those who we may find difficult, frustrating, unimportant or even threatening. Finally, we looked at the importance of personal discipline – a commitment to constructively managing our responses to our emotions and desires, rather than simply expressing or repressing them. All of these practices, attitudes and disciplines will serve anyone well when dealing with the complexity facing us in the 21st century.

9

The Seventh Practice –
Change Behaviour (and
Expand Your Comfort Zone!)

'We must continually choose between deep change or slow death'.
Robert Quinn, *Deep Change: Discover the*
Leader Within and Change the World.

Although the learning cycle is not intended to be a 'stage theory' (where one part of the cycle follows another in strict order) it is often the case, particularly in times of change, that changing behaviour comes last. A leader may have paid attention to some personal feedback, she may have successfully come through the emotional challenge this presented for her, she may have recognized that she needs to change aspects of her management style, and then . . . nothing. No change.

This phenomenon is the *behavioural lag*. The behavioural lag is another form of blind spot. It has two sources:

- the tendency to repress, distort, dismiss or fail to notice information that suggests personal changes in behaviour are necessary;

- the refusal to act on the recognition that it is necessary to change one's behaviour (the 'Hamlet' problem!).

The behavioural lag does not occur at all times. When people are leading change in a visionary learning state, spurred by hope, desire and optimism, they may readily change their behaviour. Also, when people are generally supportive of the change, in an adaptive learning state, they will tend to make small experiments in their behaviour – gradually testing out new approaches to see how they feel and how they work. However, dissonant learning that challenges your sense of identity (i.e. your core beliefs and values) is very much subject to the behavioural lag.

It is easier to see this if we take an example from the diaries. We will look at the example of Will, who, after a long behavioural lag, eventually changes his behaviour. Will's example is somewhat extreme, because the change in behaviour is radical and highly risky. But what this example does is to illustrate the different stages that people often have to go through before they eventually change their behaviour. Will's journey provides an example of dissonant learning and how the behavioural lag operates in extreme circumstances. Although Will does eventually change his behaviour, there were many cases in the diaries where people got 'stuck' during the transition, failing either to recognize the need for change or to turn that recognition into real behavioural change.

Will – To Leave or Not To Leave

When Scientific Solutions was privatized, it brought with it a new set of values around commercialism. The new emphasis placed on profitability, sales and efficiency clashed with the more scientific values based upon thoroughness, risk avoidance and expertise. For example, safety reports that previously might have been critical of 'clients', were changed in tone in order to please the customer. There was a new emphasis placed on time efficiency. Before, scientists could take as long as they believed was professionally necessary to conclude a safety report; now, there was a new pressure to produce reports according to strict deadlines. In addition, it was found that the core activities of the science organization were not particularly profitable. Suddenly, conducting safety reports was no longer 'sexy'. What *was* sexy was developing new high-margin products and services that brought in increased revenues.

This presented significant challenges for the scientists. To tell scientists who value objectivity, thoroughness, truth and expertise that what's important is pleasing clients, bringing in revenue and making profits is to challenge important aspects of their identity. Essentially, there is a tacit message suggesting that:

'what you thought was important, what you based your whole life upon, is, in fact, relatively unimportant. And what you disregarded (even maybe condemned) is, in fact, extremely important'.

During this period many of the scientists felt their self esteem dropping to new lows. It was becoming increasingly apparent that their expertise and technical skills were no longer highly valued. There was a sense that a new world had dawned, one in which people like themselves no longer had a valuable role to play.

Will was one of the scientists who had been highly respected and a leader in his field. He was also very good with 'clients', being warm, approachable and a very good communicator. He, too, felt his self esteem dropping as the organization brought in new ways of operating. Will entered a period of dissonant learning which took him on a long and difficult journey of change.

Early days – do I need to change?

When the changes were first introduced, Will tended to criticize the changes along with everyone else. Whilst he recognized the need for an increased commercialism, he felt that the scientific values were also important, and were being dangerously disregarded. He felt that this was morally wrong and potentially putting people at risk. He also felt that short-term financial pressures were being promoted at the expense of longer-term growth and sustainability.

Initially he attributed the 'mistakes' to poor management and to unintended consequences arising from the change programme. His belief was that these mistakes were 'one off' incidents rather than a sign that the organization was going to change fundamentally. He believed that Scientific Solutions would continue to value its people as important members of a scientific community, promote scientific excellence and focus on promoting science for the public good. This view is what we will term the *scientific values schema*. This is contrasted with a growing sense that the organization was becoming more commercial and focusing its priorities purely onto shareholder value. This is the *commercial values schema*.

In the early days, Will would focus on any event that seemed to support the scientific values schema, and dismiss or discount events that seemed to support the commercial values schema. He was motivated to make sense of events in a way that suggested that the organization would stay the same, and, more importantly, that he would not have to make any radical changes in his own behaviour. This, of course, is a form of blind spot.

However, it became increasingly difficult to continue to interpret events using the scientific values schema. One day, Will was told that a growth project he had personally championed would not be given funding. This project was central to his desire to position the company as a leader in a particular field. In effect, the incident was a tipping point that finally reinforced the commercial values schema. As far as Will was concerned, the triumph of the commercial values schema meant the destruction of his goals and aspirations. He was extremely angry. His anger triggered the first important recognition: *I need to change*. Will decided he could not continue as if nothing was going to change; he was going to have to make some personal changes in order to address the situation. For the first time, he contemplated leaving the organization.

Turmoil – can I change?

Despite recognizing that he might have to leave, Will did nothing about it. He reverted to trying to interpret events in light of the scientific values schema. Why?

Over the period of time in question, Will had, along with many of the other scientists, lost his self confidence. He felt that the world had moved on and his skills were no longer valued. He did not believe that he would be able to find a new job. And even if he did, would he be able to cope? Having spent over 20 years with the organization, it was tempting to wait for early retirement or to convince himself that it would probably be the same in other organizations. There were many ways of making sense of his situation in order to justify not changing.

So Will carried on. But the anger and frustration increased. Eventually, he encountered another tipping point. His professional opinion was not taken seriously by a manager who did not understand Will's professional field. He was so angry that he decided to attend a recruitment fair. This *was* a small change of behaviour but one which carried no risks or commitments – he was 'just looking'!

However, at the fair his world exploded – he discovered that he was valued! People fell over themselves to offer him jobs! His self esteem was boosted and the outside world suddenly looked very different.

Will then reached the next stage on the change journey: I am valued by others – I am a skilled, competent professional. This recognition provided the self confidence to recognize – *I can change.*

Contemplating a new future – do I want to change?

Will pursued a few job opportunities and was offered them. But he had not answered the question of whether he really wanted to change. There would be a lot of upheaval involved in moving the family; the risks of going to a new, unknown organization would be significant. It would be a lot easier to wait for retirement! Besides, with a renewed sense of his own value, he felt invigorated and ready to handle the ups and downs of life at Scientific Solutions.

However, in the face of a number of high profile resignations, senior management decided to offer a group of people a significant increase in salary. Will was not one of those people and he interpreted this event as a personal affront and a sign of how little he was valued in the company. This contrasted significantly with how he was valued by the outside world, as job offers continued to come in. His anger and frustration at this event eventually triggered the next stage on his journey: he realized *I want to change* – I really want to leave this organization.

Taking the plunge – 'I will change'

However, Will still did not hand his notice in. He continued to have concerns and doubts. Nevertheless, he received more job offers, including one that was very attractive in professional terms. Will was in a quandary. Perhaps if he were to inform Scientific Solutions that he had been offered this job, they might re-evaluate his worth to the organization and treat him differently. Then he could stay – he wouldn't have to change anything!

It did not work. In fact the management interpreted his motives as 'angling for more money' and trying to 'blackmail' them. When he heard of this on the grapevine, Will was furious that his motives could have been interpreted in a way that was so totally out of alignment with his values. Seething with anger, he finally resigned!

He had finally changed his behaviour. And, having done so, Will never looked back. He found a new life where he was both valued and happy. But it was a long time between recognizing that he needed to do something and actually doing it. This is the behavioural lag.

As previously mentioned, Will's example is extreme. He faced an irreversible decision – one that was radical and life-changing. But what this example does provide is a clear illustration of the four stages that we all encounter when contemplating behaviour change – I have to change, I can change, I want to change and I will change. Unlike Will, others will have an easier experience of these stages and traverse them more rapidly. Those in an adaptive learning state, for example, will reach the final stage more quickly for a number of reasons. First, the change is not completely out of line with their values. Second, and partly as a result of the alignment with their values, they will have more confidence in their ability to change. Third, they will want to change, for a variety of reasons, ranging from sympathy for what the organization is trying to achieve, to a realization that it is in their own self interest. Lastly, there will be energy reserves to implement the changes; unlike the dissonant learner, the adaptive learner has not been so worn down by all the changes.

There is no doubt that visionary and adaptive learners do not experience the behavioural lag to the same extent that dissonant learners do. However, it is important to point out that we all have areas where we will experience a dissonant learning state and where we are, therefore, particularly resistant to change. In the same way, we all have areas where we are likely to experience a visionary or adaptive learning state, where we will be more receptive to experimenting with behaviour change.

The point about changing behaviour is that there is no going back. It is the riskiest part of the whole learning cycle. Once we have changed our behaviour we enter the unknown. Even if the change is not as radical as Will's was, changing behaviour still involves uncertainty:

- we may fail;
- people will react differently towards us;
- we do not know what the consequences will be;
- people may mock or reject our attempts to change;
- there may be other risks associated with changing behaviour, such as financial risks or relationship risks (i.e. we may jeopardize our relationships with close friends or family who like us as we are);
- it will feel odd, uncomfortable and scary.

Changing behaviour is where the learning cycle really takes off. As we change our behaviour we translate our learning into the external world, and, once it's out, it's impossible to turn back. There will be consequences. When we change our behaviour we change how people react to us and we break with the normal chain of events – we make different things happen, which, of course, we will have to cope with. Furthermore, we don't know what those events will look like – inevitably uncertainty and anxiety will increase. It is much easier to stick to what is familiar, even if that does involve a degree of frustration.

The sheer energy, effort and emotional exhaustion involved in changing behaviour is a significant deterrent. Frustration with the present is often far more preferable to fear of an unknown future. And many people make that choice, staying in a relatively comfortable, predictable world rather than initiating change and facing uncertainty.

However, there are consequences to staying in the comfort zone:

- As the world changes, our tried and tested methods become outdated and no longer work in the way they used to.

- We lose the ability to learn – we become so used to psychological comfort that we become incapable of handling any form of anxiety or emotional tension.

- Because we are not changing our behaviour, we fail to learn the new strategies and skills that are needed to achieve our goals in the new, changing environment – as a result, we fail to achieve those goals.

- We may be seen as predictable, boring, dinosaur-like.

- Our lives become boring – we know this, but feel incapable of making any changes; somehow we miss the emotional roller-coaster associated with learning.

When we refuse to change our behaviour, despite the obvious necessity of doing so, we are subject to a blind spot. This blind spot arises from a failure to understand that whilst changing behaviour is a big step, so, too, is refusing to change behaviour. Both choices have repercussions, it's just that we often fail to examine the repercussions of *not* changing behaviour.

So what can we do to shorten the length of time taken to change our behaviour or, in some cases, to ensure we do not get 'stuck' in the process? How can we overcome the blind spots that cause us to make sense of events in a way that convinces us that we do not need to change? How can we overcome the trap where we recognize the need to change yet refuse to carry this recognition through to action? In order to answer these questions, we need to investigate the four transition points in greater detail.

1. I Need to Change

There are a number of reasons why people do not recognize that they need to change. Two that we will explore here are:

- their existing paradigms do not make sense of the world in a way that leads them to this conclusion;

- they feel anxious at contemplating an unknown future.

Existing Paradigm Use

We have mentioned before that many senior executives get personal feedback about their behaviour without ever coming to the recognition that they really do need to change that behaviour. This is because their current behaviour 'works' for them – it helps them achieve their goals in a way that makes them feel comfortable and in control. They do not see how changing their behaviour will better help them to achieve their goals.

One diarist had a role that involved influencing large numbers of people throughout the organization. He tended to have an abrupt, task-focused style that alienated people, making them angry and resentful. He did not understand the political sensitivities involved in his role and that he was 'threatening' people, without being aware of it. When he got feedback that he needed to soften his style, he rejected it. As far as he was concerned, he needed to be *more* assertive, as people were not being cooperative and, hence, they were jeopardizing important projects. Whilst he understood that many people would have preferred him to be 'softer' and more approachable, he did not see the utility of changing his behaviour. In fact, he believed that becoming more friendly would cause people to relax, thereby delaying projects even further. We can see here that part of the problem lies in the diarist's lack of 'psychological' and 'power' paradigms. He tended to view the world through his operational paradigm, seeing people as units of resource that have to be forced to work 'rationally' for the overall benefit of the organization.

If we are to overcome this blind spot, we must ensure that we develop our paradigms constantly – particularly the power and people paradigms. We must also ensure that we really listen to and probe feedback that we disagree with – it may be difficult at first to understand how it will help us reach our goals, but we can use it to expand our cognitive complexity and to encourage our acceptance of the need to change.

Anxiety at an Unknown Future

Another reason that people do not recognize that they need to change is that, like Will in the above example, they do not want to face the awful, threatening and scary truth about the changes going on around them. We come back to another diarist's point, already quoted in a previous chapter:

> *'I just felt that, I'd been feeling like that (unhappy) for a long time but . . . once I'd left this place in the evening or for the weekend, I'm one of these people that can switch off completely. Now if this seeming overwhelming uncomfortableness came with me when I did leave in the evening, then maybe I would have done something about it in the evening or at the weekend, but I didn't, because once I'd left this place, I no longer had that overwhelming motivation to do something about it, and as soon as I got out of this place, . . . I had lots of other things on that were higher priority in the short term.'*

In other words, the discomfort and frustration associated with the present has to grow to such an extent that it is greater than the discomfort involved in facing potential change. The diarist is saying here that he would only sit down and reflect upon the problem when motivated by the prospect of eliminating intrusive, uncomfortable pain. This is, in part, because he recognizes that accepting new ideas and constructs often involves deep-rooted change. Once you accept an idea, you 'have to put your whole way of life' behind the idea:

> *'and I suppose I'm the sort of person that, when exposed to novel ideas, . . . to begin with, you don't necessarily trust them. But as you live with them and have reflected upon them for a year or two, you then think of them as being the bleeding obvious, even though . . . it's taken me some time to accept that way of looking at things. And now I've got it . . .* **having put my entire livelihood now behind that way of thought, I still have to have the motivation to go through with it.'**

Somewhere inside us we know that if we really sat down and examined the changes going on around us we might have to take some very radical and scary steps – so we simply refuse to think about them. We even tolerate extremes of pain and discomfort before we're ready to face the pain of learning.

This is even more the case with people in senior leadership positions, who are often highly resistant to the idea that they should change their own behaviour. We have seen that, because they have so much to lose, they may be more anxious than others.

This can only be countered by a discipline of structured reflection, as outlined in previous chapters. In particular, it involves focusing on uncomfortable emotions and interpreting them before it is too late to do anything about them. It involves moving from a dissonant learning state to an adaptive learning state, where we may be more ready to make simple experiments with our behaviour.

2. I Can Change

People will not even contemplate change if they believe in the backs of their minds they will not be able to adapt to the required changes successfully. It is noticeable that in the diaries most people changed their behaviour after a sudden and unexpected boost to their confidence. Before Will really started looking into new jobs, he attended a recruitment fair and realized that he was indeed valued by the external world. This gave him the confidence to pursue other opportunities more actively. Another diarist successfully overcame a complex problem that made him remember that he was a highly skilled and successful scientist. Shortly after that, he handed his notice in. Another diarist received positive feedback from a client, which boosted her self belief and gave her the courage to ask for a transfer. This pattern was extraordinarily prevalent during the period of change. People do not change their behaviour until and unless they believe that they are 'valuable' people who have a chance of success. They must believe that they 'can change'.

This is just as relevant to those in senior leadership positions as it is to anyone else. There may be many reasons why those in senior positions feel that they cannot change. They, too, may be scared of failing; they may have relied on a particular management style and feel that changing that style would provoke ridicule or scorn, particularly in the early days when it feels so uncomfortable. Those in senior positions spend much of their time seeking control over events – changing behaviour feels like the opposite, it feels like you are totally out of control.

This is where some of the techniques of positive psychology have an important role to play. Instead of focusing on the problems, challenges and reasons why people might have difficulties in changing, positive psychology focuses on the valuable contributions that people bring to the change situation. It makes them feel as if they can change, that they want to change and, by providing a source of positive energy, ensures people will change.

Another way of accelerating the change process is to have regular time out with a coach, mentor or close colleague who knows your work. These outsiders can bring a calm, rational but supportive view to bear in situations that otherwise are characterized by 'hot cognition'. They can ensure that you make sense of events in a more positive and rational way than is normally possible when you are caught up in the continuous stream of events.

3. I Want to Change

However, even if people decide that they can change, they are also evaluating whether they 'want to change'. This is a highly complex area. There are many reasons why people decide they do not want to change. We have already referred to many of them:

- The changes are out of line with our values. For example, many people decide that they do not want to 'play politics', even though they realize it is necessary in order to ascend the hierarchy.

- We do not want to suffer the emotional exhaustion of changing behaviour. Changing behaviour can be emotionally exhausting – some people simply do not want the hassle.

- We do not want to take the risks. Whilst we might be up for changing behaviour if the benefits are clear, sometimes it does not seem that the benefits of change outweigh the risks of potential failure.

- We feel angry or resentful that we have to change, having developed an approach that has always worked very well up to now. Often there is an emotional block – 'why should we change?', we ask ourselves. Although we can see there might be a reason to change, we feel angry and sullen that we have to move outside our comfort zones.

- We may feel that the changes required of us will not help us achieve what we want. Whilst there might be a change of management style in the company, we may feel that becoming more of a team player will simply not get us what we want – power, independence, attention . . .

- We may choose an alternative to changing our behaviour – early retirement, relinquishing our career ambitions, focusing on our home life.

It is not uncommon for people to come to the conclusion that they simply do not want to change their behaviour – they do not want the hassle, they do not believe it is right, they do not feel it will be helpful to them and simply do not have the emotional or psychological strength to do so.

This is a common scenario for people in top leadership positions – contrast Sir Richard Greenbury's complacency at Marks and Spencer with Sir Terry Leahy's emphasis on innovation, customer focus and continual change. Even if business leaders recognize the need to change, deep down inside they may not really want the discomfort involved in changing their own behaviour. Life in the comfort zone at the top is *extremely* comfortable. One M&S board member explained to a journalist why he did not take the risk of challenging Greenbury:

> *'Well, there is the prestige of being a director of the best-loved retailer in the land . . . There is a comfortable financial package, wonderful pension, great lunchrooms, a car and a driver, company tickets to the opera and first-class travel wherever and whenever you want it, without questions'.*[1]

---

[1] Bevan, J. (2002) *The Rise and Fall of Marks and Spencer*. London: Profile Books Ltd, p. 129.

Contrast this with what *Fortune* magazine refers to as Samsung's culture of *perpetual crisis*. According to the article, Samsung cultivate a 'paranoid' corporate culture where disaster lurks around every corner and success only increases the danger of complacency and failure.[2]

However, it is not easy to live your life in 'perpetual crisis'. It is no wonder that many leaders decide that they simply do not want to change their approach, style or behaviour, no matter how pressing the need.

Refusing to change one's behaviour may be a blind spot, but it may also be a rational, valid decision. If a company changes its culture it may be rational to decide that the new values are no longer in alignment with one's own values. If you value teamwork and your company decides to bring in a culture based much more on individual performance, often in competition with others, you may decide quite validly that it is time to move on. If the company brings in new values based on teamwork and you prefer a more independent, achievement-oriented culture, you may decide quite rationally to leave. This is particularly the case if the new values are swept in by a strong visionary leader, who may be blind to the benefits of the existing values already in place.

The point is that it is important to be clear about the true motives behind a decision not to change. Are you avoiding the discomfort, are you running away, are you scared of the risks involved or are you taking a rational, principled decision based on self awareness and an honest appraisal of the situation? This form of sensemaking is again best conducted with a coach or close friend who knows you and understands your work.

Again, after a period of reflection, you may decide that 'change' is too psychologically exhausting. You may decide that it is time to step down because you do not want to change, and this may be a rational decision. The temptation for those in leadership positions is to decide that they do not want to change but, at the same time, refuse to relinquish their comfortable, status-enhancing leadership role. This, perhaps, is a matter of personal ethics – which we will

---

[2] 'The Crisis Machine.' *Fortune*, September 5th, 2005, pp. 37–43.

look at in the next chapter. Whatever forces lie behind the decision
to change or not to change, it can be quite an exhausting time, recognizing that whatever decision you make will either involve some
risk or the loss of opportunity.

4. I will Change

The 'will to change' is rather like steeling yourself for your first ever
dive off a really high diving board. OK, you've decided that you
really do need to learn to dive – maybe all your friends have cracked
it and you're beginning to look a bit stupid. You've also decided
that you really want to dive – it would be incredibly cool to be able
to dive from such a high board – it would certainly impress the
girls/boys! You know you can dive – after all, you easily dive off a
low diving board.

So, having recognized the need, acknowledged that you want to,
recognized that you can, you step onto the diving board. You walk
to the end of the board, thrust your arms forward and there you
stand, frozen.

There is a second, maybe it feels like a lifetime, where you really,
really want to throw yourself off the end of the board and yet you
are really, really not sure. You may swing your arms backwards and
forwards, saying to yourself, 'here we go'. You may even rock your
body forwards with every intention of throwing yourself off the edge,
but somehow it doesn't happen. Somehow, there you are, still on
the edge of the diving board. Suddenly, someone shouts out – 'get
out of the way, loser!' And all of a sudden you find yourself sailing
through the air, plunging into the water and coming up for breath
– relieved and elated. What was it that made you dive? Actually, it
was anger; anger at being called a 'loser'. That anger provided the
final burst of energy that overcame the fear; the anger provided the
final 'will to change'.

This was very apparent in the diaries. Over the period of a year,
many people decided that they needed to change but were stuck on
the edge of the diving board, not really ready to take the plunge.
The final impulse to change often came in the form of a burst of

energy, sometimes it was the elation of success, or the soul-searching of guilt or the surprise of shock, but often it was anger:

> 'there's an automatic assumption that I should do that because they want me to! My initial reaction was "how", excuse my French, "how f***ing presumptuous". What they've done is taken what their values are . . . to being values that I might have, without bothering to actually question or ask what it was that made me tick and what I actually liked doing . . . no seriously there's no way I want to continue to work for this company'.

Bill changes his behaviour due to a feeling of guilt:

> 'there were some really good people who were in danger of falling apart I think, and I wanted to try and do something about that personally, just because I felt responsible in a way I guess, because, if you're the person who's in many ways driven this, then you've got to take responsibility for the outcomes. Some of the outcomes were that people were feeling very, very uncomfortable'.

In Chapter 2 we saw how one manager made a presentation to his colleagues on mistakes he made in managing a difficult project. This was after a long period of denying that he had done anything wrong at all. It was guilt that finally impelled him to change his behaviour:

> 'I wanted to do it because I thought if I did that I would finally purge it from my system you know, and get rid of it, and **so I did feel happier afterwards**, I felt as though, right that's it, that's the end of it and we've done our best out of it, not only in terms of closing it out properly but also in letting people know what sort of problems we encountered, and what signs there are to look out for so they can try to avoid them in the future.' (my emphasis)

Jake changed his behaviour when he felt his vision was being threatened. A discussion involving a project that was crucial to his vision suddenly catalysed him to offer to present to the board (something he had never done before and which he had had no intention of doing):

> 'there is to be a meeting "at the highest levels" of our companies, there is major concern that our directors will not understand where

Tilco are coming from or where we are in Tilco's perceptions and where we are in terms of the site developments. I ended up tackling both Pete and Chris (two board members) on this issue, and thankfully I'm going to be given a chance to present to the board on these issues – did I say thankfully?'

All these examples demonstrate a change of behaviour that seems to have been propelled by a sudden surge of emotional energy. That energy appears to feed the courage that overcomes the fear of letting go. There has to be something that almost kicks you out of the comfort zone. At some point, if change is to be embraced, there has to be a surge of the will – a determination to jump, no matter what the consequences.

This is important for those in leadership positions, because at the highest levels you can be immune from the shocks or threats or reflective admissions of guilt that provide the energy to change. You can easily find yourself surrounded by people protecting you from the uncomfortable truth or by the ambitious, fearful of challenging your ideas and decisions. Sometimes, in order to penetrate the veil of comfortable illusion that surrounds the leader, the shock has to be so great that it is too late to do anything about it. It is possible to see the history of UK banking in this light – by the time of Big Bang, with the huge and sudden influx of professional American banks, it was too late for British merchant banks to compete. The American banks were too far ahead. Whilst the British were still painfully negotiating the phases of change, many refusing to recognize the need for change, still more not wanting to change, others not able to change, the Americans were what Steve Jobs (CEO/founder of Apple Computer and Pixar Animation Studios) terms 'hungry and foolish' – ambitious, driven and yet neither complacent nor arrogant. This is why Samsung's culture of perpetual crisis, Google's culture of empowerment and 'chaos', Tesco's focus on continuous innovation or Jobs's recommendation to be 'hungry and foolish' are the only ways forward for today's leaders. Not only do they have to discipline themselves to strengthen their will and resist the temptations of the comfort zone, they have to encourage their people to do the same.

And great change leaders often find that the more you push yourself outside the comfort zone, the bigger and more flexible your comfort zone becomes. Eventually, you find that your emotional, behavioural and cognitive repertoire is actually big enough to cope with most challenges and most change. You find that the 'stretch' required to cope with whatever change throws at you is smaller, the steps you have to take when you venture outside the comfort zone are easier to take – you've been out of control before and you know how to handle it. In fact, you might start to miss it!

Leading Change and the Behavioural Lag

Whenever change is introduced, you get the leaders, the followers, the resisters and those who are confused and unsure. The trouble is that the leaders of change experience a visionary learning state. They have recognized the need for change, they are both able and willing to change and they are impatient to do anything that would seem to support their vision. People in a visionary learning state can be highly receptive to changing their behaviour (as long as it suits them and their vision!) and get furious when they encounter others in a dissonant learning state (when the change is out of line with their values and goals). Dissonant learners need time to go through the various stages of change – I need to change, I am able to change, I want to change and, finally, I will change. Visionary learners, however, have been through all of these stages months, even years, before. All they want now is for others to catch them up – to change instantly without having to go through all the different stages. In the middle are the adaptive learners – engaged with the change but still trying to come to terms with it, slowly experimenting with new behaviours to see which work and also feel comfortable and right. This can be a recipe for disaster – with impatient visionary leaders becoming more and more angry because others are not changing their behaviour quickly enough. Yet, often enough, our visionary learners and leaders do not realize that they, too, have to change their behaviour in ways that seem to undermine their own goals and values – they have to learn to be a little bit patient, to listen, to encourage and challenge at the same time. Even visionary leaders are often resistant to changing their style when it does not suit them; even visionary leaders have their behavioural lag.[3]

Today, it feels like there is a continual pressure on everyone to change. There are limits to how much we can change and by when. There is a natural transition cycle and it takes time to traverse it. Changing behaviour is a discipline, an art, a science and a way of life – it is a crucial skill for surviving in changing times.

---

[3] This is powerfully illustrated by Bunker and Wakefield in their *Transition Leadership Wheel*. They maintain that a leader has to manage dilemmas, balancing urgency with patience, optimism with realism, being tough with being empathetic, self-reliance with trusting others, capitalizing on strengths and going against the grain. Leaders will inevitably find one side of the dilemma easier than the other, but according to the authors, leaders have to balance both. For many, this will lead them outside their own comfort zones and present them with their own behavioural challenge. See Bunker, K. A. and Wakefield, M. (2005) *Leading With Authenticity in Times of Transition*. Greensboro: CCL Press.

10

The Eighth Practice – Nurture Integrity

'I'm using the House [of Commons] *as a kind of club/ringside seat/status enhancer, not as a central mission.'*
Alan Clark, *The Diaries*

Throughout this book we have seen how values can either assist or inhibit learning. As with the other drivers in learning, such as goals, psychological comfort and self esteem, the role played by values appears to be double edged. On some occasions they can help generate deep learning, whilst at other times they can be sources of blind spots.

Values can assist learning when they prompt us to undertake new challenges. The diarists showed us that when their values were challenged, many of them entered a dissonant learning state, which led them to question fundamental aspects of their lives and careers. Some of the diarists decided to embark on a process of radical change (e.g. leaving their organizations) rather than tolerate beliefs and practices that they felt were wrong. Others decided to take action to protect long-cherished values and ways of working. In all of these cases, people stepped outside their comfort zones and expanded their living knowledge in order to protect deeply held beliefs and values. However, not everyone responded in this way. Some people were content to pursue their needs for comfort and security, despite the fact that in doing so, they did not feel they were acting in accordance with their 'values'. This led to a certain degree of dissonance, but the dissonance generated defensiveness, such as cynicism or victim behaviour, rather than learning.

Values also act as spurs to learning when they inspire leadership and followership. Leaders and followers who pursue visions infused with strong values can go through a period of intense learning as they fight for their values to be enacted in the world. One of the diarists, for example, described the struggle to achieve his vision as equivalent to a 'guerilla war'. He described his job as a 'battle for hearts and minds', and saw himself as a 'disciple' who was 'converting' people to his way of thinking. Values can trigger a highly emotional learning state, which may be manifested in metaphors of warfare or of religious conversion. However, this type of learning state can also lead to intolerance, rigidity and a narrowness of mind. In this state of mind, it is easy to exclude alternative, diverse opinions and miss opportunities for transformatory or generative learning.

Values can alert us to when we need to change our behaviour, drawing our attention to those instances when we may not have acted with complete integrity. One diarist mentions the guilt he experienced at making an older member of the team redundant:

> *'my candid approach and our discussion about how he is coping with change has paid off. Relieved at this acceptance – I really didn't think he would sign up; feel a little sense of guilt that he may not easily find a new job. Commercially will be good, he is a barrier to change, in longer term, others in the department will benefit.'*

At this point the diarist is rationalizing his guilt by referring to what he sees as the benefits to the company of the individual leaving. However, he later admits:

> *'I guess on reflection in an attempt to shake him into reality and get him to accept early release, I wasn't the usual nicey-nicey, Scientific-Solutions-pretend-nothing-is-wrong kind of person. I'm sure he will thank me in the end, although he hasn't coped well with the transition from his civil service days.'*

At this point, whilst he accepts that he could have done things differently, he is not quite prepared to embrace the full consequences of his actions for the individual concerned. It takes time and further reflection for him to draw out the full learning from the incident:

'(nowadays) I take a bit more of a people orientation and actually make sure that I'm not just asking people to do things, I'm actually paying a bit more attention to their working environment and how they feel about work and what have you.'

The diarist only learned to change his behaviour, beliefs and emotional orientation to people having had a period of time to reflect on his underlying motivations and the consequences of his actions. This involved him facing his guilt and admitting that he could have done things differently.

However, whilst guilt can generate transformatory learning, it can also provoke defensiveness and inhibit learning and change. Much depends upon how the individual handles the discomfort associated with the feelings of guilt.

It appears as if values play an important role in learning, but that role is ambiguous and uncertain. This chapter will examine the nature of values by exploring how we can use them to promote learning and integrity in three areas often characterized by blind spots:

- expanding your range of values;

- walking the talk;

- learning through your values.

Part one of the chapter will present a working definition of 'values'. Parts two to four will examine each of the above areas in more detail. Part five will offer some conclusions and recommendations for action.

1. Values

Freshwater and Robertson in their book *Emotions and Needs*,[1] list some basic human *needs:*

---

[1] Freshwater, D. and Robertson, C. (2002) *Emotions and Needs*. Buckingham: Open University Press.

- survival;
- love;
- security;
- respect;
- independence;
- power;
- sexuality.

Reese in his book, simply entitled *Values*,[2] lists some basic *values*:

- survival;
- love;
- security;
- self respect;
- individuality;
- strength;
- meaningful and meaningless sex.

This overlap between values and needs is complex. Milton Rokeach, one-time Professor of Social Psychology at Washington State University and leading figure in the field of human values, provides a useful definition of a value:

> an enduring belief that a specific **mode of conduct or end-state of existence** is personally or socially preferable to an opposite or converse mode of conduct or end-state of existence.[3]

McClelland, on the other hand, defines *motivation* as a combination of 'needs, drives and incentives' that impel a person to strive for a *particular goal or end state*. Buchanan and Huczynski[4] provide us with another definition of *motivation*:

---

[2] Reese, W. L. (2000) *Values: A Study Guide with Readings*. New York: Humanity Books.

[3] Rokeach, M. (1973) *The Nature of Human Values*. New York: The Free Press, p. 5.

[4] Buchanan, D. and Huczynski, A. (1985) *Organisational Behaviour*. Hemel Hempstead: Prentice Hall.

the cognitive, decision-making process through which the individual **chooses desired outcomes** and sets in motion the actions appropriate to their achievement. (my emphasis)

There is clearly an overlap here between our understanding of human needs, motivation and values. All express preferences for desired end-states, outcomes or goals. Values take the form of beliefs that an end-state is preferable whilst motivation has the added component that there is a will or energy that impels the individual to act in order to achieve the desired outcomes. Values are therefore more passive than motivation: we may have values that express preferences, but personally we might not choose to invest our energy striving to achieve those preferences. However, some would argue that some, at least, of our values do contain this energizing element – that if one has certain values, one is strongly motivated to act in accordance with those values. We have had glimpses of this already with the diarists. A significant number of diarists decided to change their behaviour in response to an event that triggered and challenged their values. In the following examples the diarists changed their emotional orientations, beliefs *and* behaviour in response to a challenge to their values:

'*my initial reaction was "how," excuse my French, "how f***ing presumptuous"* . . . *what they've done is taken what their values are* . . . *to being values that I might have, without bothering to actually question or ask what it was that made me tick and what I actually liked doing.*' (this diarist left the organization)

'*they've altered the results to suit themselves. I am disgusted* . . . *Quite clearly they don't give a shit about the health and safety of their workforce. Spoke to people here about it and it appears this isn't the first time this has happened. I have refused to work on any more of their projects. There is (to me anyway) such a thing as professional integrity.*' (this diarist moved to a different division within the organization)

'*I was just very angry, I thought "right, OK if that's the way they want to play it I won't be open and honest anymore"* . . . *but it's not my style, it's not my natural way of working.*' (this diarist left the organization, significantly influenced by this event)

'*I'm the only person here that ever organizes any sort of social dos, I organize things like the raft race that we get involved in, you know,*

I put in a lot of effort in ways that, you know, in trying to make this place a more pleasant place to work, but because you can't put a monetary value on it and that comes back to that, they're not interested. Unless it's pound notes, forget it.' (this diarist left the organization)

'*I'm not totally convinced that they're always the very best people that get to the top. You get some people who are extremely focused on their own goals and achievements, which might well not be the success, the optimum success of their business and the people within it.'* (this diarist started to question senior management more and gained the confidence to express his own opinions and beliefs)

We can see from the above that the everyday conceptual understanding of 'values' often contains a mix of constructs that include:

- A *subjective need or motivator* that is good or right for me – e.g. '*teamwork* is good – I prefer to work in a team, it feels right for me and there are powerful arguments that justify my personal preference'.

- A *personal ideal* that I strive to achieve because I believe it is good for me – e.g. 'I need to work on my *teamwork* in order to counter my strong preference for independence'.

- A *subjective need* or *personal ideal* that everyone should strive to achieve because I believe it is good and right for our social unit/ organization, etc. – e.g. 'we all need to work as a *team* because teamwork is obviously a better way to work'.

- A *societal ideal* that *our* society should strive to achieve because I believe it is good and right – e.g. 'we need to increase spending on social welfare in order to promote a *fairer and more egalitarian society*'.

- A *societal ideal* that *all* societies should strive to achieve because I believe it is good and right – e.g. 'all societies need to become democracies because *democracy* is obviously the best way to organize society'.

A general definition of values that includes all of the above constructs would look as follows:

a set of personally or socially defined preferences regarding end-states and modes of conduct which inform beliefs as to what is 'right' and 'good'.

However, sometimes, in order to separate out the notion of values as needs, personal ideals and societal ideals, it can be helpful to differentiate further. For example, it is common for the popular psychology and self-help literature to use the word 'values' when referring to a subjective need or motivator. According to this perspective, we act in accordance with our values in order to meet deep, personal needs. Values such as 'independence', 'achievement', 'getting things done' are expressions of personal needs and preferences, and, as such, they are part of our personality. These may be innate or may be learned as part of early socialization. In this chapter we refer to these types of values as *motivational values*.

In the philosophical, ethical and political literature, we see a greater focus on values as ideals. Ideals such as 'justice', 'equality' and 'fairness' are not necessarily personal needs, but are something we strive to attain and can, in fact, contradict our needs and desires. These kinds of values are often learned via socialization and derived from historically and culturally specific *systems* of norms. They tend to be encompassed within larger systems of thought, and are sometimes superseded by time and the evolution of ideas. Examples would include: 'the divine right of kings'; 'communism'; 'equal rights for women'; 'democracy'; 'Christianity'; 'Islam'. Alternatively, they may be expressed in more abstract terms, such as 'freedom'; 'equality'; 'justice'; 'peace'. We refer to these as *idealistic values*. Idealistic values also include personal preferences that are not innate or part of our personal motivational profile. When we strive to live up to an ideal that does not come naturally to us, we are attempting to live by an idealistic value.

Idealistic values are often the most difficult to question as to their moral 'rightness'. Today, it is difficult to question the rightness and goodness of 'democracy' or 'freedom'. Idealistic values tend to carry an aura of ultimate goodness and unquestionable, obvious 'rightness' about them. When I stand up for my idealistic values I feel morally justified, there is a feeling of heroism and self sacrifice. This 'heroic' approach derives from the philosophical, political and ethical traditions whereby values are distinguished from self interest and may be associated with acts of self sacrifice conducted for the sake of the 'common good'. However, we often make the mistake of carrying over this sense of rightness and goodness to our motivational values. It is important to remember that our motivational values are simply personal preferences. When we act in support of our motivational values we can, in some small way, be acting out of selfishness – following our preferences at the expense of others. There is nothing 'right and good' about teamwork. It is simply a preference, at the expense of independence. There is nothing 'right and good' about achievement. It is simply a preference, possibly at the expense of teamwork or helping others. We often forget this when talking of our values, and rarely do we question whether our values are 'right'.

Of course there are often overlaps between idealistic and motivational values, and it is sometimes difficult to tell the difference, but nevertheless the distinction can be useful when exploring how values affect the learning and behaviour of leaders. This is because the actions and decisions of leaders may result from a conflict between personal goals (e.g. making profits), motivational values (e.g. being liked, expressed as 'teamwork') and idealistic values (e.g. customer service). A person with this set of goals and values might find that her motivational values make it difficult for her to negotiate with a client, as she tries to balance the goal of maximizing profits (driving her to push a hard bargain), her motivational value of being liked by her team (feeling she must not agree to taking on too much additional work from the customer) and her idealistic values of prioritizing the needs of the client (causing her to put his needs first). These clashes in goals and values can cause a lot of frustration and confusion. They can also lead to blind spots and, sometimes, when we pursue goals at the expense of our idealistic values, a perceived lack of integrity.

All of us manage these conflicts daily as we make a flow of decisions that seek to balance our self interest, our needs and the ideals we strive to live by. But the process is often managed subconsciously and, as a result, is susceptible to cognitive biases such as rationalization. For example, we may decide not to include a highly talented individual in our team. We tell ourselves that he would disrupt the dynamics and potentially destabilize the team. In fact, if we were to examine our motives more closely, we might have to acknowledge that our decision was driven by a dislike of being challenged, a need to be in control and a determination to ensure that the 'disruptive' individual would not succeed in gaining power or influence in the organization. But whilst we may be able to hide these motives from ourselves, when we are in leadership positions, they can be very apparent to those around us. Unless we are honest with ourselves about some of our underlying drives and motives, we are in danger of being subject to blind spots that undermine our integrity, the effectiveness of decisions and, ultimately, our leadership. The simple process of bringing our conflicting motivations into conscious awareness can significantly address typical leadership blind spots such as intolerance, expediency and complacency.

The following three sections offer some ways in which we can do this.

2. Expanding your Range of Values

Much one-to-one coaching focuses on helping people to identify and act in accordance with their motivational values. This involves becoming aware of one's motivational values and developing the necessary confidence to take leadership on issues that one believes in profoundly and passionately. The process often encourages a visionary learning state, as individuals construct visions rooted in their personal values and a sense of what is 'good and right'.

However, there is another process which involves going beyond one's natural inclinations, instincts and preferences and exploring the 'other side' – the truths that we ignore or exclude because they are not part of our motivational profiles and, hence, do not come to us naturally. As we develop into more and more senior roles, our motivational values can limit us. We are then called to explore the world beyond our values in order to make decisions that are more rounded and reflect the more complex world we are dealing with. This involves seeing that other people who have very different values from us also have valid preferences and ways of operating in the world. It is difficult for someone who naturally values teamwork to see the value in independence; it is sometimes difficult for someone who values 'supporting others', to see the value in being task-focused and tough. However, the more senior and more complex the leadership role, the more the leader is required to appreciate values beyond his or her own preferences. Sometimes teamwork is appropriate, sometimes not; sometimes consultation is appropriate, and sometimes not. A wise leader is able to see the truth outside his or her own value set.

Paul

Paul was a gifted manager and a popular leader amongst those who reported to him. He had been promoted regularly over the past six years and had recently been offered a senior position running a large division within the international accountancy firm for which he worked. He had refused. His reason was that he did not like the politics that he observed taking place at this level.

In Paul's view, 'playing politics' was the opposite of everything he valued. People who were good at politics were deceitful, dishonest, manipulative and untrustworthy. They were flatterers and liars, and made decisions based on their own self interest rather than that of the firm or of the people who worked for it. Paul's values were centred on openness and honesty. He believed in people being promoted according to their talent rather than because they fitted into certain leadership cliques or alliances. He believed in telling things as they were rather than hiding the truth in order to help a senior partner save face. He simply was not prepared to play their game. If it came down to sacrificing his career or sacrificing his integrity, he would rather do the former.

It was clear that whilst some partners were pleased at this refusal, other partners were disappointed. Some people saw Paul as a person of great courage and integrity who could help alleviate some of the political infighting that often took place at senior levels. Other partners, however, saw Paul as politically naïve and a 'loose cannon', and were relieved that he had declined the offer.

After some coaxing from his boss, whom he respected greatly, Paul agreed to undertake some coaching with regards to the issue. During the coaching sessions he began to recognize that one of the problems with the firm was that those who disliked the politics tended not to compete aggressively for promotion. This left the way open for the more Machiavellian employees to climb the career ladder, making it inevitable that political infighting would thrive at senior levels. This had a negative impact on the firm and on the people working for it. Everybody recognized this, but did not know what to do about it.

Furthermore, there was a strong tendency for people with values around teamwork, meritocracy and professionalism to denote any behaviour that involved so-called 'self-promotion' as 'politics'. These 'meritocrats' felt that their work should speak for itself. This was naïve. When it came to getting oneself known, it was necessary to put names to faces, to build relationships of trust with people and to build networks throughout the organization to help open doors and get things done. Politics was simply the art of getting to know people in large organizations, and building networks of trust and mutual respect.

Paul had never seen 'politics' in this light before and he could see the sense of it. If people like himself did not take leadership, then senior management would always be dominated by the Machiavellian and the expedient. In fact, if no-one made a stand, even the decent people who accepted promotion would have to adopt 'political' behaviour simply in order to survive. Moreover, he could see that his blanket disapproval of 'politics' also masked a discomfort he felt with the whole notion of networking and, what he called, 'schmoozing'. Part of his dismissal of politics was a rationalization of his own preferences for remaining task-focused and his discomfort with small talk and relationship-building. He could see that he had used the idea of playing politics to justify the fact that he did not want to step outside of his comfort zone to work purely and simply on developing and improving his relationships in the firm. He had rationalized his own discomfort and made himself feel good by claiming that his avoidance was based on his integrity, rather than personal preference.

Looking at the situation in this way made Paul think again about accepting the promotion. He could see that the promotion would be a challenge and would require him to step outside his comfort zone, change his attitude and expand his range of behaviours. However, it would be for a good cause. Perhaps he could use his new-found political awareness to make a difference in some small way. He decided to accept the position. He also decided to retain his coach in order to help him develop his political awareness and relationship-building skills.

This simple example shows how we often hide behind our values in order to justify a refusal to embrace new ways of working. Paul pretended to himself that his refusal to question his exclusive emphasis on 'achievement' was, in fact, a morally justified stance that demonstrated his openness, honesty and integrity. He confused his motivational and idealistic values. What he believed was his discomfort at the lack of senior management integrity was, in fact, discomfort at the prospect of learning and coming outside of his comfort zone.

As people enter more and more complex environments, it is more and more likely that they will face dilemmas such as Paul's. It is unlikely that one's motivational values are going to be effective in all situations. Sometimes consultation will be right; sometimes a more directive style is appropriate. Sometimes teamwork is right; sometimes a more independent style works better. Sometimes a coaching and supportive style is effective; sometimes a harder, discipline-oriented style gets better results. It is important for leaders not to be imprisoned by their motivational values, but to recognize situations that require them to work in ways that, at first, may feel uncomfortable and unnatural. A leader has to learn that just because it feels uncomfortable does not mean it's wrong! Just as a golfer would not go into a tournament with only one or two clubs, nor should a leader go into a complex situation with only one management style. It may take time to develop a more broad selection of management styles, but this flexibility and range is what makes an effective leader.[5]

---

[5] Goleman, D. (2000) 'Leadership That Gets Results'. *Harvard Business Review*, March–April, pp. 78–90.

3. Walking the Talk

Remember our M&S director who admitted that he was not prepared to challenge Sir Richard Greenbury:

> ' *"We suffered years of brutalization in the boardroom," (he) grumbled to an analyst over lunch one day. "So why stay?" asked the analyst. "Well, there is the prestige of being a director of the best loved retailer in the land," replied the director. "There is a comfortable financial package, wonderful pension, great lunchrooms, a car and a driver, company tickets to the opera and first-class travel wherever and whenever you want it, without questions".* '[6]

This leader had sacrificed any idealistic values he might have had because he was fulfilling his motivational values so nicely. This is why leaders do not walk the talk. Because, in a classic conflict between their motivational values and their idealistic values, they, like many of us, pursue their motivational values – they do what they want rather than what they should do.

Invariably, when organizations publish sets of values, many of them are idealistic, aspirational values. Values such as openness, honesty, customer focus and continuous learning are often published on posters and in magazines as guides for action. However, when these idealistic values get in the way of motivational values and goals, they are dropped. If work/life balance involves missing an important deadline, then it will be sacrificed and staff will be asked to work late. This is regarded as being 'realistic' and nothing more is thought about it.

Walking the talk is about making the difficult choices to follow idealistic values, even when it may be difficult or even not in your own self interest. Walking the talk often involves making difficult choices (for example, it may involve asking staff to work late but being aware that you are contravening an important value around work/life balance and therefore taking steps to make amends – for example, offering time in lieu). It is about being conscious of the idealistic

---

[6] Bevan, J. (2002) *The Rise and Fall of Marks and Spencer*. London: Profile Books Ltd.

values of the organization and putting them into practice, even when it is inconvenient or frustrating. More than anything, it is about constantly striving to live according to one's idealistic values and avoiding the traps of expediency or complacency.

Peter

Peter worked for a government department and had just been appointed to manage the unit responsible for community relations, diversity and social cohesion. Peter had entered the civil service on the graduate 'fast track', and since leaving Cambridge University he had risen rapidly through the hierarchy. This was not surprising. Peter seemed to represent the ideal fast tracker. He had come from a family who had produced a number of outstanding civil servants. He had attended a famous public school where he had received an excellent education and a good-quality, influential network. He was confident and articulate. His confidence sometimes bordered on the arrogant, but this was countered by his extroversion and wit, which made him popular with his peers and bosses.

Peter was a 'doer'. The combination of a quick mind and his unerring confidence helped him get to the bottom of an issue and decide rapidly what needed to be done. He prided himself on his decisiveness and leadership abilities. He saw his leadership style as being clear, confident, articulate and charismatic. He seemed to have that great gift of being able to combine an emphasis on the task with an ability to influence and be liked by people. He knew what to do and how to get people to do it.

It was partly as a result of his reputation for action that he had been appointed to his latest role. His boss hoped that he would be able to bring energy and determination to his new role. The department for community relations, diversity and social cohesion (or CU – community unit – for short) had a reputation for being slow to deliver. Furthermore, the people on the ground were known to 'go native', coming back to the unit as representatives of the various factions rather than managing to bring them together to reach much needed agreements. Peter's boss, Sue, believed that Peter would be able to get to the bottom of these issues and speed up delivery, so that the department would be seen as being more productive. Sue was anxious because the community unit was beginning to be seen as the lame duck of the organization. She wanted to improve its image as well as its performance.

Peter quickly threw himself into the role, approaching it as he had many others before. He prioritized four key projects that the department was working on, and pulled resources out of other, less important areas. Within each project, he set six measurable targets and emphasized to each team the importance of accountability and delivery. He held regular team meetings with each of the project leaders to monitor progress on each target. He constantly emphasized the importance of delivery, along with the need for tangible results which could be seen by other people in the organization. The team, on the other hand, tended to stress the need for gradual progress as the only way to gain commitment and long-lasting, sustainable change. Peter saw this as prevaricating and resistance to change. He did not have time to wait for results that would only emerge after years of negotiation.

It was not long before the unit was in uproar. One project team was devastated when its project was halted just as an agreement between three organizations who represented important minority interests in the area was about to be signed. At least three members in the team had specialist backgrounds and had been allocated to projects where their specialism was not needed. One team had been in the middle of persuading an important religious group to come to the negotiating table when their funding had been halted. Project teams were insulted by the crudity of the targets that had been set, which clearly did not recognize the complexity of the issues they were dealing with. Furthermore, they distorted activity, focusing resources on areas that were relatively easy to address but which did not address the central problems. Peter soon acquired a reputation for being a typical 'fast tracker'. Fast trackers were seen as only interested in pursuing their own careers. They were people who came into departments, set themselves easy targets, achieved them and then moved on elsewhere before the consequences of their decisions were fully apparent. They never fully engaged with the complexity of the issues, because they were neither interested in nor concerned about the issues themselves or the people affected by them. They simply wanted to please their bosses. This meant agreeing to do anything that was asked, not challenging any requests and never representing the views of the department to their bosses.

News of the disruption, anger and disappointment soon reached Sue's ears. She was surprised. Nothing like this had ever happened to Peter before. She decided to investigate further, and soon realized that a rift had taken place between Peter and his staff. Sue felt that this would be a good learning experience for Peter. She decided to have a one-to-one session with him.

During the session she asked Peter to describe the past six months and how he felt it had gone. Peter was very happy with his performance. He was on course to achieve all his targets and he felt that the department now had some tangible results to show. When asked about relations with his staff, he acknowledged that these had been difficult at times but he put this down to resistance to change. At this point, Sue decided to tell Peter how he was viewed by his staff. She described the image of the fast tracker as seen by other people in the organization. The fast tracker was only interested in himself and his career. He preferred to address symptoms rather than focus on the complexity of the issues and their causes. The fast tracker was not interested in his staff or the people directly affected by his decisions. He was only interested in power, ambition, status and career. Sue ended her description by adding:

> *'Peter, you are seen by your staff as being a typical fast tracker.'*

Peter was appalled that he could be seen in this light by other people, including, it seemed, by his boss. This was totally unfair. He had focused on results, but only in order to help the team perform better and, ultimately, to increase their reputation in the organization.

As the conversation continued, Peter became aware of another set of feelings – frustration, anger and also guilt. Was there an element of truth in what Sue was saying? Had he stressed short-term results at the expense of longer-term, sustainable results because it was easier and looked better on his CV? He felt embarrassed and exposed.

Sue felt some sympathy for Peter. He had been faced with a series of apparently irreconcilable dilemmas. There was no doubt that his unit interfaced with some hugely complex social and cultural systems. However, they had to perform within a target-oriented culture that was not sympathetic to the complexity and sensitivity of these types of issues. She didn't envy him the challenge he faced. They had a long discussion which included an exploration as to why Peter wanted to go into the civil service in the first place. In fact, this conversation did reveal some of Peter's idealistic values. Peter wanted to make a difference to society and felt that this was an area in which he could achieve that. He did believe that the role played by the executive was crucial, and if done well could contribute towards the overall wealth and welfare of society. On reflection, he admitted he had changed since immersing himself in work. He had allowed his desire for personal career success to dominate and had all but forgotten why he had joined the civil service. He had, without realizing it, begun to treat people as units or resources, getting frustrated when people did not agree with him or when they brought up problems. He had begun to adopt a formulaic approach to his work – thinking that he knew the answer to the problems without attempting to probe and understand them. He could see why he might be seen as someone who avoided the complex issues, which was ironic as he was intelligent and good at getting to grips with complexity.

Sue and Peter agreed an action plan. Peter needed to regain the respect of his staff and needed to listen to their concerns. There was an element of truth in what they were saying about long-term sustainable change, and Peter would have to acknowledge this without denying the importance of improving results in the short term as well. The team would have to get together and really get to grips with the issues. Peter would call a team meeting where he would acknowledge his past failings and apologise. He would stress the need for both short-term and long-term sustainable change and would listen to and consult the team more. He would not be giving up on his determination to improve the unit's output and performance, but would be involving his people in the decisions regarding this. Most of all, Peter recognized the traps of complacency and of allowing himself to be too strongly driven by his personal motivations, desires and needs. This would take some personal discipline, but he was determined to be seen as someone with integrity, who could be trusted to handle the complex issues. Mastering this now would provide a good foundation for his leadership in the future.

Peter's story illustrates how easy it is to confuse one's ideals and one's motivations and goals. In Peter's case, there was an underlying set of idealistic values that were important to him and which could provide a 'moral compass', pointing to what was 'right' as opposed to what was simply 'good for me'. Too often we are driven by our motivational values that cause us to aim for what is 'good for me'. We smother our idealistic values, which are the source of our conscience and which tell us what we are doing is not 'right'. The Marks and Spencer director quoted at the beginning of the chapter provides a good illustration of this. Whenever there is power, wealth, status and influence, we often ignore what is right and simply do what we want, creating 'reasons' why what we want is, in fact, right and good. It takes character, self discipline and integrity to really 'walk the talk'.

4. Learning Through Our Values

Joseph Badaracco, Professor of Ethics at Harvard, writes about 'defining moments' in leadership.[7] These are times when we are called to

---

[7] Badaracco, J. L. Jr (1998) 'The Discipline of Building Character.' *Harvard Business Review*, March–April, pp. 115–124.

make a decision that involves choosing between a set of alternatives which are neither right nor wrong. In making this choice, we reveal previously hidden aspects of our personalities, both to ourselves and to others. We make a choice based upon deeply felt, personal values and, in doing so, enact those values in a way that inspires others to follow suit. When we act in this way, we help others make sense of events by defining what is 'right' in often messy and confusing situations. In effect, we act as beacons illuminating the path ahead for others to follow. Leaders who act in this way are generally recognized as having both courage and integrity.

Badaracco researched a cross-section of leaders and found that those who dealt most satisfactorily with these defining moments were those who recognized the need to take time out to learn through their values. We can best illustrate this through an example.

Martin

Martin had been made CEO just over two years ago. He now found himself faced with a difficult choice. One of his senior board members, Chris, was underperforming and depressing the whole company's performance as a result. Chris had been in position for just over 18 months, and during this time his region's results had continued to slide. Occasionally, Martin heard reports of difficulties in the region, but it was not easy to speak to people directly without undermining Chris's position.

Having discussed the situation with a number of people, including the HR director, Martin felt that Chris had probably been overpromoted. He was beginning to feel that he should remove Chris and put him in a less exposed (and less senior) role. However, there were a number of new hires on his board, all of whom had been in place for less than two years. He sensed that if he removed someone from the board at this stage, it might undermine the confidence of the other directors, and could encourage internal rivalries to develop. He was also unsure as to whether he should be giving Chris more time to rectify the situation. It felt a bit ruthless to remove someone in such a senior position after a relatively short period of time. Martin had spent a lot of time coaching Chris, and he had improved a lot over the past year. However, if Martin let the situation deteriorate for much longer, the company could suffer and relations with investors could be seriously damaged. What should he do?

Martin decided to take some time on retreat to think the situation through. He thought back over his career to see whether he had come across any situations like this before. Suddenly, he remembered an old boss of his from over 15 years ago. This boss, Alison, had acted as an informal mentor when Martin had achieved his first management position. Alison had a reputation for being tough but fair. She intimidated many people with her challenging style and her determination to seek out the truth. But Alison had a clear philosophy – her job was to make the tough and difficult decisions that no-one else wanted to make. On one occasion, this had involved shutting down a loss-making factory in a town that relied on the factory for much of its employment. Alison had known that this was necessary in order to steer the company onto a sound financial footing, but she had not enjoyed making the decision.

Once Alison had made the decision, however, she did everything she could to help the people affected. She had provided career guidance for many, and had partnered with the local council to provide help in retraining, job hunting and setting up small businesses. The company had provided good redundancy packages and had paid for personal financial advisors to come and speak to the people involved. Martin remembered how Alison had turned a difficult situation into one where she had earned grudging respect from many people involved. This had not been easy. Alison's methods had made the redundancies more expensive than they needed to be, and she had fought many battles inside the organization to achieve her aims. But Alison had always been motivated by the recognition that although being in business involved making tough decisions, this did not mean that those decisions could not be implemented fairly and compassionately.

Having thought this through, everything seemed a lot clearer to Martin. His primary responsibility was to the company – it was his job to look after its interests, and this meant it was his job to make tough and difficult decisions. That was what he was paid for and he could not, in conscience, avoid those decisions. He knew that Chris had to go. Even as he made this decision he felt a sense of relief, a sense of certainty that this *was* the right decision.

However, he would do everything in his power to ensure that Chris was handled fairly and compassionately. He wanted to help Chris and to ensure that he left with as positive an outlook as was possible. He also wanted others to recognize that the decision was based on a sensible analysis of the facts and not a knee jerk response to difficulties. Martin decided to contact HR as soon as he returned to the office to discuss the best way of handling the situation.

Martin's example shows us how sometimes we have to dig deeper to discover our own personal values. Sometimes the right response to a situation is not clear. Another person in Martin's situation might have made a different decision based on a different set of experiences and personal values. But what Martin did was to take time out to discover what *he* believed was right and what *he* stood for. This then gave him the clarity to act with conviction and courage. It also served as a defining moment for both him and his board, signalling his values around performance and responsibility to the company's stakeholders.

Sometimes this is not easy. Martin took time out to explore his past in order to guide his future decisions. Often, however, we make decisions on the spur of the moment or in the midst of events. In these situations, we may be driven by all sorts of motivations – desires, fears, motivational values, personal goals, needs, etc. – and it is easy to make decisions that are out of line with our idealistic values. We saw this with Bill in Chapter 6, who, on reflection, discovered that he had acted in a way that had contravened his values. Despite believing in teamwork and consultation, he had made decisions in isolation and imposed them on the team with no consultation. However, it was only by taking time out to explore his feelings of guilt that he had recognized this. His guilt, in turn, had been triggered by feelings of compassion for his team. Bill had opened himself up to these feelings of guilt and compassion by listening to their expressions of confusion, anger and anxiety. Bill puts it graphically:

> *'we got that wrong because I'm learning. The trouble is, you're learning in a living environment, so things happen and you're not at that level of knowledge to actually deal well with the decisions you're making sometimes. You're always at the edge of your knowledge boundaries when you're making decisions, but it's only when you gain more knowledge that you realize those decisions weren't quite as good as they could have been.'*

Sometimes learning from your values involves taking time out to explore and clarify what you believe. Sometimes it involves reflecting on the past and facing difficult emotions such as guilt or a sense of damaged competence. However, time spent exploring these feelings does, as Bill suggests above, yield rich learning. It expands the complexity of one's living knowledge and, in particular, enables the individual to adapt in morally and ethically complex situations.

5. The Discipline of Integrity

Jeremy Paxman, in his book *The Political Animal*, quotes a politician, Humphrey Berkeley:

> *'Most politicians are simultaneously cynical and idealistic, self-centred and disinterested, candid and cunning. They are susceptible to the grossest flattery; they rival actors in their sustained ability to talk about themselves and ruthlessly to wrench any discussion into an examination of their own ego and its relationship to the matter being discussed. I recognize all these qualities in myself . . . In many cases . . . they are jealous of their contemporaries. This feeling I have fought and overcome. Jealousy is poison. If you are embarked upon an enterprise where the stakes are as extreme as Downing Street or the gutter, you must rid your system of poison'.*[8]

---

[8] Paxman, J. (2003) *The Political Animal*. London: Penguin, p. 280.

Leaders will never be great, and we will never be well-led until we face a fundamental fact about human nature – one which our humanist and post 1960s culture has tried for so long to deny – that human beings contain a potent mixture of good and bad – altruism, self sacrifice, generosity, kindness, patience and love are intertwined with greed, lust, pride, jealousy, anger and self pity.

This is something that was acknowledged and recognized until relatively recently. Covey points out that up until 50 years ago, leadership development was focused on the notion of developing 'character'. He cites Benjamin Franklin's autobiography as representative of the 'character' literature – emphasizing the importance of virtues such as: integrity, humility, fidelity, temperance, courage, justice, patience, industry, simplicity and modesty. These are virtues that have to be worked at, precisely because they are 'idealistic' values – not behaviours that come naturally to us. These are not values that express our needs, goals and desires. They need to be worked at because we are constantly tempted to do the opposite, especially when we are in positions of power. Pick up any political autobiography and you will see signs of falsehood, arrogance, infidelity, excess, avoidance of what is right, impatience, laziness and pride. Not all the time of course! But they are all there at different times – and nowhere is this more clear than in Alan Clark's diaries. One of the reasons his diaries are so admired is that he paints a picture of human nature as it really is, and which is rarely publicly admitted to.

Covey then describes the literature of the last 50 years, which shifts from what he calls the *character ethic* to the *personality ethic*. The personality ethic focuses on the skills and behaviours you need to adopt in order to gain success – and can be 'manipulative, even deceptive'. Alternatively, it encourages a 'positive mental attitude', which, in turn, is often at the root of our denial of the darker side of our human nature. Covey summarizes the main message of the personality ethic literature as consisting of 'quick-fix influence techniques, power strategies, communication skills and positive attitudes'.[9]

---

[9] Covey, S. R. (1999) *The 7 Habits of Highly Effective People*. London: Simon & Schuster, p. 9.

This focus reflects a deeper change in the values promoted in our Western society. In previous ages we would have learned about values such as 'love for others', 'temperance', 'humility', 'obedience', 'patience', 'gentleness' and 'self control'.[10] Now, we simply recoil with disgust at the 'weakness' of such words. Our society has merged idealistic and motivational values, so that the motivational values of success, status, power, independence, achievement and individualism become the idealistic values of consumerism, self expression, personal freedom, competition and self fulfilment. With the decline of challenging idealistic values, we have no constraints on our behaviour, unless we are disciplined enough to restrain ourselves.

If leaders are going to be able to expand their range of values, walk the talk and learn from their values, we need to introduce notions of duty, morality, discipline and integrity into our leadership development processes. Leaders need to develop self awareness and self discipline to ensure their words, decisions and behaviour are in alignment. This is an ongoing, lifetime task, which is difficult to undertake without some help. This is why some leaders have taken to the idea of having spiritual directors. Many spiritual directors are people who have devoted themselves to the challenge of putting the really difficult idealistic values into practice, e.g. monks or nuns. These people are able to support, challenge and gently point out those areas where we are liable to blind spots and self deception. Furthermore, they hold us accountable to ourselves, making us focus on those areas in our lives where we know (but do not like to admit) we have moral and ethical weaknesses!

This chapter has focused on the last of our learning practices – nurturing integrity. It is hoped that, far from being an innate tendency that someone simply has or lacks, integrity is recognized as a skill that can be nurtured and strengthened like any other skill. We have seen that, when necessary, people can expand their range of values and go beyond their own definition of what is 'right'. Often, our definition of 'right' is simply a personal preference that suits us, rather than a moral absolute that is appropriate for all times and places. When in

---

[10] Father Dermot Tredget, a Benedictine monk based at Douai Abbey in Berkshire, runs workshops and retreats where he helps people apply these spiritual values to develop balance, wisdom and meaning in their professional and personal lives. His clients include a range of public, private and not-for-profit organizations.

leadership, it is important to recognize when you are called to question your values to adapt to the values of others, and when you are called to stand firm on your values. This is not always easy to do.

We have also seen the complexities involved in 'walking the talk'. It is difficult to walk the talk, as, like all human beings, we are driven by a conflicting melee of goals, needs, desires and motivational and idealistic values. Often, in the battle of the drivers, idealistic values come last. People with integrity are those who are prepared to choose idealistic values, often at the expense of their own self interest. Looking back at Chapter 3, we remember Dr Stephen Bolsin, who decided to bring a powerful group of doctors to the attention of the authorities in order to save the lives of sick children. He had nothing to gain from such an action and everything to lose. In fact, he lost much of what he valued; he was unable to find a job in his own country and eventually emigrated to Australia. He sacrificed his own self interest for the sake of others – this is an example of integrity. Most of us are not called to make such sacrifices. For most of us, integrity simply involves being aware of our more selfish drivers and ensuring that our decisions do not negatively affect the interests of those we represent.

Finally, we looked at the challenges involved in learning from our values. We examined those 'defining moments' when we are called to choose between right and right. These are moments where we discover our deeper values, revealing to others who we really are and what we stand for. In doing so, we help others make sense of complex situations, demonstrating what we believe is right and important. We also looked at the challenge of learning from guilt, when we may have contravened our values. Though not pleasant, learning from guilt can yield rich insights and change if we are courageous enough to confront the truth.

Nurturing integrity involves re-examining the values which we promote in our organizations and societies. It involves going back to an older tradition, where leaders were encouraged to develop humility, fidelity, temperance, courage, justice, patience, industry, simplicity and modesty. Integrity has to 'work' – in other words, people who manifest it have to be valued and promoted. Unless integrity is embedded within our systems, it will be difficult to nurture – but it will take people of courage and integrity to ensure those systems are changed.

11

Equipping Leaders in Complex Times

THIS BOOK HAS EXAMINED A VARIETY OF BLIND SPOTS, demonstrating how they permeate our decisions and actions. The construction of our living knowledge emerges from the interplay between prior learning, interpretation of personal experience and subconscious blind spots. These blind spots influence our attention, emotions, sensemaking and behaviour, infusing everything we think we know and understand. They are manifested in what we listen to and what we ignore, in what we do and what we avoid doing, in the people we like and those we dismiss. They are constantly active, steering us away from elements of reality we would rather not see.

Our blind spots are many and varied. Some are cognitive biases (a preference for certain kinds of knowledge over others). Some are emotional aversions – to people, to certain emotions (such as guilt) or to facing aspects of ourselves that we have not yet come to terms with. Some are behavioural blind spots – for example, where we say one thing but do another. The blind spots we have covered in this book include the following:

- *Visionary blind spots* – the tendency towards intolerance, rigidity and rejection of complexity that may characterize the visionary leader; a similar intolerance may be seen in people who have goals they are strongly committed to.

- *Self awareness blind spots* – refusing to face aspects of yourself that are negatively affecting your behaviour, emotional health and/or your relationships.

- *Complacency blind spots* – acting to meet your personal goals and desires rather than actively pursuing the interests of the stakeholders you represent.

- *Ethical blind spots* – not acting in accordance with your idealistic values.

- *Complexity blind spots* – refusing to develop your cognitive complexity by absorbing new and/or different paradigms, beliefs or constructs.

- *Emotional blind spots* – refusing to learn how to handle your emotions effectively – e.g. refusing to confront emotional prejudices, succumbing to hot cognition (excessive emotion) and cold cognition (repressing emotion), and continually avoiding negative emotions.

- *Values blind spots* – refusing to recognize the legitimacy of other people's motivational values and rejecting non-preferred values in all situations and circumstances.

- *Attention blind spots* – being overly focused or too broad in one's attention patterns.

- *Behavioural blind spots* – a resistance to changing one's behaviour, leading to the continual implementation of ineffective strategies.

Looking at these blind spots, we can see that they are ubiquitous. In fact, it may appear naïve to suggest that we could ever rid ourselves of them; they are part of what it is to be human. Blind spots affect how we make sense of reality; they modulate our emotional responses to events and, in so doing, shape our identity and culture.

This can lead to a sense of hopelessness. How can we hope to master something so subtle and so pervasive? The Max Planck quote we saw in Chapter 1 voices that sense of despair that we experience when contemplating the need for *other* people to overcome *their* blind spots and change *their* mind-sets:

> '*A new scientific truth does not triumph by convincing its opponents, but rather because its opponents die and a new generation grows up that is familiar with it*'.[1]

---

[1] Planck, M. (1936) *Philosophy of Physics*. New York: W. W. Norton and Company Inc.

There is a sense that all we can do in the face of these deeply engrained psychological processes is to shrug our shoulders and observe with bemusement whilst they are played out in history time and time again. Maybe this is the reason that we can never learn from history; we are condemned to learn only from our personal experience. As a result, we seem destined to repeat previous generations' mistakes over and over again.

It does not have to be this way. It *is* possible to confront and overcome our blind spots and to achieve a depth and breadth of learning more than capable of embracing the complexities of our age. The research on which this book is based consistently reveals remarkable examples of creative and productive learning and change. The real challenge lies in incorporating this into our daily practice – to become *super learners*.

The belief underpinning this book is that it is the *duty* of people in leadership positions to attempt to overcome their blind spots. Blind spots contribute towards inferior decision making, and a leader's flawed decisions can lead to detrimental consequences for many people. Leaders are constantly making decisions; some are 'big', like the decision to invade Iraq; others are small, like the decision to cancel a meeting. But every decision a leader makes helps to enact the future. It is, therefore, incumbent on leaders to ensure their decisions are as free as they can be from blind spots.

The effectiveness of decision making rests upon the accumulated living knowledge of the decision maker, which, in turn, depends upon his ability to learn – both from his own actions and those of others. These qualities are further dependent on both the ability to forge relationships and the development of personal 'character'. We have seen that relationships are the main sources of learning, as, through dialogue, they contribute towards the increasing complexity of living knowledge. Character is important, as we have also seen that the ability to learn requires the discipline to control natural desires and restrain instinctive human responses.

In order to lead effectively, therefore, a leader has to develop her *living knowledge*, her *relationships*, her *character* and her *ability to learn*. If a leader's living knowledge (cognitive, emotional and behavioural) fails to reflect the complexity of the world in which it is applied, it will generate poor and possibly harmful decisions. If the leader has stunted, unbalanced or poor relationships, decisions will be impoverished and cold. If the leader's character is flawed and subject to uncontrolled pride, greed, impatience or anger, decisions will be weak and misguided. If the leader cannot learn, her decisions will reflect a rigid and intolerant mind that sees only what it wants to see.

The aim of this book has been first to focus the attention of leaders, and those who advise and develop them, on a simple set of practices and disciplines which will help to accelerate and deepen leaders' learning. It has also attempted to provide some ideas and start a dialogue within the learning profession regarding the most effective techniques and approaches for doing this (the last chapter provides initial ideas for tools and interventions). We recognize that this is only a beginning, but our hope is that by incorporating this approach into leadership development and supporting it with a new ingenuity of method, we will be able to expand the learning capacity of leaders. In fact, we believe that the 21st century will demand nothing less.

We cannot afford to have leaders at the helm of our organizations and societies whose decisions reflect weaknesses in living knowledge, character, relationships and learning. Political leaders even now are making decisions that could lead to global conflict. Their decisions about the environment could have devastating consequences in decades to come. Business leaders make decisions daily within complex social, political, technological and economic systems. The complexity handled by our leaders and the speed at which they have to act will continue to increase exponentially. This is multifaceted. In addition to technological and commercial complexity, research has shown that 'social complexity' has increased rapidly, and will continue to do so as leaders have to implement policies through large, multicultural, multifunctional teams that are dispersed geographically throughout the world.[2] The stakes are high, and although many leaders are coping with these challenges, we need leaders who can handle them positively – with the wisdom, honesty and determination that will help to enact a future that we all aspire to.

---

[2] Jones, P. and Holton, V. (2006) 'Teams Today.' *The Ashridge Journal*, Spring.

So, how can we all contribute towards the task of encouraging our future leaders to develop these skills? The eight practices and the underlying learning theory presented here are all designed to offer a framework that can help better equip leaders to handle the challenges of the 21st century. Whilst there may be nothing new about this approach to learning, what it does offer is a more integrated approach, bringing together traditions that have, in the past, generated separate and even competing communities. This integration offers a more complex approach to learning and development and is more suited to the more complex world in which we live. In addition, the focus on blind spots emphasizes the importance of humility with regards to our living knowledge, whilst recognizing that this humility must not be allowed to undermine the confidence to act. It offers a basis for the development of the skill of *learning agility*, perhaps the key to surviving in today's challenging environments.

So, what would a leader be doing differently if she were implementing these eight learning practices on the job? Let's see what this might look like.

Effective Leadership in the 21st Century

An effective leader in the 21st century will appreciate that his own understanding of a situation is limited, subject to blind spots and in constant need of updating. He will seek out a range of views and opinions, always striving to build more comprehensive and subtle views of reality. He will be able to handle diversity, recognizing the different truths contained in different parts of the system. He will be known for his power to listen to, absorb and reconcile conflicting and contradictory views. A learning leader will go into a new situation and not assume that he knows how to handle it. He will talk to people and readily experiment with different constructs in order to build up a better guide to what will work in the new circumstances. He will be keen to check his beliefs against reality by putting in place a number of different feedback systems.

The 21st century leader will prioritize learning – taking regular retreats either alone or with her team. She will ensure that her people have regular personal and team retreats in order to hone their judgement, deepen their insights and encourage greater creativity, challenge and vision in the organization.

A learning leader will face difficult aspects of himself in order to avoid being controlled by unconscious fears and anxieties. He will understand his own defensive patterns and be able to manage them. As a result, he will be seen as an honest, open individual willing to listen to bad news as well as good.

A learning leader will be able to learn from her emotions – surfacing them and exploring their meaning. She will also be willing to change her mind about people, accepting that she might have developed unjustified prejudices. She will be able to live by her own values but, at the right times, she will be receptive to alternative values and preferences.

She will regularly monitor what she is paying attention to, ensuring she is focused on key priorities but also being open to new and emerging developments and trends.

A learning leader will be prepared to make decisions that are not necessarily in his personal interests. He will be acutely aware of his responsibilities to all the stakeholders in his leadership. A learning leader might have a spiritual director to help develop his moral compass and personal discipline.

He will be able to change his own behaviour and develop his leadership style in tune with the changes in the environment. He will encourage innovation through creativity, experiments and skilled risk management.

It is likely that a learning leader will have a coach or mentor in order to help her on her learning journey. The learning leader will be able to enhance a group's ability to learn by accessing the latest tools and techniques for both individual and group learning. She will be familiar with tools for systems thinking, dialogue, positive psychology, creativity and innovation, reality checking, etc.

The 21st century leader will understand the nature of power – both how it enables and how it corrupts. He will be able to monitor its effect and manage himself to ensure he employs it for the good of his stakeholders. He will have the wisdom and moral courage to resist its temptations and distortions.

This may sound too good to be true. But this picture of the learning leader represents an ideal to which we need to aspire – even if this is a lifelong task. There is a growing recognition that, in the context of rapid change and growing uncertainty, what worked even three years ago, will not necessarily work in the present. Leaders have to learn and change continuously if they are to keep up. In highly complex environments, it is unlikely that the leader will know the answers; indeed, it is highly unlikely that *anyone* will know the answers. All we can do is to learn to listen to different perspectives from within the system and develop a growing, evolving understanding of the situation in which we find ourselves. This will entail patience, tolerance, courage, discernment, self discipline and many of those qualities commonly associated with 'character' or wisdom. Leaders will increasingly need to access appropriately what Zen Buddhism refers to as the *beginner's mind*. This is a quality of mind that is highly receptive to learning – open, attentive, eager and willing to suspend judgement and prejudice. The Zen teacher Shunryu Suzuki has a famous saying: 'in the beginner's mind there are many possibilities; in the expert's mind there are few'. The challenge facing leaders in the 21st century is how to combine and utilize both their expert *and* their beginner's minds.

Having looked at the implications of this framework for leaders, what are the implications for those whose job it is to develop current and future leaders?

Implications for Leadership Development

The implications of this framework for those in leadership development are both personal, relating to how we manage our own learning, and content-based, relating to how we approach and what we include in the leadership development agenda.

Personal Challenges

The most obvious challenge is that we, too, have our blind spots! Many of us are wedded to traditions, tools and techniques that in some way suit us rather than our clients. If we have grown up using an approach based on Gestalt, we tend to regard this as 'true' and 'right'. If we feel more comfortable with a cognitive approach, we tend to see this as 'true' and 'right'. The trouble is that we bring our own blind spots into the learning environment, and this can itself inhibit the learning of our clients. If we are expecting busy executives to identify and address their blind spots, we have to lead the way and address our own. This does imply that ongoing supervision is extremely important, especially for coaches. It also stresses the need for ongoing professional development. The learning model presented here suggests that we may need to broaden our approach and take on board a variety of traditions – cognitive, emotional and behavioural.

We need to pass on our understanding of learning theory, so that we encourage our managers and leaders to develop their own meta-learning skills. We need to be more open about the difficulties and pain involved in learning, in particular the links between learning, identity, personal needs and self esteem. It is useful to understand the different learning states, appreciating the different kinds of learning that take place on and off the job. This also implies that we need to be more open about the techniques we are using and why and how they are relevant. We need to be alert not just to facilitating leaders' learning, but also to facilitating their meta-learning skills.

One of the biggest problems facing coaches is knowing how and when, and even if, to challenge a client's living knowledge. Many leaders taking advantage of coaching today are highly successful and skilled. In many cases they have a well-articulated view of the world, which the coach will be invited to share. Yet, we have also seen that this view of the world may be biased and self-serving. A leader's world view, having been previously very successful, may be quickly outdated. However, because of delayed feedback, the consequences may not yet have manifested themselves. Successful leaders may want coaches to bounce ideas off, to listen, support and reassure them in tough times. They may not want or welcome challenge. A critical challenge for the coach is how to identify when a leader's view of the world is significantly out of kilter with those around him. The coach is continually invited to collude with the client's view of reality – and may unintentionally prop up a view of the world that is causing harm and damage to others. Coaches need to understand more about these dynamics. In particular, we need to explore how to get beyond the living knowledge of the learner without simply resorting to our own constructs of reality. This has to involve constant reality checking and an ongoing dialogue with other stakeholders in the system.

Content Issues

When running leadership development programmes, we could afford to spend more time focusing on the nature of knowledge and truth. We need to encourage leaders to hold their knowledge more lightly. One question facing leaders today is how and when to develop their 'beginner's mind', or how to develop the Keatsian notion of 'negative capability'. This is the ability to act whilst accepting uncertainty and avoiding the temptation to reach for premature closure. Developing a beginner's mind or honing one's negative capability are complex skills for leaders to develop, as they must not undermine confidence or action. There is a lot of work that needs to be done in this area.

We need to explore the dynamics of decision making more deeply, particularly in terms of how our decisions reveal our own preferences and blind spots. These dynamics are best explored in the context of meaningful action, hence the increasing emphasis on real life challenges (both on and off the job) as crucibles for learning and leadership development. In addition, we could do a lot more to further leaders' understanding of decision-making styles, cognitive biases, group defence mechanisms, hot and cold cognition and the effects of power on decision making.

We need to understand more about the role of attention. Brain science is increasingly alerting us to the problems associated with our biased attention patterns and consequent blind spots. In a recent article on 'attention' for *Scientific American Mind*, Engel, Debener and Kranczioch summarize their research findings thus: 'The healthy brain is . . . anything but a passive receiver of news from the environment. It is an active system, one that controls itself via a complex internal dynamic. Our experiences, intentions, expectations and needs affect this dynamic and thus determine how we perceive and

interpret our environment'.[3] Leaders making decisions need at least
to understand more about this dynamic.

We need to focus on developing 'character'. This means a number
of things. First, we need to reintroduce the ideas of the 'disciplines'
back into leadership training. Whilst it is important to focus on
authenticity in leadership, it is also important to recognize the need
for self development and self restraint. Power magnifies character.
Hence, an impatient individual, when in power, becomes reckless;
an intolerant individual can become a bully. A complacent individual
can, if appointed leader, lead an organization to its downfall. There
are certain qualities that are necessary for effective leadership, and
we discover those qualities in the whole notion of 'character'. Second,
we need to understand more about the nature of 'integrity' – what
it is and how to develop it. There is much we can learn here from
the spiritual and monastic traditions of many of the world's religions.[4] Unlike the humanist approach, that believes mankind is
characterized by innate goodness combined with a constant desire
for learning, the spiritual tradition openly acknowledges and seeks
to train those aspects of human nature that we rarely like to
admit to.

We also need to teach about and focus more explicitly on 'defensiveness' – both at an individual and a group level. Defensiveness is
probably one of the commonest reasons for organizational underperformance, particularly as it is manifested in groups; it is wide-
spread, corrosive and incredibly difficult to eradicate. All of us need
to understand more about our own defensive reactions, how to
manage them and how to manage those of others. In particular,
managers and leaders need to develop the confidence to confront
defensive behaviour that is undermining the values and ethos of the
organization. After so many years of management development
influenced by 1960s style humanism, many people in senior positions are afraid of adopting a 'directive' leadership style. We need
to emphasize the validity of using the full range of leadership styles,

---

[3] Engel, A. K., Debener, S. and Kranczioch, C. (2006) 'Coming to Attention'.
Scientific American Mind, August/September, p. 46.
[4] See Zohar, D. and Marshall, I. (2001) *Spiritual Intelligence, The Ultimate Intelligence*. London: Bloomsbury. Dermot Tredget, a Benedictine monk based at Douai
Abbey in Berkshire, also runs retreats and workshops on this subject.

including the directive style, and help leaders develop the judgement, confidence and skill to employ them. Defensiveness has to be managed.

We need to pay more attention to the quality of learning 'space' we create for leaders. The processes described in this book require a 'deeper learning'. This involves the periodic use of individual and group retreats to help people assess and reconstruct the patterns of sensemaking that contribute towards their living knowledge. This is a sensitive and complex process, and requires a special type of environment.

Another complex skill is making sense in a group. As leaders increasingly lead through virtual groups or teams, we need to understand more about how best to make sense and reach meaningful consensus in this environment. Skills such as dialogue and listening (understanding the four different levels of listening from downloading and debating to reflective and generative listening) will be vital elements in a leader's toolkit. There are many other tools available for making sense – from skills-based tools such as dialogue, to processes such as scenario learning, to IT tools such as systems mapping. When dealing with the levels of social complexity facing them today, leaders need access to an array of sensemaking tools and skills.

Effective leaders in the 21st century will be disciplined learners and will be found in a variety of positions and roles. These people will realize that powerful learning is not something that occurs naturally and effortlessly, but relies on discipline, self awareness, openness to challenge and a determination to listen – really listen – to diverse views and opinions. They will be aware of their natural blind spots and will have a range of strategies to overcome them. As a result, they will be in a better position to match the environmental complexity with their own emotional, behavioural and cognitive complexity. They will be highly effective decision makers, able to absorb, analyse and critically handle large amounts of data. Our best leaders will be super learners with a finely honed ability to learn from experience.

The challenge that currently faces us, is how to develop the ability to learn from experience, so that we can accelerate the pace and the depth of learning in both ourselves and in others. There is a massive agenda here for the profession, and we are keen to engage with people interested in addressing this. At Cass Business School, as part of the Centre for Leadership, Learning and Change, we are seeking to establish a community of practice interested in further research in this area. At Waverley Learning, we are exploring new methods and interventions, specifically in the area of leadership retreats, 'deeper learning' and organizational learning.

The last chapter offers some ideas and exercises based on the eight learning disciplines. However, it is recognized that the task of accelerating learning is huge and ongoing. It is hoped that many more people will contribute new and innovative ideas that will help everyone, in a range of both formal and informal leadership positions, to accelerate their learning.

12

The Exercises

SO FAR WE HAVE LOOKED AT SOME OF THE CHALLENGES involved in overcoming blind spots and have hinted at how they might be addressed. This last chapter is intended to offer some exercises that can help you apply the learning practices and experiment with ways of accelerating learning, both on and off the job.

The chapter is divided into eight sections, each one dedicated to a particular learning practice. Obviously, each learning practice represents a huge, underlying body of knowledge and range of techniques that we cannot possibly reflect here. However, the exercises provide useful, illustrative support when introducing these ideas and practices, as well as being practical tools for accelerating learning on the job.

The First Practice – Direct Attention

1. Extend My Paradigm Use

Identify the paradigms that are important for your organization. You can do this by visiting and listening to as wide a range of stakeholders as is possible. Listen to the paradigms and constructs they use. Once you have done this, rate your familiarity with the paradigm. Next, rate its importance in relationship to your organization, your stakeholders and your role (this is best done in consultation with all your stakeholders, particularly your boss, peers and direct reports). Where there is a mismatch, identify what actions you will take in order to expand the number and range of the paradigms you use. Overleaf is a blank pro forma to start you off. This is followed by an example of a completed paradigm review.

Using Paradigms to Expand the Complexity of Your Thinking

1. Read through the paradigms described below.
2. Identify any paradigms that are not covered and which are important in your organisation. For example there may be technical and sector specific paradigms such as a 'scientific' paradigm or a 'fund raising' paradigm.
3. Go through each paradigm and rate your familiarity with it out of 10.
4. Assess the importance of each paradigm for your role but remember to consult key stakeholders in your role for their opinions on this (it may be that you have a blind spot here!).
5. Devise an action plan based on the results – in what areas would it be beneficial for you to expand your cognitive complexity? How are you going to do this?

Paradigms	Familiarity Out of 10	Importance Out of 10	Action Plan
Business			
Clients – knowing individual customers' strategies, needs, issues and concerns			
Strategy – knowing your strategy and how that relates to environmental trends			
Competitors – knowing them as individuals, understanding their strategy and positioning			
Commercial – knowledge of current opportunities, risks, deals			
Suppliers – knowing them, understanding their issues, monitoring the relationship			
Global – socio, political and economic trends			

Paradigms	Familiarity Out of 10	Importance Out of 10	Action Plan
Ethical			
Environment – trends, stakeholders demands and actions, internal policies			
Social responsibility – organisation's wider role in society and in the world.			

People	Familiarity Out of 10	Importance Out of 10	Action Plan
Power – where does it lie, who has it, how to increase it, how is it being used, your own			
Staff – understanding individual needs and motivators; focusing on people strategies			
Climate – thinking about the mood in your organisation and how to improve it			
Leadership – defining, spotting, developing and rewarding leadership			
Relationships – monitoring, extending, improving your relationships			
Self – your goals, hopes, strengths, development needs, how you are perceived by others. Are you learning and changing?			

Organisational	Familiarity Out of 10	Importance Out of 10	Action Plan
Structure – latest thinking/ practice, what's working, what isn't, what are you doing, what do staff want			

Continued

Paradigms	Familiarity Out of 10	Importance Out of 10	Action Plan
Organisational			
Marketing – latest thinking/ practice, what's working, what isn't, what are you doing in this area, what are the views of the marketing professionals			
Processes – latest thinking/ practice, what's working, what isn't, how do you know? How are you gathering information			
HR – latest thinking/practice, what's working, what isn't, what are the views of the people in HR			
Culture – latest thinking/ practice, what's working, what isn't			
Governance and ethics – latest thinking/practice, what's working, what isn't; who's working in this area?			
Goals and measures – what you pay attention to and measure			
Technology – latest thinking/ practice, what's working, what isn't, what are the views of the professionals working in this area?			

Finance	Familiarity Out of 10	Importance Out of 10	Action Plan
Stockmarket – how are you viewed by the markets, how do you want to be viewed			
Management accounting – what processes do you have for supporting decisions, are they adequate, what do staff think/want			

Paradigms	Familiarity Out of 10	Importance Out of 10	Action Plan
Other			

Conclusions – My Attention Profile

EXAMPLE: Completed Paradigm Review

Paradigms	Familiarity Out of 10	Importance Out of 10	Action Plan
Business			
Clients – knowing individual customers' strategies, needs, issues and concerns	8	10	Visit EEplc with Clive next week
Strategy – knowing your strategy and how that relates to environmental trends	7	7	
Competitors – knowing them as individuals, understanding their strategy and positioning	3	7	
Commercial – knowledge of current opportunities, risks, deals	8	8	
Suppliers – knowing them, understanding their issues, monitoring the relationship	3	5	
Global – socio, political and economic trends	8	9	

Ethical	Familiarity Out of 10	Importance Out of 10	Action Plan
Environment –trends, stakeholders demands and actions, internal policies	3	7	Visit Carol and see what we are doing
Social responsibility – organisation's wider role in society and in the world	3	7	Sign up for corporate charity scheme

Paradigms	Familiarity Out of 10	Importance Out of 10	Action Plan
People			
Power – where does it lie, who has it, how to increase it, how is it being used, your own	4	8	Go on a course!
Staff – understanding individual needs and motivators; focusing on people strategies	8	8	
Climate – thinking about the mood in your organisation and how to improve it	5	7?	Talk to HR about this.
Leadership – defining, spotting, developing and rewarding leadership	9	10	
Relationships – monitoring, extending, improving your relationships	6	10	Get a coach
Self – your goals, hopes, strengths, development needs, how you are perceived by others. Are you learning and changing?	10	10	

Organisational	Familiarity Out of 10	Importance Out of 10	Action Plan
Structure – latest thinking/ practice, what's working, what isn't, what are you doing, what do staff want	8	5	Spend less time on this
Marketing – latest thinking/ practice, what's working, what isn't, what are you doing in this area, what are the views of the marketing professionals	4	5	
Processes – latest thinking/ practice, what's working, what isn't, how do you know? How are you gathering information	4	7	Delegate to Yvonne

Paradigms	Familiarity Out of 10	Importance Out of 10	Action Plan
Organisational			
HR – latest thinking/practice, what's working, what isn't, what are the views of the people in HR	8	7	
Culture – latest thinking/ practice, what's working, what isn't	7	7	
Governance and ethics – latest thinking/practice, what's working, what isn't; who's working in this area?	6	8	
Goals and measures – what you pay attention to and measure	4	9	Spend time planning my week
Technology – latest thinking/ practice, what's working, what isn't, what are the views of the professionals working in this area?	2	8	Spend time with IT manager

Finance	Familiarity Out of 10	Importance Out of 10	Action Plan
Stockmarket – how are you viewed by the markets, how do you want to be viewed	7	9	Spend time with some key investors
Management accounting – what processes do you have for supporting decisions, are they adequate, what do staff think/want	8	9	

Conclusions – My Attention Profile

I'm very focused on myself and my own goals and this shows in my concentration on the business paradigms. Perhaps I don't concentrate as much as I should on the softer issues, particularly my relationships with others and 'power' (both are connected). I need to explore this more.

I'm ashamed that I don't think more about my ethical and social responsibilities. I don't have much time to do this (I'm too selfish!) but I can at least give money using the organisation's scheme.

2. Leadership Attention Profiling

This exercise is particularly useful for making sure you are disciplining yourself to ensure you are focusing on the right things. It is best done at regular intervals once you have identified a focus for your attention.

Remember you cannot pay attention to everything. Your attention has a limited capacity. Think of it, therefore, as like a cup, glass, bottle, vase or anything that has a limited capacity. Draw this vessel. Now divide the vessel up to reflect what you pay attention to (in terms of how you use your time) over a typical month, e.g. 10% of your time might be spent on finances; 7.5% on administration; 20% on your direct reports, etc. Try to be as specific as possible. You may want to check your figures by keeping a diary for a month.

Once you have filled your vessel with all the things you pay attention to, focus on one area at a time. Identify what makes you pay attention to this area. There will be inner drivers and outer drivers. First identify the outer drivers – these may be people who tell you that these things are important or legislation that states that you, and only you, have to focus on these areas. Then identify the inner drivers – these are the voices in your head that tell you to do these things. For example, you might spend a lot of time in meetings with your direct reports. One of the drivers for this might be that for you it is important that your team is happy. Having done this, refer back to the focus you identified in the last exercise.

Now evaluate your attention profile. What is central to what you want to achieve, what is relatively important and what is irrelevant? Take an area that takes up a lot of your attention but is not central for your vision. Look at the drivers – can you challenge these in some way? Are you doing these things because you feel comfortable or you cannot let go of control or you cannot trust others to do them?

Having examined your attention profile, identify what you are going to do differently to shape it more in accordance with your vision and in accordance with how you see your role. Is it really a useful investment of your time to spend 20% of it doing admin? What do you need to do to let go of this? How can you focus your attention on areas that are crucial but which you are currently ignoring?

3. Focusing Attention

As a leader, you need to balance the needs of your stakeholders with your own sense of what is important and what is not. If you listen too much to yourself in isolation from your stakeholders, you may be missing important information. If you listen too much to your stakeholders and not enough to yourself, you are not doing your job. Difficult decisions may have to be made, and stakeholders will often encourage you to avoid them. In addition, Jim Collins emphasizes that it is important to develop your focus in collaboration with your team, rather than before you bring your team together. Not only will these people be responsible for implementation, they will also have important insights which will enrich your perspective. Developing your leadership voice is an important skill that involves listening to others, listening to yourself and constantly adapting to changing circumstances. The exercise below can be done by yourself or in collaboration with your team.

1. Identify all the stakeholders in your leadership. Use the list of paradigms at the beginning of this chapter to help you. Do not leave anyone out – from the government to impoverished farmers in Africa to vociferous environmentalists!

2. Contact all of them. Use this as an opportunity to listen and develop your own knowledge, constructs, paradigms and value set. If you find yourself becoming irritated or angry – listen even harder. Map out the arguments of all your stakeholders, noting key constructs and values that they refer to.

3. Go on a leadership retreat (see the fourth practice). There should, by now, be many voices in your head! The most important task now is to discover your own voice. For this you will need a calm, quiet atmosphere and a skilled facilitator. You will probably find you have many different inner voices talking to you. There will be an excited, passionate voice; there will be a doubtful, uncertain voice. There will be emotional voices and rational voices. There will be voices from the past and voices

calling you to the future. All of these voices need to be acknowledged and looked at.

4. Having done this, time is needed to get perspective on your situ-
    ation, and you need to reconnect to your own values and dreams.
    You need to ask yourself questions such as, 'where does this
    organization need to go?', 'where would I and my people like to
    take it?', 'what common dream do most of us share?', 'what diffi-
    cult decisions need to be made?', 'what are the most significant
    challenges and opportunities facing us right now?', 'where is my
    natural alliance and how powerful is it?', 'what would I like my
    legacy to be?', 'what would I love to achieve in my time as leader?',
    'what is actually possible given the circumstances?' As you ask
    these questions, you will feel a sense of excitement as the leadership
    challenge becomes clear to you, and the journey that the organiza-
    tion needs to take opens up before you.

5. Finally, imagine yourself in two years' time and write down your
    achievements as if you have already fulfilled them. For example: I
    have helped people to recognize the need for change and already
    people have become more client-oriented. I have a great team in
    place who are brilliant at implementing change by getting people
    behind them. The organization feels energized and enthusiastic.
    Unfortunately, we did have to make a number of staff redundant,
    but having done that, people now feel much more positive – they
    recognized that difficult decisions had to be made and were relieved
    when they finally were. I have the respect of my peers in the sector
    and am looking forward to increasing our reputation for quality
    with our clients.

6. Having done this, you should now be able to describe your
    future desired state and your key priorities for getting there. This
    will help you focus your attention.

7. Remember that this exercise can just as easily be done with a
    team, and even if you decide to do it alone, you will probably
    need to repeat some of it with your team.

8. However, remember that having a focus can narrow your
    attention too much. Put in place strategies for broadening atten-
    tion that will help you learn on the way, talking to your stake-
    holders and constantly adapting your strategy to meet changing
    circumstances.

The Second Practice – Harness Emotion

1. Interpretive Biases

This is a fun exercise. Take a subject around which there is a lot of emotion. See if you can identify the interpretive biases that you commonly use. Catch yourself and others using them. Take time to reflect on and challenge your interpretations. You can also seek feedback from people to see if they feel you are succumbing to a particular bias or not. If you are addressing an issue as a team, you can ask the team if they feel the team is subject to any of the biases.

Cognitive Distortion	How often do I use it? My assessment (10 is a lot and 1 is hardly ever)	How often do I use it? Other person's assessment. (10 is a lot and 1 is hardly ever)
Confirmation bias Only paying attention to and believing data that confirm what you already believe.		
Black/white thinking Seeing the world in terms of a few extremes – if it is not black then it must be white.		
Mind reading Assuming you know the motivations, thoughts and feelings of others.		
Flooding If emotion is felt strongly enough, it must be justifiable; strong emotions are always right.		
Overgeneralization Taking one event or piece of evidence and making general rules based upon it.		

Continued

Cognitive Distortion	How often do I use it? My assessment (10 is a lot and 1 is hardly ever)	How often do I use it? Other person's assessment. (10 is a lot and 1 is hardly ever)
Personalization Believing that the motives for other people's behaviour concerns how they affect you – 'I know he said that to hurt me'.		
Stereotyping Classifying people in crude and often negative ways. Blaming them for problems.		
Self-serving bias Taking credit for events that are successful and denying responsibility when they are not.		
Mood bias Evaluating a situation according to how one feels.		
Recency bias Paying more attention to data that was most recently brought to your attention.		

2. Emotional Inventory

Many people cannot respond when asked what emotions they feel. They often refer to what they think or what they want. However, there is a separate truth inherent in emotions – one that cannot be apprehended except through the open acknowledgement of the emotion. As soon as we begin to recognize and name our emotions, a whole new world opens up in front of us. Emotions are integral to learning, and if we cannot name them, this will inhibit our ability to learn, change and grow.

From the following list of emotions, identify which ones you tend to feel in your everyday life; categorize them into those that you experience a lot (high frequency), those that you experience occasionally (medium frequency) and those you experience rarely (low frequency).

Emotion	Frequency (High, Medium, Low)	Emotion	Frequency (High, Medium, Low)
Happiness		Anxiety	
Calmness		Fear	
Contentment		Boredom	
Relaxation		Frustration	
Excitement		Anger	
Optimism		Disgust	
Curiosity		Sadness	
Hope		Stress	
Joy		Depression	
Interest		Pessimism	
Puzzlement		Guilt	
Peace		Envy	
Love		Jealousy	
Warmth		Contempt	
Generosity		Regret	
		Hate	
		Coldness	
		Disdain	
		Distance	
		Resentment	

Now, over a period of time (this will require some reflection), complete the following table. I have started the table off, but you will notice that, done properly, this should take a long time to complete. The more detail you go into, the more insights you will gain about your emotional responses. Ideally, this should be done in a journal, but the briefer, table format is a good start!

Frequency	Emotion	Context – circumstances in which emotion is experienced
High experience of emotions	Hope Optimism Frustration Anger	Hope: I often feel hope as I am leading a big change project and I believe it's going to make a big difference. I feel hope particularly when I am giving presentations to people and when I talk to senior management who are 100% behind me. Anger: I often feel anger, particularly when I talk to people in the customer service department. They don't have a clue about what I am trying to do and what's more, they don't seem to care. I also feel angry when . . . Optimism . . . Frustration . . .
Medium experience of these emotions	Happiness Puzzlement Interest Curiosity Stress Pessimism	I feel curious when I talk to Charles; he's interesting and has an unusual perspective on things. I think I can learn a lot from him. I get stressed with all the work I am getting and when I have to work at home.
Low experience of these emotions	Joy Disgust Sadness Depression	I don't experience joy much at all. The last time I experienced this was when I was working with my old team and we clinched the deal with ROOTco. Also, when Grace was born. Sadness: I don't really feel sad in my life. I do get sad when I think of the type of world my kids are growing up in. I also get sad when I see people wasting their lives, when they have so much to offer.

Now explore what these emotions are trying to tell you. For example, if you experience a lot of boredom, it may be that you dismiss this on a day-to-day basis. You shrug it off as 'inevitable when you reach middle age' and then forget about it. Actually, your boredom is probably telling you something quite profound about your life, and it may be that you are frightened of exploring what that truth might be. Typically, people do not explore emotions because they are scared of losing something else that they value or desire. For example, the bored middle-aged executive might really want to set up his own business, but is scared because he fears losing his wife, his wealth, his status and the admiration of his peers. As a result, he does not even entertain the idea. Yet, if he faced his boredom, he could ask a set of more probing questions:

- 'How could I establish my own business whilst limiting the downside?'

- 'What does my wife really want in her life?'

- 'Why am I so obsessed about the admiration of my peers? Actually, there are only two that I really respect and I know they would support my decision.'

- 'Is it that I am more concerned about how my parents would take it – I've always wanted them to be proud of me? Isn't it about time I grew out of this?'

- 'How do I want to live my life from now on?'

- 'Would I regret not trying if I stick to the safe route?'

Try taking one emotion that you feel or sense is important, and exploring its meaning. Write down your thoughts in a journal. This will probably take some time to bottom out, and will be the beginning of an important emotional journey for you.

3. Take One Person

We are surrounded by people. Every person we know generates an emotion in us, even if that emotion is simple indifference. You can learn a lot about yourself, your values and your relationships when you examine the emotions that different people evoke in you. Try the following exercise.

Choose a selection of people that you interact with. Take each person in turn and describe the mixture of emotions you feel with regards to them. Take time to identify as many emotions as possible. You can go further and explore sensations and thoughts as well.

Now repeat the exercise but with people who have 'stakes' in your learning. This includes people who need your input in order to do their work properly and people who are affected by your behaviour and your decisions. This may very well include people with whom you experience conflict and disagreements.

Tony

Admiration. Happiness. Laughter. Warmth. Excitement. Hope. Optimism.
'He seems to know the way forward.'
'He seems a kind guy, honest and genuine.'
'He doesn't seem a fake. He's got good relationships with his team and is also a good family guy.'
'I sense I can trust him; he won't let me down.'

David

Dislike. Suspicion.
'He's only in it for himself.'
'Obsequious, dishonest, self-interested.'
'Loves himself, arrogant.'
'Weak – no integrity.'
'I wouldn't trust him as far as I could throw him.'
'How come he's got so high in the hierarchy?'
'What does this say about the people who have promoted him and who work with him?'

Jessica

Indifference. No strong emotions either way.
'She's quiet.'
'I don't really know her that much.'

'She's actually quite important to the team but we take her for granted.'
'I dismiss her because she's not extrovert and in your face.'
'I shouldn't!'

As in the last example, identify how your feelings for each person affect your relationship – with them, their friends and teams and also amongst your own team and circle of friends.

Challenge your feelings – are they creating self-fulfilling prophecies, are you seeing only what you want to see? Empathize with these people (very much like Rob did when he realized that he had picked up an unwarranted prejudice). See the world through their eyes. Imagine what it must be like to be this person. Articulate your insights – speak them out loud or write them down. Conduct this exercise as if you were someone else looking at you, e.g. what emotions does a colleague associate with you? See if you can change your feelings towards the individual concerned. Ask yourself the following questions:

- On what evidence have I based my emotional reactions?

- What is it that makes me feel this way towards him or her? (identify behaviours, body language, words, image).

- What does this say about me and how I judge people? What does this say about my values?

- How fair is my emotional reaction towards people?

- How is my emotional reaction affecting me, my work, my relationships with others?

- What would it take for me to change my emotional response to this person?

When you have done this for a number of people, ask yourself the following questions:

- What values am I ignoring by dismissing certain people?

- What values am I attracted by?

- What am I afraid of in others?

- How can I develop greater tolerance of others?

The Third Practice – Overcome Defensiveness

We can approach defensiveness from two different vantage points – what to do about my own defensiveness as a leader (to prevent me from generating a defensive culture) and what to do about the defensiveness of those around me.

My Own Defensiveness

1. Recognize your own Defence Mechanisms

We are all defensive; we need to protect our self esteem from the setbacks and failures that experience regularly throws at us. We all have our favourite defence mechanisms. So the first step on the road to self discipline is to recognize your favourite defence mechanisms. Have a go at completing the following inventory. You can get some fun out of this if you do it in a group, laughing good humouredly at each other's characteristic defence mechanisms.

Put a tick against the defence mechanisms you use and show how often you use them. Remember, we all use defence mechanisms at some point, so do not be afraid of being honest with yourself! Analyse the costs of using your favourite mechanism, together with the benefits. Are you using some behaviours that do not really generate many benefits and may possibly lead to more problems?

The Defense Mechanisms Inventory

Type of Defence Mechanism	Not at all	Rare	Often	Very Often	Cost/ Benefit
Denial Refusing to face unpleasant facts					
Aggression physical and verbal					
Blaming Avoiding responsibility by blaming others					

Type of Defence Mechanism	Not at all	Rare	Often	Very Often	Cost/ Benefit
Flippancy Using humour to avoid serious discussion					
Conformity and Self Censorship suppressing doubts; conforming to the group					
Rationalisation Hiding your emotions behind logical arguments					
Withdrawal Going into your shell; aloof					
Playing Victim Seeing yourself as a victim & not responsible for your behaviour					
Illusion of Invulnerability Belief that you are always right. Exaggerated belief in one's abilities					
Dependency Being self critical to elicit pity from others					
Cynicism Channelling anger, bitterness, disappointment into overly negative assessments of situation/people					

Continued

Type of Defence Mechanism	Not at all	Rare	Often	Very Often	Cost/ Benefit
Stereotyping Classifying people in crude ways and blaming them for problems					
Excuses Denying responsibility					
Harmonization Suppressing conflict; asserting that people's interests are in accordance					
Avoidance Avoiding disagreements, risk or conflict					

2. Recognize what Triggers your Defences

Complete a defence mechanisms diary – in written form or quite simply in your head. Over the next month, be alert to your own defensiveness. Every time you catch yourself being defensive, make a note of what triggered it. Keep these notes and once the month is finished, go back over them and see if you can identify any patterns as to when you become defensive and what type of defence mechanism you use. Are there any patterns in terms of what triggers your defensiveness, or, maybe, who triggers your defensiveness?

Now take some time to explore these defensive patterns. The next exercise will give you a start.

3. Face your Fears and Challenge Them

There is a quotation from a science fiction novel called *Dune*. Like Luke Skywalker in the *Star Wars* films, the hero is trained in the latest forms of mind and body control. Part of his training includes learning to face and control his fears. Part of this involves reciting the following mantra:

> '*Fear is the mind killer. Fear is the little death that brings total obliteration. I will face my fear. I will permit it to pass over me and through me. And when it has gone past me, I will turn to see fear's path. Where the fear has gone, there will be nothing. Only I will remain.*'

Facing our fear is the only way to overcome its power over us – in fact, it frees us to address the problems that, if we are not careful, will make those very fears come true. Facing fear is the only way to regain control.

Take one of your examples of defensiveness and examine it. Ask yourself the following questions:

- How was I feeling?
- What triggered the feelings?
- What was I thinking whilst I was experiencing the feelings?
- Why was I feeling – angry, hurt, upset . . .?
- What was I afraid of?
- Was I feeling a threat to something dear to me – my self esteem, my competence, my values, my goals, my interests, my feelings of comfort and control?

Notice how you feel as you raise these questions. What bodily reactions are being stirred – for example, sensations in your stomach, gut, face, throat? These can be signs that defensiveness is being triggered and that some reflection might be required in order to handle the situation.

Now, imagine the fear as something that you wish to get rid of – like a gremlin or a sore or an irritant of some kind. Name it – for example, this is my 'what will they think of me' gremlin. Or, this is my 'I'm afraid this person is better than me' gremlin.

Now imagine yourself dealing with your gremlin in whatever way is best for you. For example, you can acknowledge your gremlin (thank you for warning me about the risks in this situation. I will now handle it better if you go away). You can fight your gremlin (oh no; you are not going to win this time. I know you want me to dismiss this person, but I will look ridiculously defensive if I do this. No, I am going to rise above my wariness of him and behave calmly and rationally). You can call upon an alternative, more rational 'voice'. For example, if you are wary of someone because you think they are better than you (an extremely common form of defensiveness), you can call upon the inner voice that we talked about in the last chapter – your 'learning' voice:

> '*I am not going to fall into the comparison trap. I know that we all compare ourselves to others and find ourselves wanting. I know what it is that people appreciate about me; I am just going to enjoy being that person and doing what I do best. I am not going to compare myself to anyone – just perform at my best knowing that people appreciate the genuineness, warmth and honesty that I bring.*'

Remember, it is not possible for anyone to be perfect. The more someone tries to be perfect, the more they will have to defend themselves from reality, and hence the more likely they will make a big mistake!

4. Monitor Key Performance Indicators and Discuss in Team Meetings

Identify what is critical to the organization's success and measure it. Ensure the information is available to others and to your team. Regularly hold team sessions where it is considered normal to celebrate successes and openly confront and deal with problem areas. Make this an opportunity for creative thinking, brainstorming and team building.

Handling Others' Defensiveness

As a leader you have two roles with regards to defensiveness – preventing it and confronting it. It is surprisingly easy for organizations to succumb to the virus of defensiveness, and once it is in, it is difficult to eradicate.

1. Be Kind

When asked the most powerful thing he had learned in the last few years, a senior leader told the audience:

'everyone is insecure'.

We may not be insecure all the time, but most of us are insecure at least some of the time. Good leaders know this, and know, too, that the power they wield is a potential source of defensiveness in others. No matter how amenable leaders are, there will always be an element of fear in the relationships they have with those who report to them.

So remember this: everyone is insecure. Go out of your way to reassure that you are not a threat; that you are sympathetic, understanding and tolerant. This does not mean that you are a walkover or that you will avoid making difficult decisions in your organization. Nor does it mean that you will eliminate the fear that others have of you; you will simply reduce it. And by reducing it in others, you will cultivate a healthy organizational climate where people can concentrate on the task, because they no longer have to concentrate on their personal survival.

Show you are human – for example, talk about your hobbies, your family and what you did at the weekend. Admit mistakes, past errors and current weaknesses. Enable people to relate to you as a normal human being rather than an aloof power figure. Never underestimate how the power that is invested in you permeates and affects every single relationship you have.

2. Confront Defensiveness

Remember, defensiveness in certain individuals can get out of control. Often, these people have psychological issues they need to address. They need to be dealt with, because if they are not, they can affect the whole organization. The one problem that we have when dealing with defensive personalities is that many people are frightened of conflict –

that includes very senior people (who often do not have to deal with conflict because it is suppressed). This is the single most powerful weapon in the armoury of the defensive personality. So:

- Ensure all your managers are highly skilled in performance management; ensure they understand, recognize and know how to deal with defensiveness.

- Whenever defensiveness is encountered, confront the unacceptable behaviour – gently but firmly, e.g. 'do not shout at me'; 'I will not talk to you unless you lower your voice'; 'do not threaten me'.

- Take the defensive individual to one side and have an open discussion; try to get the individual to be explicit about his or her concerns and anxieties. This should be in the style of a coaching or even counselling discussion. It may be that you are able to deal with the situation by adopting a coaching approach.

- Recruit a coach to help. If you decide to do this, ensure:

  —you are explicit with both the coach and the coachee about what outcomes you are expecting from the coaching;

  —you put in place monitors to check that the outcomes are being achieved (e.g. six-monthly peer/direct report feedback processes);

  —if necessary, check that the coach has a counselling background.

  If this does not help, you may need to adopt a more directive approach, as described below.

- Be specific, explicit and clear about what you want the individual to do and what you want the individual not to do. This means focusing on specific behaviours:

  —I do not want you to raise your voice to anyone in the team;

  —I want you to pass your client files to Debbie when she asks for them;

  —I want you to be helpful to clients on the phone; this means asking them questions about their concerns, checking that you have understood their concerns correctly, adopting a helpful tone of voice and being clear about when you will get back to them with an answer.

- Being clear about measures. For example, how will you find out if your expectations have been met?

- Ensure there are consequences for non-compliance, e.g. 'If you do not do this, I will have to bring HR into the conversation and we will consider disciplinary action'.

- Constantly monitor the situation. Regularly check that the individual is complying with your wishes.

- Offer counselling if necessary.

- Remember there are often deep, complex emotional reasons why someone is defensive. They may not be susceptible to reason because they are acting to meet more emotional needs. You can explain why their behaviour alienates clients, but the defensive individual may not really care about clients. They often have one over-riding need – e.g. control – and all their behaviours are designed to achieve it. Sometimes you need to adopt more directive, 'power'-based tactics, showing the individual that unless they comply, they will lose control (ultimately by losing their job). Always remember that you are doing this to save and preserve important organizational values.

- Don't give up. The defensive person relies on the fact that people will tire of confrontation and the energy that this involves.

- Having followed the correct disciplinary procedure, if all else fails, ask the individual to leave.

The Fourth Practice – Deepen Sensemaking

1. Self Assessment

Before you begin to deepen your sensemaking, why not conduct an analysis of where you are at right now?

The Learning Cycle

Are you giving each part of the learning cycle appropriate emphasis? Do you monitor and shift your attention patterns? Do you focus on and learn from your emotions? Do you manage your emotions in order to learn in a mature and balanced manner (do you gain 'sophrosyne' – wisdom achieved through a balance between reason and emotion)? Do you spend time in the sensemaking part of the cycle – taking time out to reflect in a deep and creative way? Do you change your behaviour when necessary? Are you good at adapting your style to the circumstances? Do you step out of your comfort zone?

Your Learning State

Do you find yourself adopting a particular learning state? Think about how often you find yourself in a visionary, adaptive, dissonant or reflective/meditative learning state. What are the implications of this?

Your Listening Practices

How do you listen? Assess how much time you spend in the four listening states:

Listening state	Time spent and people I adopt this mode with	Action
Downloading – putting across what I think. Not interested in diverse views.		
Debating – listening to other views but mainly for their faults or weaknesses.		
Reflective – really listening for what the person believes and feels and why.		
Generative – really listening for how this view fits into the system as a whole. Trying to understand the system as a whole.		
Notes		

Drivers

How do your individual drivers affect your learning? Complete the
following table.

Driver	Implication	Action
Goals – how do your goals affect your learning? Are you impatient, determined, excited, dismissive, overly focused?		
Values – how do your values affect your learning? Are you inspirational, dismissive, combative, judgemental?		
Self Esteem – how does self esteem affect your learning? Are you avoiding difficult issues, managing your emotions, developing yourself? How are you developing your self esteem? Do you need to develop a bit more humility?		
Psychological Comfort – how do your emotions and needs affect your learning? Are you avoiding painful issues, focusing on areas you feel comfortable with, rejecting difficult views? When was the last time you felt uncomfortable?		
Notes		

Having done this, take time to reflect upon your answers. Are there
any conclusions you come to with regards to how you are making
sense of your environment? Think about:

- Your focus – are you focusing on the right areas, do you need
  to broaden or focus your attention?

- Completing the learning cycle – do you get stuck in a certain part of the cycle? Are there areas where you are particularly strong?

- Are you listening in order to learn? Do you use other people to learn from?

- Have you got stuck in a particular learning state, e.g. very visionary but not reflective enough?

- Where and how could you deepen your learning?

2. Learn from Dialogue

In a fast-moving world, the main source of new intelligence, ideas, insights and perspectives will be people. We do not learn from people as much as we could. This is because we judge and dismiss rather than listen and learn. If we are to listen and learn from people, we have to approach our conversations in an entirely different way.

I recognize that it is extremely frustrating to talk to someone who has the opposite point of view from you, and for this reason we are not going to eradicate conversations based on mutual fighting and the battle for influence. However, at times it is important to go into a conversation where the intent is simply to learn. When you do this, you decide that the objective of the conversation is to expand your own living knowledge. Once you have decided that the objective is to learn from the individual rather than influence them, it becomes a lot easier to listen. Use conversations to steal constructs! Just listen to the other person's constructs, mental models, experiences and sensemaking processes. Also . . .

- Read the learning dialogue in Chapter 8, page 148. Gain a sense of how a learning dialogue looks and feels different from a normal dialogue.

- Ensure you are in the right frame of mind for the dialogue. The right learning state for a learning conversation is the reflective/ meditative, or sometimes the generative, learning state. A learning dialogue has a slower pace than normal dialogue – you need to have both time and space in your mind. Being in a strong visionary learning state, for example, might hinder a learning conversation, which requires patience and tolerance. Also, make sure you choose an environment that is conducive to a more reflective, discursive conversation.

- Develop some of the skills and techniques associated with learning dialogues, especially: reflecting back what the individual has just said, checking understanding, probing for the underlying experiences that have led the individual to her conclusions, suspending judgement, focusing on key constructs, sensing how the person is feeling, encouraging them to voice their feelings, spotting the values they use to make sense of their experience.

- Reflect on the conversation. Repeat back what you heard from the individual, trying to represent their view as accurately as possible. Try to see where and how this perspective has emerged from the system. Highlight key constructs from the conversation. How do these fit into your own living knowledge? Can you incorporate them into your living knowledge? Can you spot any dilemmas? If so, how would you best reconcile them? How will your living knowledge change as a result of this conversation? What have you learned about the system?

- What are you going to do as a result of the conversation?

It would be a good idea to attend a course on dialogue. These skills are important elements of successful leadership, and vital for building healthy relationships. Courses on coaching would help develop some of the basic skills, whilst more focused courses aimed specifically at dialogue would impart a degree of expertise.

3. Map the System

We all live our lives within highly complex, multilayered, overlapping systems. You may think of your activity as being confined to a particular geographic region or function or profession, but, ultimately, your activities will have consequences for people outside the world that is represented within your living knowledge.

Often, we have no idea of the consequences of our actions, because we do not understand how the different pieces of the system interlink. The only way to overcome this is to gain a more complex picture of the system within which you work – in other words, to visit and talk to participants in the system.

Try and spend quality time with people in a different part of the system. Spend a day out visiting clients with your sales staff; spend a day in the factory or in the shop doing the jobs alongside staff. You will learn a lot about how various systems (finance, marketing, operations, HR) work themselves out in different environments. Visit little-known operations – even if they do not seem to have a very strong connection to your job. Spend some time with an industry expert and catch up with the latest thinking and practice in other companies. Form a consortium of companies facing similar issues to yourself and find out what they are doing in the area. Meet with politicians to discuss areas of mutual interest. Attend conferences. Find people in the system who disagree with you. Listen to their arguments and concerns (don't debate, just listen!). All the time, think about what people are thinking, feeling and doing. Find ways of developing your cognitive complexity by talking to different, challenging or disempowered people who participate in some way in your system. As you are doing this, you will be building networks of people who will help to provide your industry 'intelligence'. Nurture these people and ensure you listen to them in the right state of mind. Even if their insights do not appear to be relevant, note them in some way. It may be that they are experiencing new forces that will only manifest themselves in your part of the system later.

Find out about systems thinking. Bring in consultants who specialize in the area which is most relevant to you. Look at different ways of mapping systems and explore ways of using these maps to aid decision making. In a recent *McKinsey Quarterly* article, it was proposed that management has evolved from an art to a science.[1] What the authors were referring to was the increasing use of IT-based tools to support decision making, and also an increasing reliance on experts. Systems mapping techniques are part of these new decision

---

[1] Davis, I. and Stephenson, E. (2006) 'Ten trends to watch in 2006'. *McKinsey Quarterly*, July.

support tools; however, face-to-face dialogue will always be the most important source of information and insights into how your systems work in practice.

The Fifth Practice – Engage Creativity

1. Create Time for Generative Thinking

The generative learning state that characterizes creative thinking has to be nurtured. Some organizations, such as Google, manage to encourage this state of mind as part of their corporate culture.[2] Other organizations arrange time off the job in order to think creatively about their activities. It is difficult to cultivate creativity when you are focusing on deadlines and financial targets; that is not to suggest that these things are unimportant, it is simply that creativity requires head space, time and permission to dream and play.

Think about how you can create time for generative thinking. Creativity often arises from interplay with diversity, so is best done in groups or in conversation with others. Find a consultant who specializes in creativity to advise you as to how you can encourage creativity, generate creative ideas and embed creativity into your organizational culture.

2. Ask Creative Questions

Senge refers to a *creative tension* that arises when a vision of the future is juxtaposed with the state of current reality. It is all too tempting when encountering dilemmas, problems and obstacles to abandon the vision or to simplify the problem. Simplifying the problem helps, because an action can then be devised that will seemingly resolve the issue. However, more often than not, this addresses the symptoms rather than the underlying causes. One way in which we can resolve these creative tensions is to ask creative questions.

---

[2] 'Chaos at Google.' *Fortune* (Europe edition), October 2, 2006, **154**(6).

As we saw in Chapter 8, examples include:

- Both . . . and questions – how can we encourage *both* risk-taking *and*, at the same time, respect values around risk avoidance?

- Connection questions – how are problems a, b and c connected?

- Brainstorming questions – how many ways can we find to . . . or how many options can we generate . . .?

- Hypothetical questions – what would happen if (we did the opposite of what we were thinking or if we didn't do anything right now)?

- Dream/visioning questions – what would 'ideal' look like in two years' time?

Creativity is often stifled by the frustration that builds in the desire for a quick solution. So it has to be recognized that time is needed when asking and answering these questions. It can feel like you are going off on a tangent, especially if you are strongly goal-oriented. For this reason, it is best to prepare people for creative thinking sessions, ensuring there is time, people are relaxed and the purposes of the session are perfectly clear.

3. Use your People

Creative People

Some people are just more naturally creative. Sometimes they will not be the most practical of people, and this can be highly frustrating for task-oriented, goal-focused leaders. The question is, how can you tap their talents in a way that contributes towards the overall goals and purposes of the organization? This is, in part, about valuing their contributions, despite the fact that their way of working might be very different from yours.

Again, a good starting point is to identify the ideas and talk to the people in a more generative frame of mind. Listen to them, encourage them and let them experiment – within given constraints identified by you.

There is a multitude of systems that encourage both creativity and innovation in organizations. A good way to explore these ideas is to engage a consultant who specializes in this area, and to belong to a consortium of organizations who are good role models or who are trying to improve their own organizational innovation.

Tap the Creativity of All your Employees

There are some wonderful processes that help you to tap the creativity of *all* your people. Scenario planning is one such system that helps large groups of employees envisage and enact potential futures.[3] Future search is another such system that helps people take a step back from their current situation, put it in perspective, envisage a positive and empowering future and take steps to enact it. The more people that are engaged in identifying and connecting with the future direction of the company, the more grounded the vision and the easier it is to enact.

The Sixth Practice – Reality Check

1. Regular Reviews

This book has focused on how easy it is to avoid reality. So how do we ensure that we are truly facing reality? And how do we ensure that it is the right reality as opposed to the comfortable reality? These are questions that need to be raised by you and your people on a regular basis. Typically, you will be asking:

- What are our goals? Do our goals challenge us and keep us up to date? What do other stakeholders think our goals should look like? Do our goals reflect the interests of a range of stakeholders?

---

[3] See Ringland, G. (2006) *Scenario Planning*. Chichester: John Wiley & Sons, Ltd. For information on future search, see www.futuresearch.net.

- What do we need to measure – are we getting good, solid feedback to measure our progress, especially in some of the really difficult areas? Are our measures both soft and hard?

- What are we measuring – are we measuring what is easy and avoiding what is difficult? How relevant are our measures in relation to our goals?

- Are we tracking competitors, new entrants into our market, new technological developments and underlying changes in our markets?

- Do our measures challenge us? Do they bring in the perspectives of people we would rather not listen to – for example, environmentalists, institutional investors, competitors?

- How are we interpreting our feedback? Do we minimize difficulties and focus on only the good news?

If we do not bring in hard and soft evidence, it is too easy to reassure ourselves and see everything as 'fine'. It is difficult to create that sense of urgency or Samsung's culture of 'perpetual crisis', that drives innovation and risk taking. If we do not measure the right things, we can cultivate a culture of complacency, even though, whilst we are pursuing our goals, it may not feel like it.

It is worth taking time out to examine some of the challenges associated with your reality checking processes.

2. Spend a Day

One way to check reality is by spending a day with staff. It is easy to forget the realities of delivering a service or manufacturing products on a day-to-day basis. Figures may tell you one thing, but you cannot beat being there on the ground with the people involved in the delivery. Every director of Tesco's has to spend time working as a general assistant in the stores. Every week Sir Terry Leahy, Tesco's CEO, visits a competitor's store, talking to staff and customers. Of course, we saw with Sir Richard Greenbury that visiting competitors does not necessarily cure complacency – we do only see what we want to see – but, done in a learning frame of mind, this 'back to the floor' type of exercise is one of the most powerful ways of checking reality.

3. How Do You Know?

When relying on facts, opinions and ideas regarding forthcoming decisions, ask yourself 'how do I know these are true?' When others assert facts and opinions, ask them 'how do you know these are true?'

Encourage a desire for evidence when it comes to important decisions and influential opinions. It is not enough that people simply draw on their own experience in their own part of the organization. Whilst this may generate useful insights, it does not necessarily apply throughout the organization. Encourage your people to support their views with evidence – this can be anecdotal, soft evidence (based on surveys and opinion polls) or hard evidence based on different forms of data. Hard evidence does not outweigh soft or anecdotal evidence. Anecdotal evidence may signal a shift or a change that is not yet apparent throughout the system. However, we do have a tendency to generalize on our personal experience, so it is important to seek out supporting evidence – soft, hard and anecdotal.

But balance scepticism with receptivity. It is easier to dismiss important, challenging evidence than it is to accept it. Think about the implications of the evidence if it were true. If someone is suggesting that there is a new trend which implies a lot of change, ask yourself 'if this is true, what are the implications?' Then, go out of your way to check the evidence – on the ground, with competitors, with clients – and come to your own point of view. So that when someone asks you 'how do you know?' you have a range of statistics, stories, examples and illustrations to support your opinion.

The Seventh Practice – Change your Behaviour

1. Map your Comfort Zone

To help people accelerate their learning, and in particular to take risks with their behaviour, it is helpful to get them to map their comfort zone. This helps them become aware of when they are spending time inside the comfort zone and when and why they might need to step outside of it.

First, draw a large circle. This is your comfort zone. Now, put inside the circle all the elements that seem to fit. Think of:

- preferred paradigms – areas where you feel comfortable and in control;

- people you like to spend time with;

- activities you enjoy and are good at;

- places you like to be;

- values you feel comfortable with.

Now draw a series of rings on the outside of your comfort zone. Place in each ring paradigms, activities, people and places that you are less comfortable with. The more discomfort you feel, the further away from the original comfort zone you should place them.

Now take an item outside your comfort zone. What do you need to do differently in order to move it closer towards the centre? Take time to brainstorm all the ideas that occur to you. Once you have done this, put together an action plan, with goals, steps and milestones. Now implement it!

Remember, when you are venturing outside your comfort zone, do not be hard on yourself; indulge yourself with rewards. Change and learning are both exhausting. It might be good for business having a culture of perpetual crisis, but I am not so sure it is good for the individual to be living in a perpetual crisis! Get a coach; go on retreat; spend weekends away with the family; spend a day at a health farm. It is vital that you look after yourself physically, emotionally and mentally. Whatever helps you to relax, make sure that you do it frequently and regularly.

2. Regularly Step Outside your Comfort Zone

Practise stepping outside your comfort zone. Whenever you come across a challenge that you have never undertaken before, do it! Join an acting class, learn how to dance, make a presentation in a different style, do an abseil for charity. Whenever someone suggests you do something and you feel that sense of nervousness, take that as a sign that this is something you ought to do!

On a smaller scale, make sure that you try and practise 'changing your behaviour' every day. In part, this is about strengthening your willpower. Don't simply react in response to your feelings or desires; strengthen your will and resist a bar of chocolate or a glass of wine. Force yourself to make the first move in resolving a conflict. Walk to work instead of driving. Regularly find small ways to strengthen your willpower and change your behaviour.

3. Make Behaviour Change an Ongoing Part of your Management Development Strategy

Assignments and new roles should be regularly appraised in terms of how much behaviour change they demand. Executives should expect to have to change their behaviour when encountering these challenges, and should be trained in the skills associated with it. Eventually, behaviour change should be considered natural and inevitable; executives should be trained in the 'meta' skills of learning how to learn and change.

4. Provide Both Support and Challenge – For Yourself and Others

Sometimes change just takes time. As we have seen, a person is more likely to change when the discomfort associated with the present appears greater than the discomfort associated with change. Once the pain associated with the current situation pervades your whole life, bringing inescapable tensions and anxieties, the risks of change diminish. Anything is better than staying in the present situation. But it does take time for the discomfort to grow and for the realization that the pain is not going to go away.

When leading change, it is important to ensure people realize that you mean it – keep up the pressure until people realize that the pressure will not go away. Ratchet up the discomfort, but also provide support to enable people to collectively and positively make sense of what is happening to them. Also, provide training and development to help people take the first experimental steps.

If leaders have blind spots and are refusing to change, there is a range of methods to encourage them to take the first steps, again coming under the rubric of support and challenge. Coaching, of course, can provide both support and challenge. 360° feedback is another source of challenge. Leaders throughout the organization have to know that they cannot escape the discomfort of change – that it is going to affect them, their roles, their people, their jobs, their security, their bonuses. All of the usual paraphernalia associated with change management is applicable here.

If the leaders are at the top of the organization, it is very difficult to dislodge them from the comfort zone. The tactics below might help to highlight the *need to change*:

- Speakers at conferences that challenge leaders, e.g. looking at what competitors are doing, examples showing how markets are changing.

- Company surveys giving feedback on how clients and employees see the company's performance, and reasons for this.

- A 'back to the floor' exercise where the Chief Executive visits factories, plants, clients, retail outlets – both their own and those of benchmark companies.

- An awayday, led by an external facilitator, where the Chief Executive and the board can face uncomfortable issues in a safe environment.

- A yearly challenge whereby people declare one area in which they are going to change their behaviour, possibly based on their 360° feedback. They attempt to change their behaviour in the area specified, and people can go online and give them anonymous feedback on their efforts. At the end of the year, a brief survey could be completed to get feedback on how the individual has done. Various rewards could be linked to success!

The Eighth Practice – Nurture Integrity

1. Weekly/Monthly Reflection

This exercise is inspired by a Benedictine reflection that helps to aid 'confession'.[4]

Find a peaceful time at the end of a day or week when you can reflect honestly and openly on the following questions.

Have I been proud or conceited? Do I hate some people?
Have I dismissed people who have tried to help me?
Have I ignored people who have tried to bring something to my attention?
Have I been ungenerous?
Have I been stubborn?
Have I been uncooperative or ungrateful with people who are trying to help me?
Have I been irritable, sulky, jealous or angry?
Have I avoided someone who has needed my help?
Have I failed to speak out against things I know to be wrong for fear of becoming unpopular?
Have I prevented justice from being done?
Have I told lies to get myself out of trouble or to make myself appear better than I am?
Have I refused to apologise when I hurt someone?
Have I said unpleasant things about other people?
Have I bullied people or used them for my own purposes?

---

[4] *Saint Benedict's Prayer Book for Beginners* (2006), fifth edition. York: Ampleforth Abbey Press.

Do I make friends with people simply because they have power,
   influence or reputation?
Have I led others to do something which I know is wrong?
Do I live only for myself or do I have higher ideals that I am
   trying to strive for?

Now, obviously, the purpose of a confession such as this has
traditionally been to repent, atone and receive forgiveness. If one
believes in a God (from whatever religion or in whatever form,
such as 'a higher being'), this is easier to do than if one is an
atheist. However, the process of being forgiven is as important as
the process of repentance. Without forgiveness, unacceptably high
levels of guilt can accumulate, leaving the individual with a low sense
of self worth. If you are an atheist and wish to occasionally reflect
on these questions, find your own way of making atonement and
seeking forgiveness. This could take the form of making reparation
to the people who you may have wronged. Perhaps the hardest thing
for us to do is simply to say 'sorry'. Find the person you have
wronged and apologise – you will find this a lot harder to do than
you might anticipate! If it is not possible to make direct reparation,
find other ways to atone, such as giving generously to a relevant
charity. Sometimes it is good to 'confess' to a friend – just openly
admitting you have been wrong can relieve you of the sense of
guilt.

When you have reflected on this, try another reflection:

Find a peaceful time at the end of a day or week when you can
reflect honestly and openly on the following questions.

Have I been kind?
Have I expressed appreciation of people?
Have I gratefully accepted help from people?
Have I gone out of my way to listen to people who have tried
   to bring something to my attention?
Have I been generous?
Have I changed my mind in response to someone else's
   opinion?
Have I been positive, open and grateful to others?

Have I helped someone recently without any expectation of benefit for me?

Have I expressed courage in speaking out against things I know to be wrong?

Have I helped ensure justice has been done?

Have I told the truth, even though it might have got me into trouble?

Have I apologised when I hurt someone?

Have I said pleasant things about other people or brought the helpful actions of others to the attention of their bosses?

Have I really attempted to listen to people, even though I might have been irritated by them?

Have I made friends with people who do not have power, influence or reputation?

Have I led others to do something which I feel is right, even though there has been risk to me?

Have I said 'thank you'?

Have I, in some way, lived out my higher ideals?

It is important to balance the recognition of our good behaviour and the acceptance of our faults. If we focus on one to the exclusion of the other, it can cause blind spots to develop (not seeing our faults) or unacceptable levels of guilt and low self worth. This exercise is particularly important for those in positions of power. When in power, it is unlikely that others will point out our faults, so we have to ensure that we do this ourselves. If we do not, we can be lulled into a false sense of security, which may lead us to abuse our power without being aware of it.

2. Define your Goals and Values

Take time out to discover your goals, motivational values and idealistic values. A table of values is provided to help stimulate your thoughts. Some of these values will be motivational values for you (they are part of your personality and come naturally to you), some will be idealistic (you believe they are worthwhile and, although you find them difficult, you strive to achieve them). This list is not intended to be exhaustive!

What's important to you?

Achievement	Action	Affiliation	Assertiveness
Authenticity	Authority	Beauty	Belonging
Caring	Challenge	Change	Citizenship
Commercialism	Community	Compassion	Competition
Conformity	Convention	Courage	Creativity
Democracy	Discipline	Diversity	Duty
Efficiency	Empowerment	Enjoyment	Entrepreneurialism
Environmentalism	Equality	Excellence	Fairness
Family	Fitness	Flexibility	Forthrightness
Freedom	Friendship	Giving	God
Happiness	Harmony	Helping Others	Honesty
Honour	Humanitarianism	Humility	Humour
Impact	Inclusion	Independence	Individuality
Influence	Innovation	Integrity	Justice
Kindness	Knowledge	Leadership	Learning
Logic	Love	Loyalty	Making a Difference
Mastery	Meaning	Moderation	Modesty
Nurturance	Obedience	Openness	Order
Patience	Peace	Perfection	Personal Growth
Pleasure	Possessions	Power	Pragmatism
Prestige	Principles	Recognition	Relaxation
Risk	Security	Self Actualization	Self Sacrifice
Sincerity	Social Inclusion	Spirituality	Status
Strength	Survival	Team Spirit	Tolerance
Tradition	Trustworthiness	Truth	Understanding
Wealth	Wisdom		

Now write down your goals (and what drives your goals), your motivational values and your idealistic values. Can you spot any areas of synergy or tension? Assess your integrity quotient – to what extent are you acting in alignment with your idealistic values? To what extent are you allowing your goals and motivational values to dominate your idealistic values?

My assessment

Goals – identify what you want to achieve. Then ask 'why' do you want this? When you ask why you will identify deeper goals and underlying needs and values.	What is really important to me is succeeding in my career. I want to get as high as I can in the organizational hierarchy. Why do I want this . . . ? I think one reason why this is important to me is that I need visible signs of success. These signs give me confidence that I am valued and that I have something to contribute. I know I need to be recognized by others. I can't just do a job for the sake of it.
Motivational values – what values motivate me?	Recognition, status, loyalty, leadership, order, tradition.
Idealistic values – what values do I strive to achieve but find difficult?	Fairness, justice, family.
Integrity quotient – to what extent am I prepared to sacrifice my goals, needs and values for the sake of others/the organization? – to what extent do I walk the talk? Give yourself a mark out of 10	I'd give myself 5 out of 10. I'd like to aim for a 7!

Notes:

I didn't realize that 'family' was an idealistic value, but it is! I talk about it but I don't do much to show how important it is to me. This is because I spend too much time devoted to my career goals and motivational values. I am going to change this. From now on, I will devote my weekends to spending time with the children and with my partner.

When you have finished this exercise, you can, if you are brave enough, seek feedback from others as to how they see you! This will give you some idea of how you are viewed in terms of your integrity.

3. Expand your Range of Values

Take one of your preferred values. Identify a value which appears to challenge it. For example, if your preferred value is loyalty, take a value such as 'challenge'. Now think of circumstances when 'challenge' might be appropriate. Identify someone you know who embodies this value. Talk to them and learn about what motivates them, why they think this value is important and what they think are some of the problems associated with your preferred value. Learn to appreciate differences in values and continually challenge your own preferences by talking to people with different value sets.

References and Further Reading

General References

The following books and articles have been particularly helpful to me in writing about leadership blind spots.

Badaracco, J. L. Jr (1998) 'The Discipline of Building Character'. *Harvard Business Review*, March–April, pp. 115–124.

Bevan, J. (2002) *The Rise and Fall of Marks and Spencer*. London: Profile Books Ltd.

Bristol Royal Infirmary Inquiry (2001). Norwich: The Stationery Office Limited, July.

Charan, R., Drotter, S. and Noel, J. (2001) *The Leadership Pipeline – How to Build the Leadership-Powered Company*. San Francisco: Jossey-Bass Inc.

Collins, J. (2001) *Good to Great*. London: Random House, p. 72.

Conger, J. A. (1990) 'The Dark Side of Leadership'. *Organizational Dynamics*, Autumn, 44–55.

Covey, S. R. (1999) *The 7 Habits of Highly Effective People*. London: Simon & Schuster.

Damasio, A. (1999) *The Feeling of What Happens – Body and Emotion in the Making of Consciousness*. London: Heinemann.

De Geus, A. (1988) 'Planning as Learning'. *Harvard Business Review*, March–April.

Engel, A. K., Debener, S. and Kranczioch, C. (2006) 'Coming to Attention'. *Scientific American Mind*, August/September.

Goleman, D. (1996) *Emotional Intelligence*. London: Bloomsbury.

Goleman, D. (2000) 'Leadership That Gets Results'. *Harvard Business Review*, March–April.

Goleman, D. and The Dalai Lama (2003) *Destructive Emotions*. London: Bloomsbury.

Harmon-Jones, E. and Mills, J. (1991) *Cognitive dissonance – progress on a pivotal theory in social psychology*. Washington: American Psychological Society.

Hyman, P. (2005) *1 out of 10*. London: Vintage.

Jamison, Abbot C. (2006) *Finding Sanctuary – Monastic Steps for Everyday Life*. London: Weidenfeld & Nicholson.

Kahane, A. (2004) *Solving Tough Problems: An open way of talking, listening and creating new realities*. San Francisco: Berrett-Koehler, p. 98.

Kelly, G. A. (1955) *The Psychology of Personal Constructs*. New York: Norton.

LeDoux, J. (1998) *The Emotional Brain*. London: Weidenfeld & Nicholson.

Leeson, N. (1996) *Rogue Trader*. London: Little, Brown and Company.

Luft, J. and Ingham, H. (1955) 'The Johari window, a graphic model of interpersonal awareness', *Proceedings of the western training laboratory in group development*. Los Angeles: UCLA.

Mitroff, I. and Linstone, H. A. (1993) *The Unbounded Mind: Breaking the chains of traditional business thinking*. New York: Oxford University Press.

Paxman, J. (2003) *The Political Animal*. London: Penguin.

Rawnsley, J. (1995) *Going for Broke – Nick Leeson and the Collapse of Barings Bank*. London: HarperCollins.

Rodgers, C. (2007) Informal Coalitions – Mastering the hidden dynamics of organizational change. Basingstoke: Palgrave Macmillan.

Senge, P. M. (2004) 'Creating Desired Futures in a Global Economy'. *Reflections – The SoL Journal on Knowledge, Learning and Change*, **5**.

Senge, P. M., Scharmer, C. O., Jaworski, J. and Flowers, B. S. (2005) *Presence – exploring profound change in people, organizations and society*. London: Nicholas Brealey.

Sterman, J. D. (2002) 'All models are wrong: reflections on becoming a systems scientist'. *System Dynamics Review*, **18**(4), 501–531.

Sutherland, S. (1992) *Irrationality*. London: Constable and Company Limited.

Zohar, D. and Marshall, I. (2001) *Spiritual Intelligence, The Ultimate Intelligence*. London: Bloomsbury.

Academic References and Further Reading

The following references were influential in my PhD research and provide further information for those interested in pursuing some of the ideas contained in this book in greater depth.

Abelson, R. P. (1976) 'Script processing in attitude formation and decision making', in J. S. Carroll and J. W. Payne (Eds) *Cognition and Social Behaviour*. Hillsdale, NJ: Erlbaum, pp. 33–46.

Ajzen, I. (1988) *Attitudes, Personality, and Behaviour*. Milton Keynes: OUP.

Argote, L. (1993) 'Group and organisational learning curves: Individual, system and environmental components'. *British Journal of Social Psychology*, **32**, 31–51.

Argyris, C. (1976) 'Single Loop and Double Loop Models in Research on Decision Making'. *Administrative Science Quarterly*, **21**, 363–375.

Argyris, C. (1982) *Reasoning, Learning and Action: Individual and Organisational*. San Francisco: Jossey-Bass Inc.

Argyris, C. and Schon, D. A. (1978) *Organizational Learning: A Theory of Action Perspective*. Reading, MA: Addison Wesley Publishing Co.

Bandura, A. (1977) *Social Learning Theory*. Englewood Cliffs, NJ: Prentice-Hall.

Bandura, A. (1986) *Social Foundations of Thought and Action*. Englewood Cliffs, NJ: Prentice-Hall.

Bannister, D. and Mair, J. M. M. (1968) *The Evaluation of Personal Constructs*. London: Academic Press.

Barr, P. S., Stimpert, J. L. and Huff, A. S. (1992) 'Cognitive Change, Strategic Action and Organizational Renewal'. *Strategic Management Journal*, **13**, 15–36.

Bartunek, J. M. and Moch, M. K. (1987) 'First-Order, Second-Order, and Third-Order Change and Organization Development Interventions: A Cognitive Approach'. *The Journal of Applied Behavioural Science*, **23**(4), 483–500.

Beckhard, R. (1969) *Organization Development: Strategies and Models*. Reading MA: Addison Wesley Publishing Co.

Best, S. and Kellner, D. (2001) *The Postmodern Adventure*. London: Routledge.

Bieri, J. (1966) 'Cognitive complexity and personality development', in O. J. Harvey (Ed.) *Experience, Structure and Adaptability*. New York: Springer.

Bion, W. R. (1961) *Experiences in Groups*. London: Tavistock.

Boje, D. M. (1994) 'Organizational Storytelling: The Struggles of Premodern, Modern and Postmodern Organizational Learning Discourses'. *Management Learning*, **25**(3), 433–461.

Boje, D. M. (1996) 'Management Education as a Panoptic Cage', in R. French and C. Grey (Eds) *Rethinking Management Education*. London: Sage.

Boland, R. J. Jr, Greenberg, R. H., Park, S. H. and Han, I. (1990) 'Mapping the Process of Problem Reformulation: Implications for Understanding Strategic Thought', in A. S. Huff (Ed.) *Mapping Strategic Thought*. Chichester: John Wiley & Sons, Ltd.

Boydell, T. (1994) *The Eleven Characteristics Questionnaire: Basic Data from 10 Organisations*. Case Paper Number 1. The Learning Company Project, Sheffield, UK.

Brewer, W. F. and Nakamura, G. V. (1984) 'The nature and functions of schemas', in R. S. Wyer, Jr and T. K. Srull (Eds) *Handbook of Social Cognition*, volume 1. Hillsdale, NJ: Erlbaum, pp. 119–160.

Brewis, J. (1996) 'The "Making" of the "Competent" Manager: Competency Development, Personal Effectiveness and Foucault'. *Management Learning*, 27(1), 65–86.

Brown, J. S. and Duguid, P. (1991) 'Organizational Learning and Communities of Practice: Towards a Unified View of Working, Learning and Innovation'. *Organizational Science*, 2(1), 40–57.

Buckler, S. A. and Zien, K. A. (1996) 'The Spirituality of Innovation: Learning from Stories'. *Journal of Product Innovation Management*, 13(5), 391–405.

Burgoyne, J. (1994) 'Managing by Learning'. *Management Learning*, 25(1), 35–55.

Burgoyne, J. (1995) 'The Case for an Optimistic, Constructivist and Applied Approach to Management Education'. *Management Learning*, 26(1), 91–96.

Burgoyne, J., Pedlar, M. and Boydell, T. (1991) *The Learning Company: A Strategy for Sustainable Development*. London: McGraw Hill.

Burrell, G. and Morgan, G. (1979) *Sociological Paradigms and Organizational Analysis*. London: Heinemann.

Cangelosi, V. E. and Dill, W. R. (1965) 'Organizational Learning: Observations Toward a Theory'. *Administrative Science Quarterly*, 10, 175–203.

Carroll, J. S. and Payne, J. (Eds) (1976) *Cognition and Social Behaviour*. Hillsdale, NJ: Lawrence Erlbaum Associates.

Chaiklin, S. (1992) 'From Theory to Practice and Back Again: What Does Postmodern Philosophy Contribute to Psychological Science?' in S. Kuale (Ed.) *Psychology and Postmodernism*. London: Sage.

Charmaz, K. (2000) 'Grounded Theory: Objectivist and Constructivist Methods', in N. K. Denzin and Y. S. Lincoln (Eds) *Handbook of Qualitative Research*. Thousand Oaks CA: Sage.

Chia, R. and Morgan, S. (1996) 'Educating the Philosoper-Manager: Designing the Times'. *Management Learning*, 27(1), 37–64.

Claxton, G. (1998) 'Knowing Without Knowing Why'. *The Psychologist*, May, 217–220.

Cohen, M. D. and Sproull, L. S. (Eds) (1996) *Organizational Learning*. Thousand Oaks CA: Sage.

Colledge, R. (2002) *Mastering Counselling Theory*. Basingstoke: Palgrave Macmillan.

Colquitt, J. A. and Simmering, M. J. (1998) 'Conscientiousness, Goal Orientation and Motivation to Learn During the Learning Process: A Longitudinal Study'. *Journal of Applied Psychology*, 83(4), 654–665.

Cook, S. D. N. and Yanow, D. (1993) 'Culture and Organizational Learning'. *Journal of Management Inquiry*, 2(4), 373–390.

Coopey, J. (1994) *Crucial Gaps in the 'Learning Organisation': Power, Politics and Ideology*. Management Working Papers No. 1, University of Dundee, May.

Cornelius, R. R. (1996) *The Science of Emotion: Research and Tradition in the Psychology of Emotion*. Englewood Cliffs NJ: Prentice-Hall.

Cossette, P. (1992) 'Mapping of an Idiosyncratic Schema'. *Journal of Management Studies*, **29**(3), 325–347.

Craib, I. (2001) *Psychoanalysis – A Critical Introduction*. Cambridge: Polity Press.

Crockett, W. H. (1965) 'Cognitive complexity and impression formation', in B. A. Maher (Ed.) *Progress in Experimental Personality Research*, volume 2. New York: Academic Press.

Crockett, W. H. and Meisel, P. (1974) 'Construct connectedness, strength of disconfirmation and impression change'. *Journal of Personality*, **42**, 290–299.

Crossan, M., Djurfeldt, L., Lane, H. W. and White, R. E. (1994) *Organizational Learning – Dimensions for a Theory*. Working Paper Series No. 94-09R. London, Canada: Western Business School, The University of Western Ontario.

Crossan, M., Lane, H. W., Rush, J. C. and White, R. E. (1993) *Learning in Organizations*. Monograph from 1992 Workshop. London, Canada: Western Business School, The University of Western Ontario.

Csikszentmihalyi, M. (1990) *Flow: The Psychology of Optimal Experience*. New York: HarperCollins.

Cunliffe, A. (2002) 'Reflexive Dialogical Practice in Management Learning'. *Management Learning*, **33**(1), 35–61.

Daft, R. L. and Weick, K. E. (1984) 'Toward a model of organizations as interpretation systems'. *Academy of Management Review*, **9**, 284–295.

Daniels, K., Johnson, G. and de Chernatony, L. (1994) 'Collective Frames of Reference, Recognition, and Managers' Mental Models of Competition: A Test in Two Industries'. Paper submitted to *Academy of Management Journal*, November 1994, Centre for Strategic Management and Organisational Change, Cranfield School of Management.

De Board, R. (1978) *The Psychoanalysis of Organizations*. London: Tavistock/Routledge.

De Geus, A. (1988) 'Planning as Learning'. *Harvard Business Review*, March–April, 70–74.

Dodgson, M. (1993) 'Organizational Learning: A review of some literatures'. *Organization Studies*, **14**(3), 375–394.

Driver, M. J. (1993) 'Learning, Cognition and Organization', in M. M. Crossan *et al.* (Eds) *Learning in Organizations*, Western Business School, the University of Ontario, Ontario.

Driver, M. J. and Rowe, A. J. (1979) 'Decision Making Styles: A New Approach to Management Decision Making', in C. L. Cooper (Ed.)

Behavioural Problems in Organisations. Englewood Cliffs, NJ: Prentice-Hall.

Duhaime, I. M. and Schwenk, C. R. (1985) 'Conjectures on Cognitive Simplification in Acquisition and Divestment Decision Making'. *Academy of Management Review,* **10**(2), 287–295.

Eden, C., Jones, S. and Sims, D. (1979) *Thinking in Organizations.* London: Macmillan.

Eden, C. and Spender, J-C. (Eds) (1988) *Managerial and Organizational Cognition, Theory Methods and Research.* London: Sage.

Edwards, R. and Usher, R. (2001) 'Lifelong Learning: A Postmodern Condition of Education'. *Adult Education Quarterly,* **51**(4), 273–287.

Ekman, P. and Davidson, R. J. (1994) *The Nature of Emotion: Fundamental Questions.* New York: Oxford University Press.

Elliot, A. (2000) 'The Ethical Antinomies of Postmodernity'. *Sociology,* **34**(2), 335–340.

Ellis, A. (1993) 'Reflections on rational-emotive therapy (RET)'. *Journal of Consulting and Clinical Psychology,* **61**, 199–201.

Esser, J. K. (1998) 'Alive and Well after 25 Years: A Review of Groupthink Research'. *Organizational Behaviour and Human Decision Making Processes,* **73**(2/3), 116–141.

Esser, J. K. and Lindoerfer, J. L. (1989) 'Groupthink and the space shuttle *Challenger* accident: Toward a quantitative case analysis'. *Journal of Behavioural Decision Making,* **2**, 167–177.

Eysenck, M. W. and Keene, M. T. (1990) *Cognitive Psychology. A Student's Handbook.* Hove: Lawrence Erlbaum Associates.

Fahey, L. and Narayanan, V. K. (1989) 'Linking Changes in Revealed Causal Maps and Environmental Change: An Empirical Study'. *Journal of Management Studies,* **26**, 361–378.

Fenwick, T. (2003) *Learning Through Experience: Troubling Orthodoxies and Intersecting Questions.* Malabar: Krieger Publishing Company.

Festinger, L. (1957) *A Theory of Cognitive Dissonance.* Palo Alto, CA: Stanford University Press.

Fineman, S. (1993) *Emotion in Organizations.* London: Sage.

Fineman, S. (1997) 'Emotion and Management Learning'. *Management Learning,* **28**(1), 13–25.

Fineman, S. (2003) 'Emotionalising Organisational Learning', in M. Easterby Smith and M. Lyles (Eds) *The Handbook of Organizational Learning and Knowledge Management.* Oxford: Blackwell.

Fineman, S. and Sturdy, A. (1999) 'The Emotions of Control: A Qualitative Exploration of Environmental Regulation'. *Human Relations,* **52**(5), 631–663.

Fiol, C. M. and Lyles, M. A. (1985) 'Organizational Learning'. *Academy of Management Review,* **10**, 803–813.

Fiske, S. T. and Dyer, L. M. (1985) 'Structure and Development of Social Schemata: Evidence from positive and negative transfer effects'. *Journal of Personality and Social Psychology*, **48**, 839–852.

Fiske, S. T. and Kinder, D. R. (1981) 'Involvement, Expertise and Schema Use: Evidence from political cognition', in N. Cantor and J. Kihlstrom (Eds) *Personality, Cognition and Social Interaction*. Hillsdale, NJ: Erlbaum.

Fiske, S. T. and Taylor, S. (1991) *Social Cognition*, second edition. Singapore: McGraw Hill.

Fletcher, K. E. and Huff, A. S. (1990) 'Strategic Argument Mapping: A Study of Strategy Reformulation at AT&T', in A. S. Huff (Ed.) *Mapping Strategic Thought*. Chichester: John Wiley & Sons, Ltd.

Forgas, J. P. (2001) 'Affect and the "Social Mind": Affective Influences on Strategic Interpersonal Behaviours', in J. P. Forgas, K. D. Williams and L. Wheeler (Eds) *The Social Mind: Cognitive and Motivational Aspects of Interpersonal Behaviour*. Cambridge: Cambridge University Press.

Forgas, J. P., Williams, K. D. and Wheeler, L. (2001) 'The Social Mind: Introduction and Overview', in J. P. Forgas, K. D. Williams and L. Wheeler (Eds) *The Social Mind: Cognitive and Motivational Aspects of Interpersonal Behaviour*. Cambridge: Cambridge University Press.

Fournier, V. and Grey, C. (2000) 'At the critical moment: Conditions and prospects for critical management studies'. *Human Relations*, **53**(1), 7–32.

Frankl, V. E. (1959) *Man's Search for Meaning*. New York: Washington Square Books.

French, R. and Grey, C. (Eds) (1996) *Rethinking Management Education*. London: Sage.

Freshwater, D. and Robertson, C. (2002) *Emotions and Needs*. Buckingham: Open University Press.

Freud, A. (1936) *The Ego and the Mechanisms of Defence*. London: Hogarth Press.

Friedlander, F. (1983) 'Patterns of Individual and Organizational Learning', in S. Srivastva and Associates (Eds) *The Executive Mind: New Insights on Managerial Thought and Action*. San Francisco: Jossey-Bass Inc.

Frijda, N. H., Manstead, A. S. R. and Bem, S. (2000) *Emotions and Beliefs: How Feelings Influence Thoughts*. Cambridge: Cambridge University Press.

Gabriel, Y., Fineman, S. and Sims, D. (2000) *Organizing and Organizations*, second edition. London: Sage.

Gallwey, T. (2000) *The Inner Game of Work*. New York: Random House.

Gardner, H. (1985) *The Mind's New Science*. New York: Basic Books.

Garratt, B. (1987) *The Learning Organisation*. London: Fontana.

Garratt, B. (1990) *Creating a Learning Organisation: A Guide to Leadership, Learning and Development.* Cambridge: Director Books.

Garrick, J. and Clegg, S. (2001) 'Stressed-out Knowledge Workers in Performative Times: A Postmodern Take on Project-based Learning'. *Management Learning*, 32(1), 119–134.

Garvin, D. A. (1993) 'Building a Learning Organization'. *Harvard Business Review*, July–August, 78–91.

Gergen, K. (1985) 'The social constructionist movement in modern psychology'. *American Psychologist*, 40, 266–275.

Gergen, K. (1992) 'Organization Theory in the postmodern era', in M. Reed and M. Hughes (Eds) *Rethinking Organization*. London: Sage.

Gheradi, S. (2000) 'Where Learning Is: Metaphors and situated learning in a planning group'. *Human Relations*, 53(8), 1057–1080.

Gheradi, S. *et al.* (1998) 'Toward a Social Understanding of How People Learn in Organizations: The Notion of Situated Curriculum'. *Management Learning*, 29(3), 273–297.

Giddens, A. (1984) *The Constitution of Society: Outline of the Theory of Structuration.* Cambridge: Polity Press.

Gioia, D. A. (1992) 'Pinto Fires and Personal Ethics: A Script Analysis of Missed Opportunities'. *Journal of Business Ethics*, 11, 379–389.

Gioia, D. A. and Poole, P. P. (1984) 'Scripts in Organizational Behaviour'. *Academy of Management Review*, 9(3), 440–459.

Goleman, D. (1996) *Emotional Intelligence.* London: Bloomsbury.

Goodwin, V. L. and Ziegler, L. (1998) 'A test of relationships in a model of organizational cognitive complexity'. *Journal of Organization Behaviour*, 19, 371–386.

Greenfield, S. A. (1996) *The Human Mind Explained.* London: Cassell Publishers.

Grey, C. and French, R. (1996) 'Rethinking Management Education: An Introduction', in R. French and C. Grey (Eds) *Rethinking Management Education.* London: Sage.

Grey, C. and Mitev, N. (1995) 'Neutrality, Critique and Quality: A reply to Burgoyne, McAuley and King'. *Management Learning*, 26(1), 103–108.

Gruenfeld, D. H., Martorana, P. V. and Elliott, T. F. (2000) 'What Do Groups Learn from Their Worldliest Members? Direct and Indirect Influence in Dynamic Teams'. *Organizational Behaviour and Human Decision Processes*, 82(1), 45–59.

Hayden, B. C. (1982) 'Experience – a case for possible change: the modulation corollary', in J. C. Mancuso and J. R. Adams-Webber (Eds) *The Construing Person.* New York: Praeger.

Hayes, R. H., Wheelwright, S. C. and Clark, K. B. (1988) *Dynamic Manufacturing: Creating the Learning Organization.* New York: The Free Press.

Hedberg, B. L. T. (1981) 'How Organizations Learn and Unlearn', in P. C. Nystrom and W. H. Starbuck (Eds) *Handbook of Organizational Design*, volume 1. New York: Oxford University Press.

Heron, J. (1992) *Feelings and Personhood: Psychology in Another Key*. London: Sage.

Herzberg, F. (1966) *Work and the Nature of Man*. New York: World Publishing Company.

Hill, R. C. and Levenhagen, M. (1995) 'Metaphors and Mental Models: Sensemaking and Sensegiving in Innovative and Entrepreneurial Activities'. *Journal of Management*, 21(6), 1057–1074.

Hirschhorn, L. (1995) *The Workplace Within: Psychodynamics of Organizational Life*. Cambridge MA: MIT Press.

Hochschild, A. (1983) *The Managed Heart*. Berkeley CA: University of California.

Hodgkinson, G. P. and Johnson, G. (1993) *Exploring the Mental Models of Competitive Strategists: The Case for a Processual Approach*. Discussion Paper No 93.22, Cranfield School of Management.

Holman, D. (2000) 'Contemporary Models of Management Education in the UK'. *Management Learning*, 31(2), 197–217.

Holman, D., Pavlica, K. and Thorpe, R. (1997) 'Rethinking Kolb's Theory of Experiential Learning in Management Education. The Contribution of Social Constructionism and Activity Theory'. *Management Learning*, 28(2), 135–148.

Honey, P. (1991) 'The Learning Organisation Simplified'. *Training and Development*, July, 30–33.

Honey, P. and Mumford, A. (1986) *The Manual of Learning Styles*, second edition. Maidenhead: Honey.

Huber, G. P. (1991) 'Organizational Learning: The Contributing Processes and the Literatures'. *Organization Science*, 2(1) 88–115.

Huff, A. S. (1990) 'Mapping Strategic Thought', in A. S. Huff (Ed.) *Mapping Strategic Thought*. Chichester: John Wiley & Sons, Ltd.

Janis, I. L. (1972) *Victims of Groupthink*. Boston: Houghton Mifflin.

Johnson, G. (1990) 'Managing Strategic Change: The role of symbolic action'. *British Journal of Management*, 1, 183–200.

Jones, A. M. and Hendry, C. (1992) *The Learning Organization: A Review of Literature and Practice*. Centre for Corporate Strategy and Change, Warwick Business School. The HRD Partnership.

Jones, A. M. and Hendry, C. (1994) 'The Learning Organization: Adult Learning and Organizational Transformation'. *British Journal of Management*, 5, 153–162.

Kahneman, D., Slovic, P. and Tversky, A. (Eds) (1992) *Judgement Under Uncertainty: Heuristics and Biases*. Cambridge: Cambridge University Press.

Kanter, R. M. (1985) *The Change Masters*. London: Unwin.

Kayes, D. C. (2002) 'Experiential Learning and Its Critics: Preserving the Role of Experience in Management Learning and Education'. *Academy of Management Learning and Education*, **1**(2), 137–149.

Kelly, G. A. (1955) *The Psychology of Personal Constructs*. New York: Norton.

Kelly, G. A. (1963) *A Theory of Personality: The Psychology of Personal Constructs*. New York: Norton.

Kets de Vries, M. F. R. (1984) *The Neurotic Organization*. San Francisco: Jossey-Bass Inc.

Kiesler, S. and Sproull, L. (1982) 'Managerial Response to Changing Environments: Perspectives on Problem Sensing from Social Cognition'. *Administrative Science Quarterly*, December, 548–570.

Kim, D. H. (1993) 'The Link Between Individual and Organizational Learning'. *Sloan Management Review*, Fall, 37–50.

Klein, J. I. (1989) 'Parenthetic Learning in Organizations: Towards the Unlearning of the Unlearning Model'. *Journal of Management Studies*, **26**(3), 291–308.

Kolb, D. (1984) *Experiential Learning*. Englewood Cliffs NJ: Prentice-Hall.

Kubler-Ross, E. (1969) *On Death and Dying*. New York: Macmillan.

Kuhn, T. S. (1970) *The Structure of Scientific Revolutions*, second edition. Chicago: Chicago University Press.

Kvale, S. (1992) 'Postmodern psychology: a contradiction in terms?' in S. Kuale (Ed.) *Psychology and Postmodernism*. London: Sage.

Langan-Fox, J. and Tan, P. (1997) 'Images of a culture in transition: Personal constructs of organizational stability and change'. *Journal of Occupational and Organizational Psychology*, **70**, 273–293.

Lave, J. and Wenger, E. (1991) *Situated Learning – Legitimate Peripheral Participation*. Cambridge: Cambridge University Press.

Lazarus, R. S. (1991) *Emotion and Adaptation*. New York: Oxford University Press.

LeDoux, J. (1998) *The Emotional Brain*. London: Weidenfeld & Nicholson.

Leicester, M. (2000) 'Post-postmodernism and continuing education'. *International Journal of Lifelong Education*, **19**(1), 73–81.

Lessem, R. (1991) *Total Quality Learning, Building a Learning Organisation*. Oxford: Blackwell.

Louis, M. R. and Sutton, R. I. (1991) 'Switching Cognitive Gears: From Habits of Mind to Active Thinking'. *Human Relations*, **44**(1), 55–76.

Lukes, S. (1974) *Power: A Radical View*. Basingstoke: Macmillan.

Lyotard, J. F. (1984) *The Postmodern Condition: A Report on Knowledge*. Manchester: Manchester University Press.

MacDonald, S. (1995) 'Learning to Change: An Information Perspective on Learning in the Organization'. *Organization Science*, **6**(5), 557–568.

Mangham, I. (1979) *The Politics of Organisational Change*. London: Associated Business Press.

March, J. G. and Olsen, J. P. (1979) *Ambiguity and Choice in Organizations*, second edition. Bergen: Universitets-forlaget.

Maslow, A. (1964) *Motivation and Personality*. New York: Harper and Row.

McGill, I. and Beaty, L. (1995) *Action Learning*, second edition. London: Kogan Page Limited.

McGregor, D. (1960) *The Human Side of Enterprise*. New York: McGraw Hill.

McMillen, M. C., Baker, A. C. and White, J. (1997) 'Cultural Analysis, "Good Conversation" and the Creation of a Multicultural Learning Organization'. *Management Learning*, **28**(2), 197–215.

Merriam, S. B. and Caffarella, R. S. (1999) *Learning in Adulthood*. San Francisco: Jossey-Bass Inc.

Mezirow, J. and Associates (1990) *Fostering Critical Reflection in Adulthood: A Guide to Transformative and Emancipatory Learning*. San Francisco: Jossey-Bass Inc.

Miller, D. and Ming-Jer, C. (1994) 'Sources and Consequences of Competitive Inertia: A Study of the U.S. Airline Industry'. *Administrative Science Quarterly*, **39**, 1–23.

Miner, A. S. and Mezias, S. J. (1996) 'Ugly Duckling No More: Pasts and Futures of Organizational Learning Research'. *Organization Science*, **7**(1), 88–99.

Mingers, J. (2000) 'What Is It to be Critical? Teaching a Critical Approach to Management Undergraduates'. *Management Learning*, **31**(2), 219–237.

Morgan, G. (1986) *Images of Organization*. London: Sage.

Nagel, T. (1980) 'What is it like to be a bat?' in N. Block (Ed.) *Readings in the Philosophy of Psychology*, volume 1. London: Methuen.

Naranjo, C. (1993) *Gestalt Therapy: The Attitude and Practice of an Atheoretical Experientialism*. Bancyfelin, Wales: Crown House Publishing.

Neisser, U. (1976) *Cognition and Reality*. San Francisco: W. H. Freeman.

Newall, A. and Simon, H. A. (1972) *Human Problem Solving*. Englewood Cliffs, NJ: Prentice-Hall.

Nichol, B. (1997) 'Group Analytic Training for Management Trainers: Integrating the Emotional and Cognitive Dimensions of Management Learning'. *Management Learning*, **28**(3), 351–363.

Nonaka, I. (1991) 'The Knowledge Creating Company'. *Harvard Business Review*, November–December, 96–104.

Nystrom, P. C. and Starbuck, W. H. (1984) 'To Avoid Organizational Crises, Unlearn'. *Organizational Dynamics*, **13**, 53–65.

Oatley, K. (1998) 'The Structure of Emotions', in P. Thagard (Ed.) *Mind Readings*. Cambridge MA: MIT Press.

Parker, M. (2004) 'Becoming Manager, or, The Werewolf Looks Anxiously in the Mirror, Checking for Unusual Facial Hair'. *Management Learning*, **35**(1), 45–59.

Pedlar, M., Boydell, T. and Burgoyne, J. (1989) 'Towards the Learning Company'. *Management Education and Development*, **20**(1), 1–8.

Perriton, L. and Reynolds, M. (2004) 'Critical Management Education: From Pedagogy of Possibility to Pedagogy of Refusal?' *Management Leaning*, **35**(1), 61–77.

Perry, J. M. and Jamieson, S. (1997) *In the Zone: Achieving Optimal Performance in Business – as in Sports*. Chicago: Contemporary Books.

Polyani, M. (1967) *The Tacit Dimension*. London: Routledge.

Poole, P. P., Gioia, D. A. and Gray, B. (1989) 'Schema Change During Organisational Transformation'. *Journal of Applied Behavioural Science*, **25**(3), 271–289.

Porac, J. F., Thomas, H. and Baden-Fuller, C. (1989) 'Competitive Groups as Cognitive Communities: The Case of Scottish Knitwear Manufacturers'. *Journal of Management Studies*, **26**, 397–416.

Prawat, R. S. (1999) 'Cognitive Theory at the Crossroads: Head Fitting, Head Splitting or Somewhere in Between?' *Human Development*, **42**, 59–77.

Raelin, J. A. (1997) 'A Model of Work Based Learning'. *Organization Science*, **8**(6), 563–578.

Raelin, J. A. (2001) 'Public Reflection as the Basis of Learning'. *Management Learning*, **32**(1), 11–30.

Rawnsley, J. (1995) *Going for Broke: Nick Leeson and the Collapse of Barings Bank*. London: HarperCollins.

Reason, P. (1993) 'Sacred experience and sacred science'. *Journal of Management Inquiry*, **2**, 10–27.

Reason, P. and Rowan, J. (Eds) (1981) *Human Inquiry: A Sourcebacked New Paradigm Research*. Chichester: John Wiley & Sons, Ltd.

Reber, A. S. (1993) *Implicit Learning and Tacit Knowledge: An Essay on the Cognitive Unconscious*. New York: Oxford University Press.

Reese, W. L. (2000) *Values: A Study Guide with Readings*. New York: Humanity Books.

Reger, R. K. and Palmer, T. B. (1996) 'Managerial Categorization of Competitors: Using Old Maps to Navigate New Environments'. *Organization Science*, **7**(1), 22–39.

Revans, R. (1980) *Action Learning: New Techniques for Management*. London: Blond and Briggs Ltd.

Revans, R. (1982) *The Origins and Growth of Action Learning*. Chartwell-Bratt.

Reynolds, M. (1997) 'Learning Styles: A Critique'. *Management Learning*, **28**(2), 115–134.

Reynolds, M. (1998) 'Reflection and Critical Reflection in Management Learning'. *Management Learning*, **29**(2), 183–200.

Reynolds, M. (1999) 'Critical Reflection and Management Education: Rehabilitating less hierarchical approaches'. *Journal of Management Education*, **23**(5), 537–554.

Reynolds, M. (2000) 'Bright Lights and the Pastoral Idyll: Ideas of Community Underlying Management Education Methodologies'. *Management Learning*, **31**(1), 67–81.

Reynolds, M. and Trehen, K. (2003) 'Learning from Difference?' *Management Learning*, **34**(2), 163–180.

Robey, D. and Taggart, W. (1981) 'Measuring Managers' Minds: The Assessment of Style in Human Information Processing'. *Academy of Management Review*, **6**(3), 375–383.

Rokeach, M. (1968) *Beliefs Attitudes and Values: A Theory of Organization and Change*. San Francisco: Jossey-Bass Inc.

Rokeach, M. (1973) *The Nature of Human Values*. New York: The Free Press.

Rowe, D. (1996) *Dorothy Rowe's Guide to Life*. London: HarperCollins.

Rumelhart, D. E. (1998) 'The Architecture of Mind: A Connectionist Approach', in P. Thagard (Ed.) *Mind Readings*. Cambridge MA: MIT Press.

Runyan, W. M. (1982) *Life Histories and Psychobiography: Explorations in Theory and Method*. New York: Oxford University Press.

Sadler-Smith, E., Allinson, C. W. and Hayes, J. (2000) 'Learning Preferences and Cognitive Style: Some Implications for Continuing Professional Development'. *Management Learning*, **31**(2), 239–256.

Schank, R. C. and Abelson, R. P. (1977) *Scripts, Plans, Goals and Understanding*. Hillside, NJ: Lawrence Erlbaum Associates.

Schein, E. H. (1968) 'Organizational Socialization and the Profession of Management'. *Industrial Management Review*, **9**, 1–15.

Schein, E. H. (1985) *Organizational Culture and Leadership*. San Francisco: Jossey-Bass Inc.

Schroder, H. M. (1989) *Managerial Competence – The Key to Excellence*. Dubuque IA: Kendall Hunt.

Schweiger, D. M. (1983) 'Measuring Managers' Minds: A Critical Reply to Robey and Taggart'. *Academy of Management Review*, **8**(1), 143–151.

Senge, P. (1990) *The Fifth Discipline: The Art and Practice of the Learning Organization*. New York: Doubleday.

Shank, G. (1995) 'Semiotics and Qualitative Research in Education: The Third Crossroad'. *The Qualitative Report*, 2(3).

Shotter, J. (1992) 'Getting in Touch: The Meta-Methodology of a Postmodern Science of Mental Life', in S. Kvale (Ed.) *Psychology and Postmodernism*. London: Sage.

Simon, H. A. (1976) 'Discussion: Cognition and Social Behaviour', in J. S. Carroll and J. Payne (Eds) *Cognition and Social Behaviour*. Hillside NJ: Lawrence Erlbaum Associates.

Simon, H. A. (1991) 'Bounded Rationality and Organizational Learning'. *Organization Science*, 2(1), 125–134.

Simon, L. (1986) *Cognition and Affect*. New York: Prometheus Books.

Sims, H. P. Jr and Gioia, D. A. (Eds) (1986) *The Thinking Organization: Dynamics of Organizational Social Cognition*. San Francisco: Jossey-Bass Inc, pp. 49–74.

Slater, S. F. and Narver, J. C. (1994) *Market Oriented Isn't Enough: Build a Learning Organisation*. Marketing Science Institute, Report No. 94–103, March.

Smircich, L. and Stubbart, C. (1985) 'Strategic Management in an Enacted World'. *Academy of Management Review*, 10(4), 724–736.

Squires, J. (Ed.) (1993) *Principled Positions: Postmodernism and the Rediscovery of Value*. London: Lawrence and Wishart.

Srivastva, S., Bilimoria, D., Cooperrider, D. L. and Fry, R. E. (1995) 'Management and Organization Learning for Positive Global Change'. *Management Learning*, 26(1), 37–54.

Stata, R. (1989) 'Organizational Learning – The key to management innovation'. *Sloan Management Review*, Spring, 63–74.

Stubbart, C. I. (1989) 'Managerial Cognition: A Missing Link in Strategic Management Research'. *Journal of Management Studies*, 26, 325–347.

Sullivan, J. S. and Nonaka, I. (1986) 'Organizational Learning Theory'. *Journal of International Business Studies*, Fall, 127–147.

Sutherland, S. (1992) *Irrationality – The Enemy Within*. London: Constable.

Taylor, S. E. and Crocker, J. (1981) 'Schematic bases of social information processing', in E. T. Higgins, C. P. Herman and M. P. Zanna (Eds) *Social Cognition: The Ontario Symposium*, volume 1. Hillsdale, NJ: Erlbaum Associates, pp. 89–134.

Tennant, M. and Pogson, P. (1995) *Learning and Change in the Adult Years – A Developmental Perspective*. San Francisco: Jossey-Bass Inc.

Thagard, P. (Ed.) (1998) *Mind Readings: Introductory Selections on Cognitive Science*. Cambridge MA: MIT Press.

The Dalai Lama and Goleman, D. (2003) *Destructive Emotions And How We Can Overcome Them*. London: Bantam Books.

Thompson, J. and McGivern, J. (1996) 'Parody, Process and Practice – Perspectives for Management Education?' *Management Learning*, **27**(1), 21–35.

Tolman, E. C. (1932) *Purposive Behaviour in Animals and Men*. New York: Appleton-Century-Crofts.

Van Maanen, J. (1978) 'People Processing: Strategies of Organizational Socialization'. *Organizational Dynamics*, summer, 19–36.

Van Maanen, J. and Schein, E. H. (1979) 'Toward a Theory of Organizational Socialization', in B. M. Staw and L. L. Cummings (Eds) *Research in Organizational Behaviour*, volume 1. Greenwich CT: JAI Press.

Vince, R. (1996) 'Experiential Management Education as the Practice of Change', in R. French and C. Grey (Eds) *Rethinking Management Education*. London: Sage.

Vince, R. (1998) 'Behind and Beyond Kolb's Learning Cycle'. *Journal of Management Education*, **22**(3), 304–320.

Vince, R. (2000) 'Learning in Public Organizations in 2010'. *Public Money and Management*, **20**(1), 39–44.

Vince, R. (2001) 'Power and emotion in organizational learning'. *Human Relations*, **54**(10), 1325–1351.

Vince, R. (2002a) 'The Politics of Imagined Stability: A Psychodynamic Understanding of Change at Hyder plc'. *Human Relations*, **55**(10), 1189–1208.

Vince, R. (2002b) 'The Impact of Emotion in Organizational Learning'. *Human Resource Development International*, **5**(1): 73–85.

Vince, R. (2002c) 'Organizing Reflection'. *Management Learning*, **33**(1), 63–78.

Vince, R. and Saleem, T. (2004) 'The Impact of Caution and Blame on Organizational Learning'. *Management Learning*, **35**(2), 133–154.

Walker, M. T. (2001) 'Practical Applications of The Rogerian Perspective in Postmodern Psychotherapy'. *Journal of Systemic Therapies*, **20**(2), 41–57.

Walsh, J. P. (1995) 'Managerial and Organizational Cognition: Notes from a Trip Down Memory Lane'. *Organization Science*, **6**(3), 280–320.

Walsh, J. P. and Ungson, G. R. (1991) 'Organisational Memory'. *Academy of Management Review*, **16**(1), 57–91.

Watson, T. (1994) *In Search of Management*. London: Routledge.

Watson, T. (1996) 'How Do Managers Think? Identity, Morality and Pragmatism in Managerial Theory and Practice'. *Management Learning*, **27**(3), 323–341.

Watson, T. (2001) 'The Emergent Manager and Processes of Management Pre-learning'. *Management Learning*, **32**(2), 221–235.

Weick, K. E. (1979) *The Social Psychology of Organizing*. Reading MA: Addison Wesley.

Weick, K. E. (1990) 'Cartographic Myths in Organizations', in A. S. Huff (Ed.) *Mapping Strategic Thought*. Chichester: John Wiley & Sons, Ltd.

Weick, K. E. (1993) 'Conceptual Options in the Study of Organizational Learning', in M. M. Crossan *et al.* (Eds) *Learning in Organizations*, Western Business School, University of Western Ontario, Ontario, pp. 25–41.

Weick, K. E. (1995) *Sensemaking in Organizations*. Thousand Oaks CA: Sage.

Wenger, E. (1991) 'Communities of Practice: Where Learning Happens', in M. M. Crossan *et al.* (Eds) *Learning in Organizations*, Western Business School, University of Western Ontario, Ontario, pp. 25–41.

White, R. E., Crossan, M. M. and Lane, H. W. (1994) *Learning Within Organizations*. Western Business School, London, Canada.

Willmott, H. (1994) 'Management Education: Provocations to a Debate'. *Management Learning*, **25**(1), 105–136.

Wright, T. and Wright, V. (2000) 'How our "values" influence the manner in which organizational research is framed and interpreted'. *Journal of Organizational Behaviour*, **21**, 603–607.

Wyler, R. (1964) 'Assessment and correlates of cognitive differentiation and integration'. *Journal of Personality*, **32**, 495–509.

Zemke, R. and Zemke, S. (1981) *30 things we know for sure about adult learning*. Training/HRD, June, 45–52.

Zohar, D. and Marshall, I. (2001) *Spiritual Intelligence, The Ultimate Intelligence*. London: Bloomsbury.

Index

Indexed compiled by Terry Halliday